Victorian Reformation

AMERICAN ACADEMY OF RELIGION

RELIGION, CULTURE, AND HISTORY SERIES

SERIES EDITOR
Jacob N. Kinnard, Iliff School of Theology

A Publication Series of

The American Academy of Religion
and Oxford University Press

Anti-Judaism in Feminist Religious Writings
KATHARINA VON KELLENBACH

Cross Cultural Conversation
(Initiation)
EDITED BY ANINDITA NIYOGI BALSLEV

On Deconstructing Life-Worlds
Buddhism, Christianity, Culture
ROBERT MAGLIOLA

The Great White Flood
Racism in Australia
ANNE PATTEL-GRAY

Imag(in)ing Otherness
Filmic Visions of Living Together
EDITED BY S. BRENT PLATE AND DAVID JASPER

Cultural Otherness
Correspondence with Richard Rorty, Second Edition
ANINDITA NIYOGI BALSLEV

Feminist Poetics of the Sacred
Creative Suspicions
EDITED BY FRANCES DEVLIN-GLASS AND LYN MCCREDDEN

Parables for Our Time
Rereading New Testament Scholarship after the Holocaust
TANIA OLDENHAGE

Moses in America
The Cultural Uses of Biblical Narrative
MELANIE JANE WRIGHT

Intersecting Pathways
Modern Jewish Theologians in Conversation with Christianity
MARC A. KRELL

Asceticism and Its Critics
Historical Accounts and Comparative Perspectives
EDITED BY OLIVER FREIBERGER

Virtuous Bodies
The Physical Dimensions of Morality in Buddhist Ethics
SUSANNE MROZIK

Victorian Reformation
The Fight over Idolatry in the Church of England, 1840–1860
DOMINIC JANES

AMERICAN ACADEMY OF RELIGION

Victorian Reformation

The Fight over Idolatry in the Church

of England, 1840–1860

Dominic Janes

UNIVERSITY PRESS

2009

OXFORD
UNIVERSITY PRESS

Oxford University Press, Inc., publishes works that further
Oxford University's objective of excellence
in research, scholarship, and education.

Oxford   New York
Auckland   Cape Town   Dar es Salaam   Hong Kong   Karachi
Kuala Lumpur   Madrid   Melbourne   Mexico City   Nairobi
New Delhi   Shanghai   Taipei   Toronto

With offices in
Argentina   Austria   Brazil   Chile   Czech Republic   France   Greece
Guatemala   Hungary   Italy   Japan   Poland   Portugal   Singapore
South Korea   Switzerland   Thailand   Turkey   Ukraine   Vietnam

Copyright © 2009 by The American Academy of Religion

Published by Oxford University Press, Inc.
198 Madison Avenue, New York, New York 10016

www.oup.com

Library of Congress Cataloging-in-Publication Data
Janes, Dominic.
Victorian reformation: the fight over idolatry in the Church
of England, 1840–1860 / Dominic Janes.
    p. cm.
Includes bibliographical references and index.
ISBN 978-0-19-537851-1
1. Ritualism—History—19th century. 2. Anglo-Catholicism—History—19th century.
3. Idols and images—England—Worship—History of doctrines—19th century.
4. England—Church history—19th century. I. Title.
BX5123.J36 2009
283'.4209034—dc22   2008034901

9 8 7 6 5 4 3 2 1
Printed in the United States of America
on acid-free paper

. . . at best a wretched, mincing, harlotry imitation of the Church of Rome.
—*Lloyd's Weekly Newspaper,* November 16, 1856.

Disgust always bears the imprint of desire.
—Stallybrass and White, *The Politics and Poetics of Transgression* (1986)

Acknowledgments

With thanks for help, support, sources, and illustrations:

    Bodleian Library, Oxford University
    Library, Birkbeck College, London
    British Library
    British Museum
    Cambridge University Library
    Delaware Art Museum
    Lady Lever Art Gallery, Liverpool
    Lambeth Palace Library
    Manchester Central Library
    Manchester City Art Gallery
    National Association of Decorative and Fine Arts Societies
    Paula Cooper Gallery
    Pusey House, Oxford
    St. Barnabas', Pimlico
    St. Paul's, Knightsbridge

I particularly thank Rev. Alasdair Coles, Rev. Alan Gyle, Rev. Steve Hardwick, Dr. Tim Hochstrasser, Duncan Horne, Prof. Jacob Kinnard, Dr. Elizabeth McKellar, Rev. Anthony Moore, Prof. Les Moran, Philip Payne, Brian Ridgers, Dr. Andrew Rudd, and Prof. Mark Thatcher for their invaluable assistance and support in the completion of this project.

Funding toward the cost of the illustrations was provided by the Research Fund, Faculty of Lifelong Learning, Birkbeck College, London.

Contents

List of Illustrations

Victorian Reformation

I

Introduction: Victorian Reformation

The important shrine of Our Lady in Walsingham in North Norfolk
was suppressed at the Reformation, only to be reestablished by the
Anglo-Catholic priest Alfred Hope Patten (1885–1958) in the early
twentieth century. An image of the Virgin copied from the seal of
the former Walsingham Abbey was carved in 1922 and first taken on
procession in 1931. The statue is now carried annually on the Spring
Bank Holiday, which has been established as the date of a National
Pilgrimage that is attended by both Anglo- and Roman Catholics, as
well as by a small group of Protestant protesters. On May 29, 2006,
the latter were arranged about the sixteenth-century pump house in
the village centre past which the statue was due to progress. Figures 1.1
and 1.2 show the statue of Mary passing the pump house and the
calling out of the opposing preacher after the procession had gone
past. Here we see a clash of ritual, material, and textual cultures. The
Catholics processed singing in English and Latin. They bore on their
shoulders the statue of the Virgin Mary adorned with lace and flowers. They themselves wore various forms of ecclesiastical dress. By
contrast, their opponents were in no special sort of uniform, which,
in the circumstances, was a ritual statement in itself. But they were
provided with a series of fascinating banners and placards, notably
one providing a pagan genealogy for Mary, and another showing a
young girl saying 'I talk to my dolly', and the Pope holding a crowned
Virgin replying, 'I pray to mine'. The opposing preacher held the
Bible in his hand as he denounced the Catholic procession for its

immorality. As one their banners put it: 'No idolator hath any inheritance in the kingdom of God', and 'be not deceived neither adulterers nor effeminate nor abusers of themselves with mankind shall inherit the kingdom of God'. The underlying accusation was that Anglo-Catholicism had attempted a form of Counter-Reformation so as to allow the flourishing of immorality.

It is important to emphasise that the majority of those on the 'Catholic' side were, denominationally at least, Protestants. The Anglican shrine at Walsingham is much larger than the Roman Catholic one, and it is the former that is the focus of the National Pilgrimage. This event, therefore, substantially concerns the legitimacy of Catholic forms of worship within the Reformed Churches. In similar fashion, this book is not a study of Roman Catholicism. Rather, it is an investigation of the Anglican use of material, visual, and liturgical forms inspired, first, by the medieval past and, second, by contemporary Roman Catholicism. My subject is the huge wave of anxiety that was produced by the first substantial appearance of such material forms in the 1840s and 1850s. This is therefore a study of fears that were not so much of the enemy without, but of the enemy within. What was at stake was the long-standing contention that Protestant England and the minds and bodies of its subjects had been fully purified by the Tudor Reformation. In this study I explore the contested emergence of the Victorian Reformation, in other words, the development of mainstream Victorian understandings of the Reformation and of its relevance to contemporary

FIGURE 1.1. Annual Pilgrimage, 2006, Walsingham. Photograph by the author.

FIGURE 1.2. Annual Pilgrimage, 2006, Walsingham. Photograph by the author.

patterns of worship. The result was not simply the rise of Anglo-Catholicism, but a considerable shift in the normative practices of devotion, such that it was a matter for incredulity in the following century that, to take one example, the legality of crosses in church had been in serious dispute only sixty years before.

The pioneers of Anglo-Catholicism thought that it was they who were returning Christian worship to a state of sanctity through the rejection of worldly forms. This movement had one of its origins in the Gothic Revival of the later eighteenth century. The publications of the Camden Society ecclesiologists were particularly important in the nineteenth-century reception of medieval models of art, architecture, and worship. What they, in the words of the society's leaders John Mason Neale (1818–66), then fellow of Downing College, Cambridge, and Benjamin Webb (1819–85), curate of Kemerton in Gloucestershire, were struggling against in the 1830s and 1840s was a Protestant place of worship that possessed galleries, a central pulpit, and an altar hidden 'under the organ gallery, as being of no use, except once a month'. It was a place for the fashionable to meet and greet. It was little more than a preaching box combined with a stage setting for social snobbery:

> People come, dressed in the full fashion of the day, to occupy their
> luxurious pue [*sic*], to lay their smelling bottles and prayer books on

its desk, and reclining on its soft cushions…see the poor and infirm standing in the narrow passages, and close their poor doors against them, lest themselves should be contaminated, or their cushions spoilt.[1]

Here the splendid visual culture is that of the well-to-do, and the sacred objects that must be protected from defilement are their dresses and persons. Neale and Webb contrast this with an exercise in their neo-Gothic visual imagination, which begins with a spire seen from afar, leads into an elaborate church, up past pinnacles, and images of saints and martyrs and virgins, all red and gold, until high above in the roof hangs 'on His triumphal Cross, the image of HIM who by his Death hath overcome death'.[2] All this draws one away from the worldly cares symbolized by the royal arms hung in the 'temples' that are so many of the Anglican churches of the day. The message was that visual splendour in art, architecture, and liturgical ritual can be returned to God and can return us to God. It also represented a significant attack on the ostentatious display of luxury commodities by the middle and upper classes. Such exaltation of the image of God might appear to lead to an ultimate renunciation of the material world. On the other hand, it might appear to represent the use of objects to assert the superiority of the corporate Church over the laity. It was from such divergences of opinion that deep-seated rifts in the Church of England were to emerge.

In 1853 W. J. Conybeare (1815–57), then vicar of Axminster, published a long elaboration of 'parties' in the Church of England.[3] An emerging struggle to assert a sacred material culture purified from the materialist commodification of the market represents one of a series of trends that gave impetus to an increasing awareness of divisions within Anglicanism. The latter process of fission was nothing new. The success of Methodism had already ensured that there was a considerable blurring of the boundaries between Anglicans and Dissenters. The same thing, with the rise of Tractarianism, was to become true of the boundary with Roman Catholicism. Much of the recently spilt ink on Anglo-Catholic ritualism concerns, first, its evolution and, second, its attempted 'repression' (as opposed to its semiotic transformation which is a key focus in this study). To deal with the question of origins first, Nigel Yates believed that 'the germs of both movements [Ecclesiology and ritualism] are contemporary with Tractarianism and, in the case of Ecclesiology, could be seen to pre-date the Oxford movement'.[4] The Cambridge Camden ('Ecclesiological') Society had, during its relatively brief life, a wide and respectable membership, which included sixteen bishops and two archbishops in 1843. It thus enjoyed much more substantial patronage than the Tractarians of the Oxford Movement.[5] These movements, originating in the two ancient English universities, were led by personalities who inspired many of the next generation of Anglican clergy. The Tractarian leaders, Newman, Pusey, and Keble, were not ritualists, but their ideas provided a theological underpinning for ritual innovation and church decoration.[6] Ritualism, a movement focussed on material and liturgical innovation, emerged in the late 1840s. Its adherents distinguished between 'Roman Catholic' and (Anglo-) 'Catholic', despite the fact that it was normal in wider society to use 'Catholic' to mean 'Roman Catholic', as A. W. N. Pugin, for example, did.[7] Those who wanted a more Catholic form of ritual led a dramatic development of Anglican High Church traditionalism into what has come to be known as Anglo-Catholicism. Nevertheless, there remained some distinction between those who were theologically inspired by the Oxford movement and those 'ritualists' who wished to give that theology novel material forms.

There is a strongly generational sense to these developments, as one group of students of theology reacted to the university teachings of their predecessors. Indeed, John Shelton Reed, a little tentatively, suggested that ritualism evolved as an early form of youth counterculture.[8] Ritualism provided a good way for people, even if they did not think of it in those terms, to express their desire to rebel. On the one hand, it was learned and drew on establishment values of tradition and respect, but on the other hand, it drove its opponents wild because it gave the appearance of questioning the value of the Reformation.

Who were those opponents? Leaving aside marginal groups, such as those espousing atheist views, there was a large body of popular opinion that was hostile to undue enthusiasm in religion of any sort. However, in exceptional circumstances, as happened as we shall see in 1850, such opinion was amenable to being swayed by fervent groups of ecclesiastical opponents. These were formed of preachers and believers across a swathe of Christian territory ranging from Dissenters to Methodists and including significant elements of the Church of England. We find the term 'Low Churchmen' rising to prominence in the 1840s as sectarian positions became more entrenched in Anglicanism.

It is important to stress that there is no foolproof definition of such terms as 'ritualist', 'Anglo-Catholic', 'Low Church', and 'evangelical' because these descriptions were used in different ways depending on the date and the author. An excellent example of this is provided by the evangelicals, a grouping that overlapped with some but not all Dissenters, Presbyterians, and Anglicans, especially Methodists.[9] So when, for instance, I refer to someone as evangelical, this essentially means that they were typically referred to as being evangelical. It tends to mean those with a powerful desire to spread the truth of a reformed faith based, not on sacraments, but upon the saving Grace of God. Boyd Hilton has commented that Tractarian 'Oxford and [evangelical] Clapham should be regarded as complementary rather than antagonistic spheres of influence'.[10]

Initially, they saw themselves as allies in a struggle against liberalism.[11] And Dieter Voll has seen these movements as evolving ultimately from the pietist revival from the eighteenth century.[12] The distinction between 'High' and 'Low' was in some senses quite misleading, therefore, because members of both parties were fervent in acts and faith, embraced ascetic approaches to life, entertainment and sexuality, wrote abundant tracts, and lauded hard work; but they tended to ignore the similarities.[13] Peter Toon has investigated the theological positions of these two sides and emphasised how much the two camps agreed: on divine inspiration of Scripture, the Trinity, the Person of Christ, the need to pursue personal holiness, hope of the second coming, resurrection of the dead, and life everlasting—but what mattered were differences in understandings of the place of tradition, authority of the ministry, nature of the sacraments, and ritual.[14] The eschatological focus of many evangelicals was also distinctive. This is of great importance to this study for there was a rising sense of apocalyptic expectation among many evangelicals during our period.[15] The Anti-Christ was expected, and many identified him with Rome and the Tractarians and ritualists who were accused of being His stooges.

Even if attendance at church and chapel was patchy (notably among the urban working classes), the vast majority of the English population regarded itself as Protestant. This word was a badge of pride. However, Anglican ritualists often took a different point of view. G. R. Portal, one of the curates of St. Barnabas', Pimlico, said, 'I know not what the "Protestant faith" is, unless it be a comprehensive system of mere negation'.[16] This is why it is important to use the term 'Anglo-Catholic' from time to time, even though it is, strictly speaking, anachronistic in the early Victorian period, in order to distinguish those Anglicans who called themselves 'Catholics' but were not (and often did not want to be) Roman Catholics. Their point was that they saw themselves as part of the Universal Church of Christ. And, similarly, I will be using the term 'Protestants' to refer to those who classed themselves in that way; thus, for example, I will talk of disputes between Protestants and Anglo-Catholics.

English anti-(Roman) Catholicism since the Reformation provides the background against which to consider these events.[17] It was spurred on by the union with Ireland in 1800 and by Catholic emancipation in 1829. Twenty years later, the unreliability of the religious census of 1851 was less important than the shock effect of its findings. Published in 1854, it revealed that there were rather more than five million Anglicans, fewer than four hundred thousand Roman Catholics, and more than four and a half million Dissenters in church and chapel on a typical Sunday.[18] The Church of England was facing the fact that it was ceasing to be the national Church but was becoming simply one denomination amongst many.[19]

One might assume, from these figures, that Dissent would have seemed the greatest danger to Anglicanism, but the fact that English nationalism partly had its roots in the assertion of independence from the Papacy meant that Rome was seen as a threat to the established Church of quite another order to that posed by Dissent. One voice that we will hear much of is that of the Rev. Michael Hobart Seymour (1800–74), ordained a priest in the Church of Ireland and sometime secretary of the Irish Protestant Association. He continued his anti-Popery efforts after settling in Bath, albeit without a parish, in 1844. He was on characteristic form when he preached on 'The English Communion Contrasted with the Roman Mass', at St. George's Church, Southwark, on Sunday evening, November 5, 1843. He engaged in a thorough denunciation of Papistry as a plot against God and England. He concluded by reminding the congregation that it was on this day that there took place 'the foul and traitorous conspiracy of the Papists to destroy the whole fabric of our Christian and Protestant Church, and to desolate this Christian and Protestant nation'.[20] Across that nation, similar anathemas rolled out from pulpits every year, reaching a climax of invective on Guy Fawkes Night.

Roman Catholicism was regarded by many Protestants as bad for personal morality, inimical to national economic and social progress, and fatal for personal liberty.[21] It was held that the claims of the Papists were manifestly absurd, although often couched in dangerously seductive and difficult language. Much of the battle was fought out in the form of tracts, many of which focussed on the supposedly carnal nature of Catholic worship. In 1846, the Society for the Promotion of Christian Knowledge, as part of its 'What Is Romanism?' series, dedicated no fewer than five numbers to dealing with 'invocation of saints and angels', assuring the reader that there was no evidence in Scripture, nor support from the early Church, for it.[22] The Virgin Mary warranted nine pamphlets, and 'image worship' ten (although this included the cross and other objects as well as idolatrous pictures).[23] The Word was not to be usurped by the Image.

John Wolffe has argued that anti-Catholicism was a 'rational, if extreme, response to contemporary circumstances'.[24] The development of Catholic evangelism, Irish immigration to Britain, the advance of Ultramontanism, the crisis of Irish Protestants, and the need in the Conservative Party for a focus for recovery after 1832 all contributed to the British allergic reaction. There was, in fact, a substantial Roman Catholic revival taking place in England, but the reality was that whilst the Roman Catholic community was growing in size and confidence, it was lacking in resources and was not the treasure house of plunder alleged by some of its enemies. It is important to emphasise, however, that this volume is not a study of Roman Catholic practice as much as of the ways in which Catholic practice was imagined either by those who wished to emulate it or by those who opposed it within the English Protestant denominations. This is a study of the cultural life of a fantasised Catholicism.

The 1840s perhaps saw the 'high-water mark of Protestant activity in the nineteenth century': from the anti-Maynooth agitation of 1845, to the frustration of Lord John Russell's plans of 1848 for British government links with the Papacy and, finally, to the 'Papal Aggression' of 1850.[25] It was the last event, the restoration of a Roman Episcopal hierarchy in England, that acted as the immediate cause for riot and disorder in the case study of early ritualism in Knightsbridge, London, that forms the third chapter of this study. The reestablishment of the Roman Catholic hierarchy, with Nicholas Wiseman as cardinal archbishop of Westminster, was a sudden and, as it turned out, provocative act that led to short-lived but intense Protestant uproar. One leading 'no popery' speaker, John Cumming (1807–81), the evangelical minister of the National Scottish Church in Covent Garden, drew such crowds that

> on the opening of the doors the rush of the crowd to procure seats
> was tremendous, and in a very few minutes every inch of space was
> occupied. Many ladies fainted and had to be removed. Hundreds
> upon hundreds of persons were unable to obtain admission at
> all…he was received with loud and general cheering…when silence
> was restored he proceeded to say, that while he regretted, on the one
> hand that some were inconvenienced by the pressure, he could not,
> on the other, avoid expressing his gratitude to God that the policy
> of Cardinal Wiseman had brought together such a large number of
> Protestants to testify against it.[26]

Meetings and associated tumult were also held against Anglican ritualists, even after the initial rumpus against the Roman Catholic episcopate had died down. On July 19, 1854, a gathering, which had taken place the previous day, was reported prominently in *The Times*. Seven or eight hundred people had assembled at the Riding School, Motcomb Street, near Belgrave Square, in a newly built and fashionable part of London. Admiral Octavius Harcourt (1793–1863), lord of Masham, and son of the late archbishop of York, Edward Harcourt (d. 1847), was in the chair. Motions against the liturgical ritual taking place at the local Anglican churches of St. Paul's and St. Barnabas' were to be put to the audience:

> Upon the arrival of the speakers on the platform a scene of great up-
> roar immediately took place in the body of the meeting, and a general
> *mêlée* ensued between the representatives of the High Church and
> the Low Church, which ended in the latter party turning several of

their opponents out of the meeting by force...amid much confusion
and, before the prayers were concluded an unparalleled scene of riot
and uproar again intervened, in which a regular fight ensued in the
body of the meeting. A large number of police-constables arrived,
and with their assistance the meeting was cleared of several of the
High Church party, who were roughly handled in the affray.

The admiral then began to speak but was interrupted by 'continued uproar,
which ended in several other persons being forced out of the meeting'. The
Hon. Charles Smith Vereker, an Irish Protestant aristocrat, then spoke, con-
demning the activities in the local churches and concluding with a 'fearful on-
slaught on the Popish faith'. The speech resulted in another scene of riot and
confusion, during which the police had again to be called in. Various people
spoke, including churchwardens. One of these, a certain Mr. George, urged
direct intervention. He said that, on learning that a procession of priests was
planned, 'he then acted on his own discretion by locking up all the surplices
(applause and increased uproar), and he threatened to lock up the organ when
the clergy were for intoning the singing (applause).'[27]

Surplices, organs, and uproar: the fight against the Anglo-Catholic revival
has a tendency to appear a little quaint at a century and a half's remove. Like
the regular disturbances at elections, it can be seen as part of the stimulating
rough and tumble of Victorian life.[28] Part of the problem is that, at first sight,
the quarrel appears to have been about little more than what was sometimes
referred to at the time as the 'mere externals' of belief. This was the position
taken by George Cotton (1813–66), then master of Marlborough and future
bishop of Calcutta, when preaching at the consecration of Archibald Campbell
Tait as bishop of London in 1856. He claimed that 'less interest and excitement
is shown in the struggle against positive wickedness, than in some dispute
about a cross, a vestment or a candlestick'.[29]

This dismissive attitude toward a heightened concern with ritual and sacred material culture can also be seen manifested by more recent authorities
such as Owen Chadwick. His magisterial *The Victorian Church* does not focus
on art and ritual. This is how it discusses, and perhaps dismisses, some of the
central issues of the present study:

A violent argument and subsequent lawsuit at St. Paul's, Knightsbridge, and its notorious chapel of St. Barnabas, drew everyone's
attention to the state of the law about ornaments...these were the
years after papal aggression. The conscience of those with invincible
repugnance was alive and pulsating; and the more they manifested
their repugnance in irreverence, the more strongly attached to these

objects grew the conscience of Tractarian priests and their flocks. Blaspheming rabbles did as much as thickets of law to establish Anglo-Catholic ceremonies with the normal practice of the Church of England.[30]

There have been a number of studies of ritualism and the early years of Anglo-Catholicism.[31] But none of them has centred on the wider cultural anxieties of the period concerning material culture so as to explain the extraordinarily intense concern about 'idolatry' that these movements produced in their opponents. Ritualism is widely understood to have evolved from Tractarianism, with the key difference supposedly being an emphasis on material forms rather than theological innovation. This has meant that ritualism has often been less highly regarded by theologians and historians of ideas. However, if one thinks in terms of the encoding of ideas in material forms, a new appreciation of the significance of the movement can be gained.

Lytton Strachey placed ritualism as one of those quaint Victorian phenomena in need of deflation by his wit. In *Eminent Victorians* (1918) he wrote that with the conversion of Newman to Rome in 1845:

> The Oxford Movement was now ended. The University breathed such a sigh of relief as usually follows the difficult expulsion of a hard piece of matter from an organism, and actually began to attend to education. As for the Church of England, she had tasted blood, and it was clear that she would never again be content with a vegetable diet. Her clergy, however, maintained their reputation for judicious compromise, for they followed Newman up to the very point beyond which his conclusions were logical, and, while they intoned, confessed, swung incense, and burnt candles with the exhilaration of converts, they managed to do so with a subtle nuance which showed that they had nothing to do with Rome.[32]

In a similar vein, E. F. Benson (son of E. W. Benson, archbishop of Canterbury 1882–96) wrote of the choice of reading matter of a character in his novel *Secret Lives* (1932) that

> deeply interesting to her as was the inner history of his soul-experience when, as a curate to an Anglo-Catholic vicar, his conscience forbade him to perform certain gaudy ritualistic ceremonies which he knew were illegal in the English Church, it would be no use attempting to concentrate on the subtleties of that complicated business until she had finished the second reading of her new romance.[33]

Even Reed, in some of the most important work on Anglo-Catholicism, has talked of ritualism as the 'ceremonial froth' that came in the wake of Tractarianism.[34] As one writer put it in 1851, 'the Church against which the gates of hell shall never prevail, is not the visible Church, but the whole body of the elect, the company of true believers out of every nation and people'.[35] But if 'externals' were 'mere froth', why did they excite such determined and uncompromising opposition? Because the material mattered if only as the counterpart to the immaterial. Iconoclasts are similar to iconophiles in that they both think images have a great deal of power.[36] Furthermore, Yates has suggested that the 'average man or woman in the pew took little notice' of theological differences between the various camps of Churchmanship, 'but what happened in the church...they certainly did notice'.[37]

In the early Victorian period, the very statement of lack of interest in 'externals' marked one out as taking the clear stand that those who were so focussed were leading the Anglican Church astray. George Poole (1809–83), Rector of Winwick, near Rugby, and a Gothic Revival enthusiast, writing in 1840 against such Protestant protestations, noted that a part of the outcry against those of a more ritual persuasion was based on the misconception that it was his party that was making externals into things of importance. 'Now what is the fact? *He* simply does what he thinks is his duty and says nothing. *They* see it done and immediately raise an outcry. Which is making it a matter of importance?' For, he argued, all sects have their visible rituals: 'When Puritans and Presbyterians make it as imperative not to kneel at the blessed Eucharist, as our Church does to receive this Holy Sacrament with that mark of devotion, why, on their own principle, is not their zeal for standing or sitting to be counted a superstition?'[38]

It was a theologically driven ideological choice amongst many Protestant groups to displace art and visual culture from ostensible concern. Similarly, the displacement of the study of Victorian material culture as being outside the remit of modern history or theology departments is also driven by culturally conditioned intellectual strategies. Nevertheless, Jonathan White has identified a 'drive toward the study of material objects as part of a dramatically expanded historical archive'.[39] Material culture is currently championed most coherently in the United Kingdom within the academic realms of archaeology and anthropology.[40] From that context, it is interesting to bear in mind a case study from Vanuatu, in the South Pacific, in which textual explanations of various objects seemed not to be on offer to anthropologists: 'The refusal [of the natives] to verbalise is perhaps because the artefact as visual metaphor does the talking in a much more profound, succinct and vivid manner'.[41] If we think in terms of an interconnection of the messages of art and text, we can then ask what disturbing things Catholic objects were saying to their opponents in Victorian England.

The social scientific understanding of ritualism (as opposed to its theo-logical comprehension) dates back to the antiquarian analysis of comparative religion, which is the subject of chapter 4 of this book. However, much of this material has hardly if ever been referred to in the more recent literature on ritualism. One of the reasons for this is that comparative religion has not become well established in modern British universities, despite such work being 'firmly and centrally institutionalised in the intellectual life of Britain in the period 1870–1914'.[42] Even the study of anthropology has a tendency to start with the later nineteenth century and ignores the supposedly 'unscien-tific' work that went on before the period when the subject became established in universities.

'Ritual' (as opposed to ritualism) as a site of intellectual activity dates to the last decade of the nineteenth century, and even then there was less interest in repetitive forms of behaviour and associated artefacts than with symbolism and worship in general. In the *Encyclopaedia Britannica* of 1771, a 'ritual' means a liturgical formulary book. What we mean by ritual was referred to under 'rite'. This division continued until 1852 and the seventh edition, after which both terms disappeared, only to reappear in more-or-less modern form in the eleventh edition of 1910.[43] My aim is to think about the use of material culture in the ritual performances of worship and about aspects of the associated visual imagination. This is not an art history, in the sense of focussing on 'the aes-thetic function of images, [which from the early modern period] at least in elite circles, began to dominate the many other uses of these objects'.[44] Rather, this is a textually informed study of the material culture of religion and of its inter-action with the wider material culture of its time. Academic context for these aspects of my approach can be found in Arjun Appadurai, *The Social Life of Things: Commodities in Cultural Perspective* (1986); Asa Briggs, *Victorian Things* (1988); Victoria De Grazia and Ellen Furlough, *The Sex of Things: Gender and Consumption in Historical Perspective* (1996) and Esther Pasztory, *Thinking with Things: Toward a New Vision of Art* (2005). This is a cultural history that seeks to understand the way in which people in the nineteenth century 'thought with sacred things' even whilst many of them sought to deny it.[45] Yet I do not simply conclude that spiritual viewpoints shaped the understanding of the material realm; I think the reverse was also taking place.

Idolatry and Fetishism

It should be clear, bearing in mind the preceding discussion, that when I in-voke the Bible, I do so not as a theologian, but with the aim of exploring how this text influenced and interacted with contemporary attitudes in nineteenth-century society:

> Then God spoke all these words: I am the Lord your God, who
> brought you out of the land of Egypt, out of the house of slavery; you
> shall have no other gods before me. You shall not make for yourself
> an idol, whether in the form of anything that is in heaven above, or
> that is on the earth beneath, or that is in the water under the earth.
> You shall not bow down to them or worship them; for I the Lord your
> God am a jealous God, punishing children for the iniquity of parents,
> to the third and the fourth generation of those who reject me, but
> showing steadfast love to the thousandth generation of those who
> love me and keep my commandments.
>
> Exodus 20: 1–6, New Revised Standard Version

The first and most important commandment forbad the worshipping of anything other than the jealous God: that could refer to a golden calf, an anthropomorphic statue or a painting. But in the nineteenth century it could also refer to the worship of an abstraction, such as power or money, because the word 'idolatry' was applied to a range of what we might now term addictions, such as alcoholism and gambling. Many people even held that the love of a man for his wife and vice versa should not come close to equalling their love of God. In the legal cases on ritualism presented as a case study in chapter 3, one of the judges remarked that the reason why we need to be vigilant about externals is that the 'whole of history, both sacred and profane, shows the proneness of mankind to idolatrous practices'.[46] It was no wonder that it was thought that it was only by the Grace of the Holy Spirit that idolatry could be avoided.

But this is not a book about idolatry as much as about accusations of idolatry. These found their most acute expression in relation to alleged adoration of the material world and 'it is precisely because Catholic theology [allegedly] threatens to conflate the created order with the sacred that Protestantism saw in it the danger of idolatry'.[47] Attitudes ultimately deriving from the Reformation played a crucial role in this focus. Idolatry was represented as a confusing of the sign for the referent. To 'discover' it one must see a universe of signs, and then chide people for not focussing on the 'reality' beyond those signs. This can be understood as being ultimately an Aristotelian critique of form versus substance, as opposed to a Platonic belief that the symbol somehow shares in its archetype. For Calvin, the sacrament of the Eucharist was merely an 'efficacious sign', but, crucially, it was 'efficacious'. The accusation of idolatry, as it appeared in the nineteenth century, signalled not only a mistaken focus of adulation but also the sense that that object was not simply inefficacious but dangerous because it involved attributing power to that which should not have it.

David Hawkes makes the important point that 'what Luther found idolatrous was not the adoration of the sign but the belief that the sign was made sacred by the fetishised actions of the priest'.[48] The discourse of idolatry, therefore, indicates the fear of fetishism, that is, the belief that the priest was able to make objects with an autonomous life of their own, thereby threatening the boundary between human spiritual agency and mere matter. To Victorians, the term 'fetishism' conjured up the practices of heathen primitives and was regarded with horror as representing the grossest superstition.[49] The word first makes it appearance in Charles de Brosses, *Du culte des dieux fétiches* of 1760, which used traders' accounts of West Africa to talk about the way in which natives believed (or we supposed to believe) in the spiritual animation of objects.[50] Auguste Comte (1798–1857) popularised these notions in the 1830s and 1840s through his three-stage model of human religious development: fetishism, idolatry, and monotheism.[51] Ultimately, his 'positivism' looked forward to a future entirely beyond religious superstition.[52]

Catholics were widely believed, by Protestants, to fetishise the wafer of the mass as an object of magical efficacy, much in the same way a 'primitive' would worship an idol and believe in its animate potency. Many people considered this devilish. Opponents thought such practices to be, at their very best, childish and feeble-minded, as illustrated by the description of the character Mrs. Light's matrimonial hopes in Henry James, *Roderick Hudson* (1875). These were presented as that 'poor old fetish' that had been so played with that it was battered but was still 'brought forth in moments of trouble, to have its tinselled petticoat twisted about and be set up on its altar'.[53]

In an important series of articles, William Pietz has examined the origins of the theory of the fetish.[54] He argues that the European traders interpreted African practices through their own cultural understandings. In other words, it was not necessarily that Africans believed that certain of their objects were alive, but that Europeans read their behaviour in this way. The eighteenth-century theory of fetishism, in other words, was a colonial interpretation of the 'other' as primitive because certain goods were seemingly not being valued according to the 'rational' framework of market exchange.

Comte was read in German translation by Karl Marx in 1842–43. The reification of objects in capitalist processes of production, in which the body of the commodity becomes more important than the body of the workers, was identified by Marx through his notion of 'commodity fetishism'.[55] For Michael Taussig, the key point of a fetish in this sense is of an object that embodies the social order.[56] Capitalism, in this analysis, is that state in which the social order is determined by the objects. Whereas fetish objects are exceptional in the precapitalist world and are typically fenced off with powerful taboos, in modern market economies they take the form of ubiquitous and all-powerful commodities.

For Marx, primitivism lay in the heart of modern society in the form of the fetishism not so much of the commodity itself, but of its value.[57] The power of these idols came from their very immateriality. There was nothing obvious to smash. In the wake of the repeal of Corn Laws in 1846, the creation of limited liability corporations in 1855–56 and the abolition of a wide variety of taxes on consumption one might conclude that commodification was rampant. Having said that, recent studies have been steadily pushing the advent of the mass market from the nineteenth to the eighteenth century, and even, although this is more controversial, to the seventeenth century (in the case of London).[58] In this study I highlight that much of the overt critique of Roman and Anglo-Catholic practices as fetishistic appears in objects that were sold, notably, newspapers and novels influenced by Gothic tropes. Belief in the truth of these objects that speak for themselves implies a primitive fetishism returning to those very people who criticised it. In other words, beliefs in fetishism at the heart of Catholicism obscured the operations of *commodity* fetishism. Because sacramental potency provided an alternative means for endowing elements of the material world with value, it was in conflict with the market.

The anxious excitement over the supposed animation of religious objects betrays a deep sense of ambivalence over material culture and betrays 'the uncanniness of things in a society that is simultaneously consumerist and fundamentally anti-materialist, afraid of locating happiness in things'.[59] The question has been posed: 'When did matter come to be seen so dead, and its animation so ghoulish?'[60] It was the very draining of belief from the material world to the immaterial realm (alienation that goes to the essence of commodity fetishism) that left the animation of material objects as increasingly transgressive and as a focus for the melodramatic imagination. The nightmare of subject becoming object haunted the later nineteenth century, as is argued in an interesting paper on mummies coming to life in late Victorian fiction.[61] Consumers feared becoming consumed by their own possessions. In sum, attacks on Catholic material culture functioned to displace fears of commodity fetishism. What was taking place was a 'desperate denial of recognition'.[62]

There is, of course, a third cultural model of fetishism: Freud's notion of the sexual fetish. The notion of sexual fetishism as a form of perverse desire focussing on a material object (other than on the human body as a whole) was advanced by Alfred Binot in 1887. Freud adopted it in 1905, adding a notion of causation that I do not employ in this study, which posited that the fetish object was the substitute for the penis that a boy-child supposed his mother had possessed. The horror of the thought of her castration (lack of penis) and, therefore, the danger of his own possible castration, leads him to create a substitute, this being a fantasy comforting to his narcissism. This substitute is known as somehow unworthy and results in a mixture of 'affection and hostility in the treatment of the fetish'.[63] Freudian insights into the role of the mother as the child's first indicator of otherness and as being the original threat to the self were key to the development of Julia Kristeva's notion of abjection as being a sense of horror at elements of moral and physical dirt that threaten the boundaries of pure selfhood.[64] But whilst she saw the abject as something that troubled everyone through the withdrawal from the mother, Freud regarded sexual fetishism as an exceptional state of compensation for a specific motherly lack.

Recent work has suggested that sexual fetishism is not, in fact, restricted to a deviant minority as Freud thought, but that eroticisation of objects and parts of the body is a feature of most modern forms of sexuality.[65] The legacy of anti-Catholic pornography (discussed in chapter 4) and the erotic associations of (literary) Gothic readings of the Middle Ages (discussed in chapter 5) meant that Protestants might regard those physical objects of Anglo-Catholic culture that looked back to medieval models as being sexually fetishistic: adjuncts, accompaniments, and alternatives to seduction. That sexually fetishistic gaze, of course, was that of the Protestants.[66] Sexual fetishism, thereby, provided the means by which Catholic religion could become abhorrently exciting, and as such, it was open to being commodified as voyeuristic Gothic entertainment through the sale of newspapers, periodicals, plays, tracts, and novels. The market was able to make use of Catholic material culture by its semiotic transformation into saleable texts. In this way, the danger of this threat to the commercial operation of modern society was purged, and 'primitive' magical fetishism was rendered into its modern commodified equivalent.

This is not to say that sincere Protestants were all whole-hearted adherents of the market, but rather that this is a chapter in the history of the interaction of faith in God and belief in the value of commodities. Hawkes has shown how, in seventeenth-century England, there was a 'homology between idolatry and commodity fetishism, insofar as they represent the same tendency of human thought applied to different objects'.[67] He was referring to a strong tradition of Protestant denunciation of beliefs in the autonomous power of money to 'grow' as being a high form of idolatry (i.e., the worship of a product of human hands that stood as a fake in the place of God). There was continued, if reduced, Protestant denunciation of Capital as a form of idolatry in the nineteenth century. However, for Marx, it was not medieval Catholicism, but its 'bourgeois developments, Protestantism, Deism, etc' which fitted best with a commodifying society.[68] Protestants spent so much energy on opposing Catholic externals that they started to forget their own faith in cash. Hawkes talks of a 'blindness' that has fallen on modernity that seems not to have noticed its own worship of commodities.[69] This would be no surprise to classical Marxists, who would point out that commodity fetishism is essentially a system of forgetting in which agency drains away to the commodities themselves.[70]

Hilton has argued of Protestantism, taken in a broad sense, that 'reduced to essentials, it was a contractual religion' in which Heaven was the ultimate merchandise.[71] It is notable, as I show in chapter 3, that businessmen and providers of professional services were prominent amongst the opponents of ritualism. A repeated refrain was of distrust of ostentatious display, which was associated with fraudulent touting for business. Roy Porter provides us with the analogy of attitudes to the performances of quack doctors, who, in another parallel, were also liable to became figures of sexual scandal and critique: 'In a Protestant nation in an age of critical reason...theatricality was widely censured—above all by those of a puritan, reformist, or utilitarian temper—as mindless artifice, magic and mumbo-jumbo, an idolatrous infatuation with tawdry tinsel and specious show'.[72]

An example of this mode of denunciation appears in the squib from 'Nestor Ironside', whose name copies the pseudonym of the satirist Sir Richard Steele, founder of the *Tatler*. 'Nestor', referring to the Roman Catholic leaders in England, denounces 'Wiseman, Ullathorne, & Co.', and complains of the greed of the Church of England in general, and of priests in particular as hucksters out to sell a dud.[73] The services and artefacts of religion, in this view, are worthless in the absence of belief. Marx's point, of course, was that the same could be said of anything in the world of capitalism. His call was to rethink the system of valuation that led to what he viewed as an oppressive and degrading society. In contrast, those who wanted to defend the bourgeois social order against revolution wished for no such recalculation. They wished to reinforce boundaries in society. Religion and science were being judged by the standards of business. The amoral secret of commerce from which distraction was needed was that the most profitable transaction was the most dishonest (that which sells something worthless at the highest cost).

It is also important to pay attention to the precise form of the discourses of denunciation and their relation to wider social pressures and processes (the subject of chapters 4 and 5). Ritualism was widely referred to as a 'pollution' of the purity of Protestant religion. I argue that in order to understand this it is important to engage with the cultural significance and functions of impurity in the nineteenth century. One can think of the prominence of the conception of corruption as deriving from what Anne McClintock, in her *Imperial Leather: Race, Gender and Sexuality in the Colonial Contest* (1995), refers to as 'the peculiarly Victorian paranoia about boundary order'.[74] The English structural anthropologist Mary Douglas has written of the production of disgust in the context of boundary transgressions.[75] Pollution fears are set up to protect vulnerable domains, suggesting the perceived fragility of the then social order. It has been argued, moreover, that the fear comes from transgression presaging the collapse of social rules: 'The problem is not the Douglasian one of things being out of place; it's that there is too much flux for fixed structures to get a grip on all the turmoil'.[76] One response to panic was classification. From social surveys of the slums, to Anglican elaboration of Church parties and comparison between religions we see an explosion of schemes of social categorisation. This proliferation of boundaries, of course, provided the conditions for all manner of new transgressions.[77] Lynda Nead has commented that 'the frame is the site of meaning, where vital distinctions between inside and outside, between proper and improper concerns, are made.'[78] Therefore, the Victorians were filling their world with meaning through the progressive identification of anomalies. Those anomalies were the refuse of the system. If we understand that system to be essentially capitalist, then the anomalous 'dirt' was that which was not yet commodified and saleable.

Dirt need not be worthless. Douglas argues that 'within the ritual frame the abomination is...handled as a source of tremendous power'.[79] It acts to validate the system and its values. Moreover, such garbage can be considered as a store of vital potential, much as various people in the mid-Victorian period schemed to make money by converting human sewage into fertiliser.[80] For the Victorians were not keen simply to classify the low, dirty, and aberrant aspects of their society, but became adept at dreaming up schemes of reformation. Just as sewage on the fields could be seen as in its place but in the streets was an abomination, so ostentatious silver plate could be seen as out of place on the altar but in place on the sideboard. Putting things into place required 'technologies of sanitation', which involved semiotic relabelling: from sewage to fertiliser and from Papist outrage to family heirloom.[81] The crucial point was that the stagnant substance had been brought back into the realm of productive circulation, so that the sewage can fertilise the field and the family silver can be pawned, sold, or inherited. Catholicism was identified as the producer of cultural and commercial anomalies in Victorian England. What was important, in the absence of the opportunity to destroy that Catholicism and appropriate its treasures as had happened at the Reformation, was to find out how to profit from those anomalies.

A crucial factor to bear in mind is that the discovery of dirt also acted to produce the clean. As Alan Robinson has argued, we may 'project our guilty sense of pollution onto scapegoats'.[82] Frank Wallis, one of the authors in the minor industry that is anti-Catholicism studies, has argued that 'theology can be seen as ideology, masking something more fundamental in human behaviour'.[83] He suggests that what took place in Britain was a process of displacement. Protestant patriarchs feared loss of control over their possessions and their women and projected that anxiety onto the persons of greedy and lustful priests. For this strategy to continue to work, of course, it was important that those priests were abused but not destroyed. Anglo-Catholics were an ideal target, even better than Roman Catholics, because they were tainted Protestants; they were a perfect symbol of inner pollution. The legacy of Christian moralism was such that the conceptual model for impurity was sin. This acted to obscure the power of social and economic forms of pollution. The concealed power of commodity fetishism thus directed distress at the progressive loss of autonomy by workers in the capitalist system onto those elements that resisted commodification and denigrated them as sinful, fetishistic, polluting idols. This involved thinking disempowered marginal elements into assuming the status of terrible threats.

If power was substantially dematerialised into money, it is still important to realise that people continued to 'think with things'. Richard Grassby, the author of two major books on capitalism in the cultural life of early modern Britain, has recently published on the relations between 'material culture and cultural history'. He argues against the straightforward reduction by historians of materiality into patterns of signs and emphasises that we need to engage with both objects and symbols.[84] In a parallel comment, Kathleen Canning, in a general survey of recent work on the body, has commented that 'most of these studies merely invoke the body or allow "body" to serve as a more fashionable surrogate for sexuality, reproduction, or gender without referring to anything specifically identifiable as body, bodily or embodied'.[85] I consider bodies to be a crucial element in the material culture of ritualism and its opponents. The tendency to think 'with' the body, such that its operations become a mode through which to understand society, is far from recent. Most famously, Ernst Kantorowicz identified its evolution via the medieval notion of the king's two bodies, the body that dies and that which does not since it is coterminous with the State.[86] Porter has commented that before modernity the socially high had a 'sense of self-contained, self-assured prepossession, utterly unlike the porous permeability of bodies of the low with their gaping mouths and anuses, ever gobbling up too much food and drink, and letting off excessively—farting, shitting, pissing, vomiting, sweating and swearing'.[87] In the aftermath of the French Revolution, by contrast, the high lost their bodily self-assurance. The inadequacies of contemporary medicine, combined with a sharp awareness of Original Sin, acted to undermine confidence in corporeal existence. It was the ostentatious bodiliness of those Catholic 'idols', those hosts, crucifixes, and en-folding robes (ghosts of the body) that gave them such potential as scapegoats for widespread fears of bodily failings.

The Anglo-Catholic body was especially ambivalent and so supremely suit-able as a target onto which to project insecurities. Was it primitive or modern? Was it Protestant or was it Catholic? And was it male or female? The image of Rome as a female prostitute has a long and venerable history, which can be exemplified by works such as Thomas Dekker's *The Whore of Babylon* (1607), which extolled the virtues of Elizabeth I and imputed treachery and bloody in-trigues to the 'Scarlet Whore of Rome'.[88] The Victorian attempt to assert clear differences between the sexes involving the elaboration of the purity of the 'good woman' as the 'angel in the house' meant that 'the underside to this model of femininity in the service of middle class and male gender dominance...[was] the unmanageable woman of resolute and intense desires for emotional grati-fication, sensual bliss, and material finery'.[89] This is precisely the combination of attributes that we see projected onto Catholicism as a masquerade with its roots in the worship of sex.

Disgust at the inescapable presence of unruly sexual desire led to a denun-ciation of the visual promptings to such sin as being an illusion that covers inner filth.[90] As with a poxy whore, one loathed oneself for feeling attracted to her grisly charms. In this aesthetic economy, 'there are no intermediate or transitional stages, only masks that are lifted to reveal the antithesis of the healthy'.[91] Anglo-Catholic practices, such as the use of the confessional, were imagined through a Gothic literary sensibility that left these as spaces of horror and desire. The commoditised world of Gothic fiction and newspaper reports perpetuated such sensational tropes, haunting the reader with the delicious fear of their own complicity, yet providing a reassuring sense that such engage-ment was the result of a mere whim of purse. Fiction, therefore, provided the comforting illusion that death and disease were elsewhere and that you were secure—just a tourist, one may say, in the lower realms. The resulting fanta-sised Catholicism was a freak that could be put to economic use as entertain-ment, so combining psychological convenience with financial profit.

Ritualism, thus, needs to be understood against the wider background of cultural desires centring on health, wealth, and sex. The movement was itself partly an attempt to address some of those pressing issues through trying to recreate premodern patterns of thinking with the material world. I begin this study, therefore, in chapter 2 by exploring the background to the early Victorian emergence of ritualism in the Church of England through a focus on romanti-cism and the Gothic Revival in architecture and its impact on Church furnish-ing. Having explored aspects of the form of Anglo-Catholic ritual, I embark in chapter 3 on a detailed discussion of the events in Knightsbridge and Pimlico in London from 1840 to 1860. I have chosen this as a case study because it provides the most prominent example of the early expression of and opposition to ritualism. This involved rioting, legal cases, and the intervention of the Prime Minister, Lord John Russell, in 1850. In chapter 4 I examine the antiquarian study of comparative religion, including Roman Catholicism, which understood physical expressions of worship in terms of fertility and sex. Then in chapter 5 I explore how these materials were employed in the constructive of sensational saleable narratives.

I regard the visual imagination of both ritualists and their enemies as being of great importance. It would be fascinating to explore other aspects of religious fantasy, such as imaginings of the Reformation, or of practices in Roman Catholic churches in England. However, for current purposes I have had to restrict myself to a specific chronological focus and to the movement that aimed for the Catholicisation of the Church of England (it did not, in the main, aim for the adoption of Roman Catholicism, even though its opponents assumed that this was its purpose). The prominence of fantastic projections of Papal despotism means that the term 'anti-Catholicism', although widespread in the secondary literature, needs to be carefully considered. Its use can be misleadingly essentialising if its employment conceals an important element of Protestant propaganda, that the complexity of Roman Catholicism was nothing more than the sign of intellectual incoherence. When individuals are anti-Catholic, it is crucial to emphasise that they are against the vision of Catholicism that they have in their heads, and this may be very different from reality.

Previous theological study of the Church of England has placed much less emphasis on the visually imaginative projects of ritualism than on the textual engagements of Tractarianism. This is quite reasonable if one's focus is on doctrine. However, in order to take the origins of Anglo-Catholicism seriously, it is vital also to think in terms of material culture, both that of the Church and that of society in general. Sacerdotal religion posed a challenge to capitalism in that it was, amongst other things, potentially a rival system for valuing the material world. This is not to say that Anglo-Catholics were unique in this, but it was their tradition, erupting from the exclusive world of Ecclesiology, that was most insistent in advancing the notion of a single aesthetic system of sacred material culture that was separate and superior to the everyday world of goods. It was this that underlay the claim of John Henry Newman, as put into the mouth of his surrogate convert hero Reding in *Loss and Gain* (1848), that 'surely the idea of an Apostle, unmarried, pure, in fast and nakedness, and at length a martyr, is a higher idea than that of one of the old Israelite sitting under his vine and fig-tree, full of temporal goods, and surrounded by sons and grandsons?'[92] The

Roman Catholic logic from this was that the bone of such an Apostle was not a 'temporal good' subject to the worldly whims of the market, but was a treasure of a very different price. Although the early ritualists did not develop a cult of relics, they did incorporate elements of the sacralisation of artefacts. The pollution that ritualism's embrace of the Ecclesiological sublime brought into the heart of English society was therefore not simply moral but also material and economic, in that, as we have seen expressed in the attitudes of Neale and Webb, it stridently asserted a rival set of material practices to those of the emerging middle classes.

The counter process of demonisation drew upon researches into comparative religion that associated Anglo- and Roman Catholicism with ancient paganism and modern Hinduism, even though ritualism originated in an attempt to recreate medieval English styles in liturgy and architecture rather than to copy those of contemporary Rome. Scurrilous traditions concerning the Whore of Babylon joined with the antiquarian understanding of paganism as a collection of fertility cults to suggest a highly sexualised image of Rome as the oriental Other. That fantasy of oriental despotism was crucial in transforming the actions of ritualists into a site of exotic pleasure that could be profitably exploited by the rapidly expanding publishing industry. Ultimately, this is a study of the (re)discovery of premodern modes of understanding aspects of the material world as sacred and the ways in which these were, after a struggle, profitably accommodated within a world of traded goods and services.

2

Art and Sacrament

Ritualism was powerfully inspired by a desire to recreate the visual and material forms of medieval worship in art, artefact, and architecture. It therefore plays a role in a larger, widely documented phenomenon known as the 'Gothic Revival'.[1] The modern consensus seems to be that Gothic, as a style of art and decoration, never quite died out in England. The stretching upward of the Romanesque arch was, driven by enthusiasm for elaboration, structure, height, and light, of sufficient allure that the competing claims of perfect classical proportion were never to entirely displace it in the early modern period. The authority of past traditions was something upon which various power blocks in society attempted to seize. The spell of antiquity was felt by ecclesiastical revivalists of various persuasions. For example, George Reginald Balleine, in his classic history of the evangelicals, talking of Wesley's early enthusiasm, said that 'probably most earnest men, who take an interest in theology, pass through a stage in which they feel strongly the glamour of Antiquity... to the end of his life Wesley was a Patristic student; he translated the Apostolic Fathers for the use of his preachers'.[2] In the absence of obvious architectural parallels from early Christian antiquity, those interested in the material evocation of the Christian past turned to the medieval churches that were scattered across Britain. That much of the appeal was romantic and aesthetic should not blind us to other resonances of Gothic style. The origins of the neo-medieval style in eighteenth-century domestic architecture lay not merely in the whims of aristocratic frivolity as has sometimes been suggested in the case of Strawberry Hill. It has been argued for the eighteenth-century Gothic rebuilding of Arbury Hall in Warwickshire, for example, that 'there is nothing light, frivolous or theatrical about Newdegate [sic: the owner, Sir Roger Newdigate, 1719–1806], nor is there about his house'.[3] Statesmen, in an age of developing nationalism, could discover in Gothic a more clearly national style than was to be found in the importation of classical models from Italy. Furthermore, the popular invention of a heroic 'age of Saxon freedom' helped to counteract negative images of the 'dark ages' that were a favourite retort of the proselytes of classical architecture.[4]

If the decorative style was associated with national pride in the eighteenth century, the moral and religious aspects of the Gothic style were to receive a major boost from the work of A. W. N. Pugin (1812–52). Pugin's effect was to magnify associations between Gothic and Catholicism in the minds of hostile Protestants. He was, arguably, the 'towering figure of the Gothic Revival'.[5] He grew up a Protestant and his exalted view of Gothic as the spiritually preeminent style was a romantic English, not an Italian Catholic, idea, for in Rome the Counter-Reformation had been expressed through baroque, and this was the focal element in ultramontine architectural influence.[6] Despite the best attempts of Pugin, it was to be the Anglicans rather than the Romanists who would most sincerely take his ideas to their hearts.[7]

Pugin was also out on a Roman limb in other ways. A High Tory in politics, he feared a destabilised society and was not fond of the Irish. His concern for contemplation and unworldliness in devotion also ran counter to a rising Roman enthusiasm for emotion, engagement, and evangelism. Cardinal Nicholas Wiseman (1802–65), archbishop of Westminster, emphasised that decorative style was predominantly a matter of taste and that the practical needs of the modern Church must predominate. Rather than being rooted in the financial realities of building new churches in a cost-effective manner, Pugin, 'as well as being a loyal Catholic, was above all a dreamer of dreams'.[8] Classical architecture was for him 'pagan', even at St. Peter's in Rome, which he thought distinctly inferior because of its style. He regretted bitterly it being 'popularly regarded as the *ne plus ultra* of a Catholic Church'.[9] Similarly, expensive new Catholic churches in Ireland were 'full of trash' because they were incorrectly designed and fitted out. Moreover, he said of much Roman Catholic ritual in England that 'men of devout minds are scandalized with the foreign trumpery that is introduced on the most solemn occasions, and the noisy theatrical effects that are substituted for the solemn chants and hymns of the Church.'[10] By contrast, he extolled the virtues of an imagined Middle Ages: '[M]en must learn that the period hitherto called dark and ignorant far excelled our age in wisdom'.[11] In *The True Principles of Pointed or Christian Architecture* (1841), Pugin examined the structural forms of Gothic and Gothic decoration in more detail. The aim was 'truth': 'The severity of Christian or Pointed architecture is utterly opposed to all deception.... Cheap deceptions of magnificence encourage persons to assume a semblance of decoration far beyond either their means or their station.... Glaring, showy, and meretricious ornament was never so much in vogue as at present'.[12] His identification was with English Catholic traditions rather than with those of the Continent. He said that despite the traumas of three centuries, Catholicism still clung to the land as its essential spirit.[13] As Pugin wrote to his patron, Lord Shrewsbury, in 1843: I have 'just [been] in the old retired Catholic part of Staffordshire full of aborigins [sic] Catholics.... I went to the cemetery at White Ladies...no Protestant has ever polluted the consecrated ground'.[14] For Pugin, that traditional landscape could be brought back to life, but only when building was carried out in the best of (moral) taste.

Wiseman was not alone among prominent Roman Catholics in thinking that Pugin's prejudices were ultimately expressions of the 'insular and anti-Roman [i.e. anti-ultramontane] attitudes which as Cardinal he was to overcome.'[15] Despite such opposition, Pugin was able to look with some qualified satisfaction on the progress of new designs, for example, in articles from the *Dublin Review* reprinted as *The Present State of Ecclesiastical Architecture* (1841).[16] But he appears never to have lost that sense of urgency that came out most strongly in *Contrasts; Or, A Parallel between the Noble Edifices of the Fourteenth and Fifteenth Centuries, and Similar Buildings of the Present Day* (1836, 2nd ed. 1841), which has been described as 'one of the nineteenth century's most heartfelt and anguished responses to the Industrial Revolution'.[17] In this work he emphasised that what was required was not simply a decorative style for a church, but also the correct liturgical forms.[18] Chris Brooks emphasizes the elements of polemic and satire in Pugin's tremendous effort of architectural evangelisation as he ridiculed those who failed to commission and design the architectural sublime.[19] His vision was one of artists transfixed by faith, building churches in cities that were pastoral communities rather than ravaged industrial landscapes. David Watkin has traced the history of moralizing architecture, that desire to get away from 'mere style', from Pugin through to modernism.[20] Watkin talks of the 'unreality' of Pugin's project.[21] It was indeed an exercise in the visual imagination. Pugin was thinking, according to Nicola Coldstream, in a 'medieval way', focussing on the building's theological meaning and liturgical use rather than on cost-effectiveness.[22] These buildings were conceived, with their fittings and congregations, as morally transcendent and complete works of art. In principle, this was perfectly orthodox. The Roman Catholic bishop of Charleston, John England, writing from the Irish College in Rome, expressed the general views of his denomination that a church was 'a Christian temple erected for the purpose of having the holy sacrifice of the mass offered therein'.[23] But the Roman Church in England was poor, and Pugin never enjoyed commissions of the scale he would have liked.

Nevertheless, the Roman openness to art can be seen from the publications of Wiseman. Invited to give a talk at an Islington supper club, the cardinal talked of 'Rome, classical, but heathen on the one hand, Rome, artistic and Christian, on the other'.[24] And, at the opening of the Catholic Institute in Liverpool in 1843, he made a strenuous attempt to connect the development of art and commerce, arguing that the artistic revival of the thirteenth century was the result of the 'happy generosity of a commercial people, who sought out whatever was good in every country and brought it home . . . the ways of art, have ever been the ways of peace, and she has travelled hand in hand with commerce which peace has created'.[25] Moreover, he detected a harmony of beauty, rather than a process of contestation, between word and image. The Bible was 'a volume, beautiful and sacred, in which the whole love of the East for nature's beauties was expressed, but with subordination to a higher love'.[26] For Wiseman, language was more 'material' in comparison with the 'evanescent, the imponderable, the impalpable, the ethereal, element of thought'.[27] In his imagination, therefore, the spiritual and the material were blended rather than opposed. His was a vision that transcended a narrowly sectarian approach to visuality and visual styles.

Such serene broadness of vision was not something that can be associated with the Cambridge Camden ('Ecclesiological') Society, which was founded in May 1839 by a group of Anglican students. As the self-appointed vehicle of 'correctness' in the revival of Gothic, the ecclesiologists found for themselves a moment of stylistic perfection, the first decade of the fourteenth century, which they referred to as the 'Early Late Middle Pointed' (!). What might be thought of as a matter of taste was, for John Mason Neale (1818–66), leading light of the society, 'a discipline akin to a holy science'.[28] For example, a pamphlet of 1841 designed as a 'preface' to *Designs for Churches* stressed that 'however great the offence may be, which the Catholick arrangement of a Chancel causes, we must bear it rather than give up an arrangement which is of the essence in a Church'.[29]

There is much debate about the precise relationships between the three predominantly Anglican phenomena of Tractarianism, Ecclesiology, and ritualism. They are clearly not interchangeable but they were interrelated. Adherents of all these movements tended to be critical of Low Church and Dissenting traditions that disagreed with sacramental approaches and elaboration of the liturgy and its attendant apparatus. There was a shared reference to ancient authority, although ritualism followed Ecclesiology in stressing the visual styles of the high Middle Ages rather than those of the early Church. Members of the society were exhorted to take archaeological care for their churches, treat them with reverence, preserve old features, and not have things amended for the comfort of the congregation.[30] Innovations had to be carefully handled. 'I hope your organ is in the right place?' is a typical question (it should be at the west end).[31]

The Camden Society's programme was understood as the careful exploration of medieval building traditions and attitudes to architecture. It was this impulse that led Neale and Benjamin Webb (1819–85) to translate the first book of the canon lawyer William Durandus's (c. 1237–96) *Rationale Divinorum Officiorum*. They employed his text to advocate a symbolic approach to architectural and liturgical forms. Furthermore, they wished to argue that craft should not be a way to make money, but an act of worship.[32] They advocated truth to materials and the principle of meaning in structure and ornament. One might think that this would place them as close allies of Pugin, despite the fact that the Camden Society was firmly Anglican. Indeed, he designed the great seal of the Society (with the crowned Virgin and Child at its centre) and stated that it had done more to revive true architecture than all the antiquaries of the last decades.[33] However in debt it was to him for his drawings and ideas, the society, in public at least, was, however, 'personally friendly, but officially cautious'.[34] Neale and Webb were critical, for example, of Pugin's advocacy of Gothic domestic decoration, arguing that stylistic 'elevation' was specifically sacramental since 'contact with the Church endues with a new sanctity, and elevates every form and every principle of art'.[35] Moreover, the ecclesiologists did not follow Pugin in the idea that only a good Roman Catholic could build a good Roman Catholic church.[36]

Anti-Catholic prejudice as well as occasional social snobbery may have been visited on Pugin by the ecclesiologists, but they, in turn, were far from receiving unanimous support from the Roman Catholic side. For example, the celebrated French Catholic historian and glorifier of the traditions of the medieval Church, Charles de Montalembert (1810–70), angrily rejected their offer of honorary membership.[37] He said that the Camden Society, in its rejection of Rome and simultaneous embrace of medieval architecture was involved in the deeply dishonest mission of constructing a 'new and fictitious Catholicism'.[38]

Nor were a number of Protestants any more enthusiastic, for quite different reasons. For the strongly evangelical Francis Close (1797–1882), then perpetual curate of Holy Trinity, Cheltenham, the Camden Society was the agent of Popery, for as 'Romanism is taught *Analytically* at Oxford, it is taught *Artistically* at Cambridge'. According to him, medieval churches were the last model to follow since they had been built for 'orgies of superstition!'[39] This perception was fateful. It was to ensure that the ritualists' models derived from medieval England, mediated via the ecclesiologists and Pugin, were popularly mistaken for copies of 'typical' Roman Catholic practice, which was by no means the case.

The stand of the Camden Society was uncompromising in the face of Roman Catholic, Low Church, and Dissenting criticism. The visual agenda, the product of medievalism, romanticism, and love of decoration in general and of symbolic forms such as the cross in particular, can be seen in published splendour in James Barr, *Anglican Church Architecture with Some Remarks upon Ecclesiastical Furniture* (first published 1842).[40] This luxurious volume radiated and displayed the values expressed in its text through its elaborate, coloured and engraved material form. The new agenda of ecclesiastical splendour is very clear. Go to a meeting house, we are informed by the Anglican clergyman, editor, and antiquarian Henry Christmas (1811–68), and there, all 'that makes worship sensuous, without making it sensual, has disappeared; the link that bound, as it were, the soul and the body in one act of devotion is snapped, and an attempt is made to establish a purely spiritual worship'. There are two traditions, 'one which attempts to purify the devotion, by abstracting it from all earthly objects; the other, which hallows earthly objects, by regarding them from a symbolical point of view, gathering them within the sphere, and making them accessory to the strength of its devotion'. This was not, however, a battle between art and its absence, but for an elevatedly Christian art. For instance, the same author ridiculed the admirals and generals, sea-dogs, tritons, and 'Britannia in every possible attitude, [which] adorn the interior of that particularly Protestant church, St. Paul's [Cathedral], in London'.[41]

It has been argued that the core of the Camden Society was Tractarian, even if some of its followers were not.[42] The Gothic Revival at the time appealed most to Anglicans, who were members of the denomination with the oldest churches in England and who, therefore, stood most to gain from the idolization of this style of architecture. The traditional view has been to downplay the interest of the Tractarians in art and architecture. John Shelton Reed has argued against this position, for example, discussing the jewelled liturgical service that was made according to a Camden Society design for Edward Pusey (1800–82) when his daughter died of tuberculosis at the age of fifteen in 1844. The plate used the girl's own jewellery together with additions given by the rest of the family, and finally employed more than two hundred gems, including diamonds, rubies, emeralds, and pearls. According to Reed, Pusey was wary of self-exaltation by the minister, rather than against liturgical splendour in general.

John Henry Newman (1801–90), whilst still an Anglican, called for more vestments and decorations. It is suggested that he was 'not hostile to ceremonial and decorative innovation; [but] he seems simply not to have been very interested in the subject'.[43] Nevertheless, he had a highly aestheticised theology, assuming a 'direct parallel between religious and aesthetic experience'.[44] He did see art as playing the role of the servant of religion.[45] Edward Wells's treatise of the early eighteenth century on the duty of the rich to build churches was reprinted in 1840 with an introduced by Newman in which he said that it was timely to do so, since

> rare and beautiful substances, the substances which He has scattered through the material world,—excellent in themselves, and brought to perfection by what is equally His providing, the genius and skill of man,—being by creation parts of a great natural temple so, when wrought by human art, rightfully belong to those spiritual shrines.[46]

William Bennett (1804–86), the early ritualist who plays a key role in the events described in the next chapter, denied that there was any such thing as mere ornament, but that beauty and usefulness were normally and naturally combined. He compared the complexity of the ritualist mass to the wing of an insect as representing a piece of both the beautiful and functional wonder that is Creation. That exaltation of the world was set forth in the altars of the Old Testament, and throughout the medieval Church and was an echo or image of heaven. In his view the close of the Middle Ages was when things, liturgically, went too far, for example, in the provision of many altars in a church rather than one.[47] For one Ecclesiological writer, Bennett's church, St. Paul's, Knightsbridge, which had just been consecrated, was 'deficient in many points of architectural propriety' but overall a great improvement on the usual run of building works in the capital. The comment, 'let Dissenters and evangelicals run up their cheap preaching-houses, but let Churchmen offer to God the best they have', is certainly a sentiment with which Bennett would have agreed.[48]

Ritualists, like Pugin, were concerned to ensure a precise combination of architecture, art and ritual. Bennett commented of the resulting visual effect that 'sometimes the sight of the altar, and those decent preparations for the work of devotion may compose and recover the mind much more effectively than a sermon'.[49] Yet he was no Romanist. He lauded the Reformation but described it in distinctively materialist terms, as being like refurbishing a building, as it were, like your 'ancient hereditary castle'. Thus, he defended what he saw as the practices prevalent under King Edward VI (reigned 1547–53) and distinguished them from later 'vandalism'. Writing a series of texts dedicated to his offspring, he says:

> Let us go together, my dear children, into some fine old church of what is generally termed the Gothic architecture. You will always know this style of architecture by the pointed arch. Do not heed those churches with square windows, or with porticoes before them; they

are sure to be modern churches, and their study will not repay you, neither will they furnish you with any of the ecclesiastical uses of a church, being generally poor and mean in spiritual things.[50]

So even though Bennett was not an Ecclesiologist, he was certainly a 'Goth' and an ecclesiastical aesthete, as the architectural style of the St. Barnabas' complex, described in chapter 3, confirms.

The relationship between word and image was to be highly problematic even within the spectrum of Anglican High Churchmen: George Herring argues that 'there was a realization among the Tractarians that some had been attracted to their movement for the wrong reasons; for these people the Oxford Movement stood more for the holiness of beauty than for the beauty of holiness'.[51] Indeed, from 1861 there were art object exhibitions at each Anglo-Catholic Church Congress.[52] Opponents dismissed ritualism as superficially ornamental, but it is important to stress that the movement was not about art for art's sake. It was about communication through a range of symbolic sensual forms: art, and architecture, movement, singing and those infamous 'bells and smells'. But it was not, as the above account aims to emphasise, the same thing as Roman Catholicism, even in material, let alone doctrinal terms.

For some Protestants, religious art in any form was a delusion, and Michael Hobart Seymour, the Church of Ireland priest whom we met in the introduction, for one, was swift to denounce religious images as the 'last extreme of knavish priestcraft'.[53] The novelist Lady Sydney Morgan (c. 1783–1859), meanwhile, condemned neo-Gothic as a blasphemous, effeminate pantomime: 'The medieval times! Which work up so well in the picturesque architecture of Boudoir-Churches, got up by fashionable *Decorateurs*'.[54] For Thomas Paley, Rector of Ufford in Lincolnshire, only faith mattered since 'whoever holds this truth in sincerity will be saved, whether he build thereon gold and silver and precious stone, or wood, hay, and stubble'.[55] Those who enjoyed the things of this world, including its visual splendours, Matthew Guthrie argued, are all worldly people and they will not enjoy heaven. They will be bored by the spiritual paradise formed of the 'Word'. Such an inheritance will be for them 'like the gift of a noble library to a plumed painted savage'. Heaven is for the (in this case Free Church of Scotland) elect: 'The heaven that purifies the saint would but exasperate the hatred of the sinner'.[56] Others were more moderate. One account, although arguing that the world of 'ceremonies, of types, and shadows' was for the Jews who were still waiting for the Good News, continued by stating that 'there is a danger of carrying this sentiment [of hostility to externals in the context of worship] too far, so as to set aside convenient and decent places for the worship of Almighty God'.[57] Moreover, it was simply not true that all Dissenters and evangelicals refused to use images. For instance, in the United States, evangelicals of the earlier nineteenth century had used didactic art as a tool in conversion, and had also used engravings to educate children.[58] But images were ever liable to be interrogated for the presence and correctness of their moral message. Aesthetic elements were prone to be challenged. Colour, for instance, was often 'considered immoral...because it is an immediate sensation and makes its effect independently of those ordered memories which are the basis of morality'.[59] Beyond this, art and ornament suffered from a gendered comparison with structure and form, such that the former was held to be feminine and the latter masculine. As such, an anonymous Protestant advised, '[L]et decoration always give place to the indispensable requirements of strength and space' when it comes to architectural design.[60] Morals and emotional temperaments were read and classified from physical and facial appearances. And, since it was widely apprehended that 'all Beauty is a reflection of the moral character of God, which is perfect, [and] so all Deformity is the reflection of the evil arising from the fall of man', severe limits were placed on the reception of visual impressions that deviated from a standard code of what was deemed pleasant.[61]

Ritualists wished to produce a perfect form of worship that would do full honour to God, and, it is true, their inspiration did sometimes come from the art and architecture of continental Roman Catholicism, but they were not alone in having such interests. Few people can have spent more time or energy in discovering how to reconcile the beauty of that visual culture with Protestant morality than John Ruskin (1819–1900), who was converted to the value of Catholic art but not to its theology. In his *Seven Lamps of Architecture* (1849), we find the evangelical conviction that the Church does not need splendours, indeed 'her purity is in some degree opposed to them'. He found such ostentation to be 'surface work...danger and evil...in its tinsel and glitter, in the gilding of the shrine and painting of the image, in embroidering of dingy robes and crowding of imitated gems; all this being thrust forward to the concealment of what is really good or great in their buildings'.[62] Yet four years later, in the *Stones of Venice* (1853) Ruskin is found musing, albeit hidden in an appendix, about the meaning of idolatry. He reproves 'the ordinary Protestant manner of regarding those ceremonies as distinctively idolatrous, and as separating the Romanist from the Protestant Church by a gulf across which we must not look at our fellow Christians but with utter reprobation and disdain'. If Idolatry concerns anything that stands between us and God then, 'which of us is not an idolater? Which of us has the right...to speak scornfully of any of his brethren, because, in a guiltless ignorance, they have been accustomed to bow their knees before a statue?'[63] This is by no means a charter for Romanism. In fact, he avers that the Roman Catholics ignore many of the visual splendours of St. Mark's in

Venice.[64] Nevertheless, Ruskin's change of heart, which occurred in the midst of the tumultuous events that are the subject of chapter 3, was one factor that helped to persuade elements of mainstream opinion in England toward the acceptance of sacred art and associated ritual.

Ritualism

Having explored the Gothic revival and its connections with Roman and emerging Anglo-Catholicism, we can now turn to sacred objects and the liturgy. Churches were locations for holy ritual, or for its violation, the details of which can be deduced from surviving remains and contemporary writings. However, we might want to bear in mind Philippe Buc's warning that 'there can be no anthropological readings of rituals depicted in medieval texts, but only anthropological readings of medieval textual practices'.[65] If this is true for medieval Gothic churches, it might be equally so for the Victorian discourses, practices, and artefacts of Anglo-Catholicism. The behaviour of the congregation is likely to have conformed to patterns of decorum both inside and outside the church, even if this is not identified in any of the texts as ritual behaviour. Some work has been done for modern Britain that attempts to examine what might be termed the wider ritual impulse in society by positing Christian liturgies as one of a series of categories of elaborate communal repeated behaviour with assigned cultural meanings.[66] In fact, the notion that elaborate performance was not simply something for Roman Catholics and foreigners was recognised in the nineteenth century. As the Anglo-Catholic priest Frederick George Lee (1832–1902) put it, 'it is sometimes asserted that the English as a nation dislike ceremonial. But this statement can hardly be adopted by those who remember how cordially any royal pageant or public ceremony is approved and witnessed by multitudes'.[67] Nevertheless, when I am talking in this chapter about English ritual, I am referring to a set of liturgical practices within the Anglican Church that have come to be known as 'ritualism', to textual traditions concerning it, as well as discussing, on occasion, the general use of ritual in society.

The effect of the Anglo-Catholic movement, both in terms of its own activities and the backlash it triggered off, was spectacular. Newman expressed the sense of the radical liturgical changes that were already taking place across England when he wrote, in his conversion novel *Loss and Gain* (1848), that 'every year brings changes and reforms. We do not know what is the state of Oxley Church now; it may have rood-loft, piscina, sedilia, all new; or it may be reformed backwards, the seats on principle turning from the Communion-table, and the pulpit planted in the middle of the aisle'.[68] This quotation appears to suggest that there were equal movements of change for and against the agenda laid down by the Camden Society, however, the use of the word 'backwards' is revealing. For Newman, the way forward was not toward the preaching house model of worship. In general, innovation was running in the direction of greater Catholicism.

The word 'ritualism' first appears in *The Times* in the printed letter of acceptance of December 9, 1850, by Charles Blomfield (1786–1857), bishop of London, of William Bennett's resignation as a result of antiritualist prejudice as will be explained in chapter 3.[69] Much of the groundwork for recovering a more elaborate liturgy had been laid by William Palmer (1803–85) of Worcester College, Oxford, in his *Origines Liturgicae* (1832), which was the product of antiquarian enthusiasm.[70] This book traced the ancient texts and traditions that underlay the practice of the Church of England and became so widely employed that a primer for students based on it appeared in 1850.[71] But what had begun as a romantic search for the ancient historical roots of Anglican practices soon became the subject of major controversy. The background to this was, of course, the Roman Catholic nature of much of the Christian past. However, many people failed to see ritualism as a recovery of the past as much as an importation of foreignness. These claims were only fostered when Wiseman was found writing to the Earl of Shrewsbury that not only were some Anglicans becoming keen on Roman Catholic practices but 'our rites and ceremonies, our offices, nay, our very rubrics, are precious in their eyes—far, alas! beyond what many of us consider them'. William Blackley (1798–1885), quoting all of these, used them to build his case for the dangers of the enemy within in relation to the aims of the reestablishment of the Roman Catholic episcopal hierarchy in Britain.[72] His was simply one of a wide range of tracts that were little more than variants on a theme. Ritualism, for many English Protestants was an inner impurity that was the result of Roman Catholic contamination of Anglican ideas, practices, and persons.

It was in the aftermath of these disturbances that ritualism as a term started to be widely used. By the middle of the 1850s, we find the American Congregationalist John Sidney Davenport referring to 'ritualism (so-called)' and alleging that 'the movement has in this country failed'.[73] Even in England the ritualists were indeed very much a small minority. In 1853 it was estimated by W. J. Conybeare (1815–57), then vicar of Axminster, that Tractarians were but 1,000 clergy out of 16,000, and those who practiced the liturgical innovations of ritualism were far fewer.[74] Nevertheless, those who favoured novelty were becoming bolder. By the mid-1860s, references were being made to the new menace of 'extreme' or 'ultra' ritualism.[75]

What ritualism was should be differentiated from what its opponents said it was. The legal cases discussed in chapter 3 provide the key definitions of the legal bases of ritual innovation (or restoration, if seen from a ritualist viewpoint). The responses of ritualists to Protestant criticism tended initially toward the defensive but became steadily more confident as time went on. Reed has given a striking picture of Anglo-Catholicism as almost like a countercultural youth movement, busy with its own arcane rules. Meanwhile, sisterhoods provided a way in which women, unable to become priests, could still embrace ritualism and rebel against parental marriage designs. These people were often the sons and daughters of the well-off who had grown up surrounded by fine furnishings. Yet they sought morally to transcend their origins through embracing such causes as the campaign against box pews that was explicitly designed to undermine the public trappings of secular rank through the abolition of private seating areas in church for the rich.[76] As Robert Liddell (1808–88), the ritualist who played a leading role in the legal cases discussed in chapter 3, put it: 'We hope that the *social relations* between all the classes of our community are gradually becoming *more close and intimate*, as the real character of our Spiritual brotherhood is brought out by our frequent acts of worship, and communion in the Blessed Sacrament of Christ's Body and Blood'.[77]

Anglo-Catholics had several stock responses to criticism. One of these was to assert that ritual was inevitable; as the Tractarian Walter Farquhar Hook, at that time vicar of Leeds, emphasised, even Quakers had ritual since 'two or three cannot assemble together for one and the same purpose, without observing some form'.[78] Those who argued for primitive simplicity asserted that there was a ritual 'more or less solemn or circumstantial' in the early Church. After all, what else was the Last Supper but an invitation to ritual commemoration? The book of Revelation did not have to be read to indicate the destruction of material things at the end of time. It could be interpreted to mean that there would be 'striking elements of a visible and audible worship' in heaven.[79] Moreover, those who objected to symbols could be refuted with the argument that nature, which was the creation of God, was full of symbols: '[I]t can be no good excuse for neglecting the use of it to say that many fail to see, or rather that few are able to discern in Art, the hidden meanings' because nature is full of them.[80]

Bennett, the most prominent early ritualist in London, was always adamant that he was not an apologist for Rome, simply observing that

> there had arisen in the English Church an important and prevailing
> party, deriving their strength principally from a revival of the ancient

discipline of the Church in her dogmatic teaching, her privileges as derived from the apostolic succession, and her beauty in the external features of public worship in ritual and order.[81]

Nevertheless, his position moved steadily away from the mainstream Anglicanism of the time. As early as 1845 he could be found arguing that the Reformation was purifying, but that the ensuing simplification of ritual had gone too far, for as 'the garment warms, protects and sustains the body, so outward rites, duly observed, help forward, and sustain the Church; warm, and, as it were, clothe her'.[82] He confessed to having been inspired by Blomfield's qualified call of 1842 for a return to earlier customs of the Church, which helps to explain the bitterness of his feelings of betrayal in 1850 when he was forced to resign.[83] He notably ignored the claims of Dissenters. He observed that 'we find the Christian religion in this country to consist of two principal divisions, both calling themselves Catholic' (i.e., Anglo-Catholics and Roman Catholics), thus leaving many Anglicans and all nonconformists out of the picture altogether.[84]

It is very interesting to compare two manuscripts by Bennett that are now in Lambeth Palace Library. Both are instructions for the Eucharist. One of them is in English.[85] The other is in Latin, with the major sections in English to be spoken out loud pasted in, as in the following section:

> according to thy Son our Saviour Jesus Christ's holy institution,
> in remembrance of his death and passion, we may be partakers
> of the most blessed Body and Blood:
> (signat super Hostiam et super Calicem)
> who in the same night that he was betrayed,
> (accipit Hostiam)
> took Bread; and when he had given thanks,
> (elevat oculos ad colum)
> He brake it
> (frangit in duas partes).[86]

It is important to note that the acts to be performed were written out in Latin. In other words, Bennett wanted to perform the service in the language of early English Christianity but was forced to do so in English, for to do otherwise would have seemed to be too 'Roman'. One might compare this with certain contemporary hostile views of Latin and Greek as 'dead languages' the use of which in church was designed to hide the truth from the congregation.[87]

Such care over the spoken words of the liturgy should, Bennett thought, be accompanied by great care with its material forms. He noted that it is sometimes said that external rites were mere shadows, and 'it is true, a shadow is nothing;

but when the sun shines forth in its brightness, and I see no shadow, I shall be compelled to pronounce that there is no substance there either'. And similarly, he agreed that ceremonies were nothing, 'but where there are no ceremonies, no order, no uniformity, no obedience, there too, very quickly, there will be no religion'.[88] He was utterly dismissive of Dissenters who 'say that nothing but the inward mind need be attended to, the body is superfluous. Things external they hold in absolute contempt, churches and architecture, and holiness of *place* they do not esteem'.[89] Such people were not simply mistaken; they were also hypocrites, since all Christians had needed sort of physical framework for worship. Just imagine the reaction, he says, were we 'to rush violently into some Dissenter's chapel...and end by some gross act of personal destruction of their property'. It was only the truly ungodly that 'pass by the house of God, [and] darkly and malignantly scowl upon it'.[90] What mattered was the complete ritual performance in all its aspects, textual, performative, and architectural. Thus, he had a vision of a practice of religion in which material forms were essential and integral forms of belief and understanding.

The continuing influence of Bennett's values can be seen from the writings of James Skinner (1818–81), who was curate from 1851 to 1857 at St. Barnabas', Pimlico, the ritualist church founded by Bennett. Like Bennett he delivered trenchant criticisms of Rome and referred to conversions thence as 'perversions'. Similarly, he was learned, relished Latin, and prayed that divisions between the Churches should decline.[91] And he was adamantly in favour of ritual. His *Why Do We Praise Externals in the Service of God?* (1856) was published by the request of both of the then churchwardens, G. Evans and A. Sutherland Graeme. It had originally been preached at St. Barnabas' during advent week 1855. The published text begins with a letter of the churchwardens that explains 'the motives which induce us to seek to retain those symbolical articles of furniture, which have been in the late judgment [of the ecclesiastical courts—discussed in chapter 3] condemned'. Skinner asserts that 'I do not care a straw for any of the things in question, save as they exhibit and set forth great and solemn truths, which I would rather die than yield'. Magnificent ritual is essential since 'you must be grossly ignorant of the nature and necessities of your own race, if feeling the *indispensable* need of a court for a king, you are unwilling to own the much greater need of pomp, and circumstance, and dignity, for the worship of God'. It is, moreover, quite wrong to even think about the legitimate boundaries of the use of physical props since 'the law of love shuts out forever that niggard calculation of essentials and non-essentials which so paralyses all worship. You cannot classify things sacred into essentials and non-essentials, as you do created things into animate and inanimate'. The only determinant of what was suitable was in the presence or absence of symbolic meaning.

Skinner is quite clear that 'there is nothing in this Church of ours for instance, which is not significant. We utterly disown ornaments for show'. Everything in the Church was ordained so as to teach us a lesson.[92] Ecclesiastical material culture, therefore, was both a sublime and an improving text.

The aim of the glories of creation was, thus, to teach us lessons of goodness, not to enable us to revel in fleshliness, since there was most definitely a serpent in Skinner's Garden of Eden. As he commented a couple of years later, in 1857:

> The disease of unclean lust may be not simply a malady, but a griev-
> ous complex affliction, including well nigh all other evils in life:
> begun, haply, through the unguarded eye, but fostered by the itching
> ear, and sustained by unchaste looks at self, and horrible sweet pollu-
> tions of the body by the hand—in the waking choice of evil thoughts,
> or the unresisted assaults of dreams...virgins are stolen away,
> families are desolated, parents are hurried to the grave, thousands of
> helpless dishonoured women after having lived in reckless crime die
> in hopeless neglect, thousands of little innocents are made away with
> by a death that prevents birth.[93]

The Church in its beauty was not the expression of hidden turpitude, as opponents claimed, but was the only defence against moral ugliness and horror. We must see turpitude not in vestments and the liturgy, but in the desiring body: '[S]ee in it a plague and a burden, and throw it off with tears and deep contrition. O Christians! What can be a burden needing the special provision of the Church—confession and absolution—if this be not?' The seriousness of this situation required that one embrace asceticism and subdue the body: we must 'pray on the cold floor!' Salvation was no joking matter. Christians were exhorted to avoid double entendres, those 'forms of speech which are thought witty and amusing, because of their double meaning' but which would lead thoughts toward impurity. One should admire the natural world with a loving not a lustful gaze, otherwise lusting men would destroy and vain women would fall in the same manner as so many of their predecessors:

> too conscious of the attractions they possessed...they became prey
> to the flatterer and destroyer. Instead of living and dying as the pride
> of their families and the blessing of their neighbours—abandoned
> by the cruelty of man and blasted by the breath of sin—they have
> become the noisome pollution which you see them now.[94]

The ritualist position was to engage with these realities through hearing confessions and setting up missions to save prostitutes, although their opponents accused them of being tainted by those very acts of compassion.

Bennett, in his *Farewell Letter*, issued in 1851 when he had been ousted from his parish, provided a resounding and heavily emotional reassertion of his values. Against the contention that he had been a Romanising force, he argued that 'men have mistaken the essential spirit of the teaching of Catholicy, based on the knowledge of the human heart in its weakness and its needs, for Rome'. And he adamantly defied attempts to denigrate externals. '*You* may make it plain', he commented, '*I* may make it beautiful. *You* put brick walls, whitewashed; *I* may paint and gild it' [emphasis original]. He had been impelled by the desire to restore the ancient customs of the Church that celebrated the world as the Creation. His practice had been 'aesthetic teaching', that is 'teaching by the imagination'. Yet churches were not theatres, for 'our representation paints a reality, and that of the stage a fiction'.[95]

Andrew Greeley has published a study called the *Catholic Imagination* (2000). He comments that Roman 'Catholicism in its better moments feels instinctually that nature does not defile spirit but reveals it'. Moreover, the Catholic imagination 'tends to emphasise the metaphorical nature of creation', in other words that the visual world is a code and we should learn from it.[96] This is not to say that Greeley's claims are incontestable, nor that they are untrue of other denominations, but it was insights such as these that informed Bennett and his colleagues.

If one wishes to gain an overview of the resulting liturgical and aesthetic culture, a good place to start is the *Directorium Anglicanum* (figure 2.1). This text was compiled by John Purchas (1823–72), at that time curate first of Elsworth and then of Orwell in Cambridgeshire, before the results of *Westerton v. Liddell* (discussed in chapter 3). As a result of the final legal judgement in that case, Purchas had to make only one small amendment (on the issue of lace edgings on altar cloths), a fact indicative of the remarkable coherence of much ritualist opinion at this date. The printed text is obviously, and ostentatiously, archaising, for instance, in the use of the obsolete form of the printed 'S' as in 'Englifh'. As the text says, 'the argument for a ritual is not within the fcope of thefe remarks. We *have* a ritual, and muft ufe it, whether we like it or not...Ritual and Ceremonial are the hieroglyphics of the Catholic religion, a language underftanded of the faithful, a kind of parable in action'. The 'modern' precision with which the 'ancient' liturgical instructions are set down is illuminated by the comment that 'ritualifm is a fcience as well as theology'. For example, item forty-eight in the exposition of the administration of the Eucharist runs for more than two pages. To give just one sentence:

Then holding the paten in his left hand, he prefents the chalice on
the Altar to the Epiftoler, who receives the wine-cruet from the clerk,

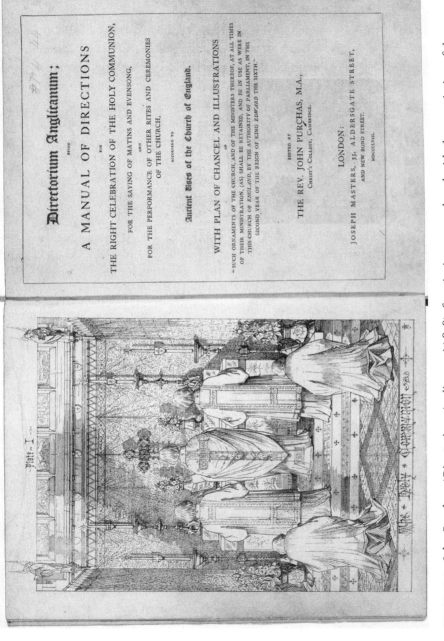

FIGURE 2.1. John Purchas, '*Directorium Anglicanum*' (1858), frontispiece, reproduced with the permission of the Cambridge University Library.

and pours fome wine with his right hand into the chalice, when the Celebrant, moving about the chalice with his wrift, in order to shake off any particles which may adhere to the infide of the chalice, drinks the wine, if poffible by the fide where the particles adhere.[97]

All of this ritual care was justified by the fact that ritualism emphasised the sacramentality of Anglicanism. This meant that great care had to be taken in the performance of the liturgy. Sanctification by the Holy Spirit was held to be via the priest rather than coming directly from God. Connected with this came the anxiety of whether the priest was to be seen as pure because of his office, and his own confession and penance, despite any personal failings.[98] Lack of faith in that purity went hand in hand with hostility toward sacramental religion amongst Protestants for whom the minister was little more than a moral guide and spokesman. Such views are expressed in an anonymous poem published in 1871, *A Christian Woman*. The writer says that she should pray for the broken hearted, for other unfortunates,

> And [for] those who bow at superstitious shrine—
> That to their priests their soul's concerns resign;
> Who with religious forms and vain display
> Fritter their precious time and life away.[99]

Hostile audiences, thus, regarded Roman and Anglo-Catholicism as only superficially alluring and as a waste of effort, time, and money. Even the staunch Anglo-Catholic, Richard Littledale (1833–90), author of *Catholic Ritual in the Church of England, Scriptural, Reasonable, Lawful* (1865), admitted that Tractarianism initially attracted aristocratic Tory supporters whose main concerns were such matters as 'black-letter learning, its pretty asceticisms, and its religious bric-à-brac in the shape of antique calf bindings, velvet faldstools and *prie-Dieus*, and engravings after Overbeck'.[100]

Ironically, the perceived danger of such decadent vanities was hugely exacerbated for opponents by the serious missionary drive within Anglo-Catholicism. The fripperies of ritualist churches such as St. Barnabas were paid for, according to critics, by a corrupt elite in an attempt to seduce the gullible. The opposite, however, could be argued, for example, by Littledale, who suggested that ritualist churches were vital in mounting a challenge to the splendours of the gin palaces in which 'internal decoration, abundant polished metal and vivid colour, with plenty of bright light, is found to pay, and to induce people to stay on drinking, just because everything is so pretty and cheerful to the eye, and so unlike the squalid discomfort of their own sordid homes'.[101] By missionary activities was ritualism to be brought to do God's work amongst the masses and so to become a religion of the people and not simply of an elite.

William Goode (1801–68), a prominent evangelical who rose through a variety of positions in London before becoming Dean of Ripon in 1860, was one of the few to try to work out a thorough refutation of the Tractarians and their ritualist relations.[102] Much hostile comment, by contrast, derived from deeply felt but ill-thought-through gut feelings toward Anglo-Catholics, their liturgical stance, and their understanding of the past. Opposition to the last of these led, for example, to the production of some bizarre versions of early British history. One such, by the Anglican priest N. S. Godfrey (1817–83), then curate of Trinity Church, Swansea, insisted that Britain was not evangelized from Rome in 597 A.D. because 'before the end of the second century, this country had generally received the gospel'.[103] Another writer of the time asserted that at that earlier date the 'British Church was entirely unpolluted by any admixture with the corruptions of Rome'. Not only that, but the Britons were supposedly shocked by the 'incipient practice of idol-worship' among the Romans.[104] As for Ireland, N. S. Godfrey asserted that 'we found them a Protestant nation (if I may anticipate the use of the term Protestant), and compelled them to receive the Roman Catholic religion' subsequent to the success of the Augustinian mission. For him, 'the Church of Rome was the first schismatic'.[105] According to Edward Harington, chancellor and canon of Exeter cathedral, the British Church slept during the Middle Ages in a 'cavern of enchantment, whose costly odours and intoxicating fumes were floating around, to overpower her senses'. It was only at the Reformation that Britain 'returned to its former faith'.[106]

The so-called 'Papal Aggression' of 1850, in which the Catholic Episcopal hierarchy was restored by Papal fiat, revealed deep fears of the vitality of Roman Catholicism, with its churches springing up across Britain and some of the most prominent Anglicans 'perverting' to Rome.[107] 'What! Convent England!', blustered the Unitarian William McCall (1812–88), 'bow the heirs of fire-tried heroes to winking pictures and bedizened dolls!'[108] These were nationalistic as well as religious fears. If England went over to Rome, it was feared that it would become a mere 'appendage to France, or a fief of the Holy Roman Empire'. But it was held that this would never happen. The flag of popish superstition would first be 'torn to rags by the strong free gale of the British soil'.[109] Yet the proximity of Ireland remained as a source of peril. In yet another November 5 sermon, this time preached before the Oxford Union, it was claimed that Romanism in England was 'comparatively innocuous', yet 'in Ireland, acting upon and with unparalleled social evils and explosive forces, it becomes both morally and politically, an active and tremendous element of change and revolution. It denies to statesmen the room or time to call sanative measures, either social, moral, or intellectual, into adequate operation'.[110] And furthermore, the rise of the Irish urban population in England in the wake of the potato famine of the 1840s spread fears for the destabilisation of the mainland.

'Puseyites', for this is how Tractarians and ritualists were often labelled, were widely, if not universally, considered to be the dupes, when they were not the cynical accomplices, of Rome. When William Bennett defended symbolical use of objects and ornaments in front of the Royal Commission on Ritual on July 4, 1867, the Baptist Thomas Beeman wrote against him stating that 'when the Papal Church turned the House of the Lord into a Theatre,—and the Passion of our Lord into a Play,—and the Priests into Performers, she plundered the requisite Dresses and Appendages from the Pagan storehouses'.[111] Moreover, we should remember that the theatre did not simply evoke frivolity. Hardline opinion saw in the stage a 'hot-bed of vice, where seeds of corruption that had hitherto lain almost unnoticed in their bosoms, have in a few hours been forced into a fruitfulness of evil'.[112] Behind the makeup was the Devil.

Opposition tapped not only anti-Catholicism, but sometimes a vein of anticlericalism that manifested particularly through wariness toward sacerdotalism. However, it is probably fair to say that many of the objections came from those who saw themselves as belonging to a party of middle-of-the-road common sense.[113] Such persons were very concerned with violations of their ideas of normality and decency and would identify with such sentiments as: '[T]he temple must be decorated, even in violation of divine law, *to make the Church attractive*. Gracious God!'[114] This relates to deeply held attitudes that understood decorative materiality as being radically divorced from spirituality. As one writer put it:

> Faith does not come by a monastic company advancing in solemn
> procession, white robed or otherwise; headed by the bearer of a silver
> cross; and after, hundreds following with candles and litany; while
> in the rear comes one who bears aloft a painting of the Redeemer,
> glowing with crimson and gold. There must be a living voice...The
> essential evil of the system is, a reliance upon that which is sensuous,
> to an almost complete distrust of that which is spiritual.[115]

Similarly, it was argued that 'we have never known a sincere Christian who would successfully pray to God with his eyes fixed on any material object; prayer is too spiritual to be contaminated with the material, and God has, in all ages of the world condemned every form of materialism, even when mixed with the truth'.[116] True Protestantism, for one Dissenter, was the 'renouncing of all human ceremonies', for 'traditions, forms and ceremonies, consist well enough with inward impurity, and offer no violence to the corrupt nature'.[117]

And the fact that the ceremonies were of considerable antiquity was no defence since, as the evangelical Cumming noted tartly, dinosaurs are old 'but they are still petrifaction'.[118] In *Yeast: A Problem* (1851), the novel by the Christian socialist Charles Kingsley (1819–75), the tragic heroine Argemone goes to a High Church vicar who tells her, whenever she objected to what he was saying, to listen to the (Anglo-)Catholic Church, 'the one and eternal Church that belonged as much to the nineteenth century as to the first'. But she left him saying that 'living in the nineteenth century, I wanted to hear the Church of the nineteenth century, and no other'.[119] Kingsley, in good Christian socialist fashion, was here emphasising the novelty of the conditions of modern life and the dangers of refusing to face up to that fact, a sentiment with which real-life ritualists tended to strongly agree, albeit with the difference that they lauded the contemporary relevance of the liturgical practices of the medieval past.

Nor was Anglo-Catholicism even held to have a monopoly of beauty. One antiritualist novel—for there were indeed such things—gloried in the Protestant beauty of English, asking 'had the fashionable worshippers in that church ever heard them [scriptures in the vernacular] before? We are apt to ask ourselves this question when the beautiful prayers of our Liturgy and the simple Saxon of our Bible are really read as they ought to be'.[120] Such arguments opposed England to Israel; for instance, it was suggested that elaborate worship had been sanctified under Leviticus, but this was the case no longer, 'the ritual economy having passed away'.[121] The image of modernity as a mature state of reason was evoked. It was commented, for instance, by the antiquary Edward Peacock of a list of goods destroyed in certain Lincolnshire churches at the Reformation that, prior to that time, people's 'childlike faith for ever mingled the visible with the unseen'.[122]

A further target of hostility for enemies of ritualism was the behaviour of incumbents, for 'we hear of these Priests instructing their congregations to look upon them as men of very superior sanctity to *others*'.[123] The key issue was the difference between the roles of priest and minister: one supposedly stood between man and God, and the other urged people toward God. According to one writer, 'hiereus' in the Bible referred to Pagan and Jewish priests who offered sacrifice. Therefore, the Church of England does not and should not have 'priests'. From such a point of view 'the main work and office of the Christian ministry is preaching'. The Christian Temple was seen as being located only in Heaven. What happened on earth was like the synagogues of the early Church; meetings centred on the Word.[124]

Anti-Semitism played a major role in the denial that the Temple and Tabernacle and priesthood of the Old Testament were to be imitated. As the prominent American medievalist H. C. Lea remarked, 'The most striking contrast between the Mosaic Dispensation and the Law of Christ is the materialism of the one, and the pure spiritualism of the other'.[125] The conversion of a Jew in 1848 by Bennett was the subject of detailed abuse that managed to combine opposition to Catholicism, Judaism, and scientific experiment, not to mention dislike of excessive facial hair:

> It is, no doubt, because the reverend incumbent of St. Paul's, Knightsbridge, does so much in his church after a JEWISH pattern, that a certain circumcised member...[a] genuine descendent from the stock of Abraham, who has more hair on his face than a bear has on his ribs, was melted down from the British Jew into the Popish Christian, in a certain laboratory in the west end of London, where a man used to preside under a Roman mask.[126]

The event referred to in this text is the baptism at St. Paul's, Knightsbridge, on July 19, 1846, of one Stephen Simons. The event was a matter for controversy because Bennett, believing Simons to be honest, had agreed to act as a character witness for him. Simons, thereby had persuaded Shout, a pawnbroker, to let Simons have one hundred pounds of goods to sell on commission. Shout told Bennett that Simons had committed fraud in the past, but the priest was adamant that the convert be given a second chance. Simons absconded and Bennett, according to Shout, would not pay the outstanding sum.[127] Bennett was wasting his time, the writer concluded, because all Jews were reprobates. Judaism quickly 'ceases to be a creed of faith. It is dissolved into fiscal association. Its god is gold'.[128]

Occasionally, hostile writers were willing to acknowledge the great efforts for the poor that ritualists had made, since they go forth and 'face the most deadly diseases, that they may give themselves body and soul to the sick and dying'.[129] But was it doing any good? For one anonymous 'Protestant', these priests were like ignorant nurses deluding with good cheer rather than healing. Such compassion and sentiment were suitable only for women, and their sermons were little more than 'emasculate polemics'.[130] Ritualists suffered from abuse from such persons as those who feared for our 'once vigorous and masculine monotheism'.[131] Decadence was to blame:

> [It is] one of the great dangers of a civilization like ours, which has reached its highest point; and, where inexhaustible wealth, and exuberant intellect, are alike taxed to minister to selfishness, and to an insatiable appetite for present enjoyment. A false gloss and refinement steals over everything—a certain *effeminacy* of mind.[132]

The supposedly effeminate Anglo-Catholics were noted for their female following, as in the statement that 'the ritualists may be proud of their successes amongst the [supposedly decadent] aristocracy, especially *the female portion*'. The frivolity of such ladies was widely excoriated. It was held that 'such women admire novelties as they admire foreign fashions; and many are those whose whole affections are divided between semi-popery and French lace.'[133] Women, in such analyses, were seen as feeble-minded and ready to be appealed to by mere surface appearance. Those who became Anglican Sisters of Mercy were accused of playing at being religious when they should be in search of a husband (figure 2.2).

FIGURE 2.2. 'Convent of the Belgravians', *Punch* 19 (1850), p. 163. Photograph by the author, with permission, from the edition held at the library of Birkbeck College, London.

Misogyny, xenophobia, and anti-Semitism were mingled in the particularly objectionable observation that one should not be surprised 'that ladies, befribbled with French tawdry and other foreign bagatelles, should resort to his [W. J. E. Bennett's] synagogue to exhibit their tuckers of *broad point*... but that men, with brains in their occiputs and honesty in their hearts... [should do so also] we are utterly at a loss to conceive'.[134] Textile splendour was thought essential in ritualism, as shown in the illustrations of vestments in Purchas' *Directorium Anglicanum* (1858) (figure 2.1). In response to the ritualist way with robes, Henry Drummond (1786–1860), one of the founders of the Irvingite Church in 1832, a banker, and Member of Parliament for West Surrey, argued that if a man 'appears in gaudy or ridiculous colours or forms, he will be treated as a light and vain man'.[135] *Punch* was to push this line of thought to the extent of directly associating vestments with ladies' dresses (figures 2.3 and 2.4).[136]

Ritualists could therefore find themselves attacked as a result of prejudices ranging from the obvious one of anti-Catholicism to anticlericalism, anti-Semitism, misogyny, iconophobia, and xenophobia. British Roman Catholics knew such attitudes all too well. Wiseman, although understandably prone to

FIGURE 2.3. 'The Reverend Augustus Cope, our High Church clergyman, has ordered a set of vestments. His pretty cousins waylay the parcel, and dress themselves up in order to astonish Mr Augustine. The Reverend young gentleman is "grieved to find they have no respect for solemn things"', *Punch* 51 (1866), p. 109. Photograph by the author, with permission, from the edition held at the library of Birkbeck College, London.

triumphalism after he became cardinal archbishop of Westminster, was, from time to time, able to make pragmatic acceptance of English realities rather than to retreat permanently into the ecclesiastical (or indeed Ecclesiological) sublime. For instance, on July 28, 1850, he spoke in industrial Salford about the glories of St. Mark's in Venice, which he saw as being the product of mercantile piety. According to him, this cathedral was evidence that: 'Venice knew how to become a great mercantile nation, and at the same time remain pious to God, and make subservient to His worship, that wonderful pre-eminence which He had given to it in the dominion over earth's treasures'. He argued that the chimneys of the factories and the spires of the churches would stand together 'great in their respective magnificence'.[137]

Bearing in mind that the cardinal was sufficiently in touch with the realities of industrial Britain to praise the grandeur of factory chimneys, we should also be wary of accepting the anti-Catholic assumption that ornamental 'frippery' sat naturally with Roman Catholics. Pugin, who was professionally obsessed with ornament, can to be found complaining of the efforts of 'well-meaning [Roman Catholic] ladies who transfer all the nicknackery of the workroom, the toilette table, and the bazaar, to the altar of God'.[138] In other words, ritualists were not being compared to what was being championed by the great

FIGURE 2.4. 'Height of Fashion. Ardent ritualist, "Oh Athanasius it's charmingly becoming"', *Punch* 51 (1866), p. 258. Photograph by the author, with permission, from the edition held at the library of Birkbeck College, London.

contemporary figures of British Roman Catholicism, but to a caricature of contemporary female devotion.

Mary Heimann has written a substantial proportion of the relatively few studies of how ordinary Roman Catholics worshipped in Victorian England. She argues that an emphasis on material props only came later in the nineteenth century. For instance, the 1859 penny catechism asked 'is it allowable to honour relics, crucifixes, and holy pictures', whilst the 1880 version said 'what honour should we give' to these objects.[139] Her picture of Catholic piety is less to do with ornament and ritual elaboration than with emotion centred on the holy family that resulted in 'a warm, direct and even childlike relationship with God'. She further comments that 'the resemblance, in vocabulary and fervour and even in method, between this new piety and what we might think of as the evangelical enthusiasm of some Protestants is striking'.[140] In other words, the reality was that Roman Catholicism and evangelicalism may have had almost as much in common as Roman Catholicism and Anglo-Catholicism.

Indeed, Heimann argues that it was not English Roman Catholicism but its Anglican counterpart that became 'more Roman than Rome' after the Restoration of the Catholic hierarchy. The Anglican vicar of Bridgenorth, George Bellett, for instance, commented in Rome that, while he deplored Romanism, he could not but note that practices such as bowing at the name of Jesus and the use of painted glass were practised by many Anglo-Catholics and were called 'Romish' in England but were not present at St. Peter's in the Holy City![141] Ritualism, therefore, represented not a copy of Roman Catholicism but an enactment of an emphasised Anglican sacramentalism expressed via the medium of a Gothic Revival version of the English sublime. It was attacked not so much by reference to the realities of the Roman Catholic Church in Britain, nor even to those of Rome in Italy, but to those of a Rome that sparkled, sprawled, and stank in the Protestant imagination. Those attacks were laced with misogynist, xenophobic, and anti-Semitic expressions of disgust. As I discuss in later chapters, this may tell us just as much, if not more, about the insecurities and desires of these Protestant writers as it does about the Anglo-Catholic objects of their polemics.

3

Riots and Trials in London, 1840–60

This chapter presents a case study of the events that took place in the 1850s in the parish of St. Paul's, Knightsbridge, in London. The purpose of this microhistory is to provide a detailed factual grounding for my exploration of wider themes in Victorian religion and society. The events in the parish involved the most prominent political controversy and the highest profile legal cases of early ritualism. This material presents the background to the ensuing thematic chapters, which engage with interpretations of these disputes through discussions of idolatry and fetishism. In chapter 2 I explored the origins of ritualism, and I should emphasise that the late 1840s represent the early years of this development within the Church of England. Precisely because ritualist clergy were few in number, their activities appeared unusual. In addition, ritual innovation took place side by side with a zeal to bring faith to underchurched urban communities. Such missionary activity to the 'home heathen' took place in the context of a swing toward urban reform, but also drew inspiration from the example of Roman Catholic missions on the Continent in the seventeenth and eighteenth centuries. The resulting building works, missions, and liturgical performances made these new ritualist clergy very visible in their localities.[1]

Opposition took many forms. Many people thought such activities to represent a return to primitive 'medieval' superstition. Dissenting, evangelical, and Low Church opinion believed that the ritualists, through their stress on the priest, the sacraments, and other physical forms, were constructing expensive, unnecessary, and dangerous barriers between holy God and sinful man.[2] The language of impurity was employed to explain, construct, and contain such developments. Opposing churchmen mounted a drive to decontaminate public worship and cleanse the service of any trace of papal pollution. The ensuing battles were marked by intense fervour and much delivering of sermons and publishing of tracts on the part of both sides. Indeed, ritualism drew some of its energy from the inheritance of the legacy of past evangelical revivals. Evangelicalism and Dissent, particularly in its more extreme forms, provided a thrill of anxiety by whipping up fears that the Judgment Day was at hand.[3] Such hard-line 'ultra' Protestant opinion regarded the emergence of Anglo-Catholicism as one of the signs of the last days.

One thing that must be made clear is that it is quite untrue to say that ritualists had a vivid material and visual culture but their opponents did not. The use of elaborately decorated Gothic churches was to become very widely diffused across most Christian denominations as the century progressed. The image of a Gothic church arising amid slums and bringing good works to the community was hymned not just by Anglo-Catholics but also by their opponents such as Charles Kingsley.[4] Moreover, with their silk hats and white ties, evangelical ministers were visually 'unmistakeable'.[5] But it was only the former that gave such grave offence. Both sides, insofar as the diversity of opinion can be reduced to those in favour of ritual innovation and those against, were concerned with purity but differed on the way it was to be achieved and how it was to be expressed. For example, a typical evangelical purity campaign was that which aimed at establishing the Sabbath as a day of taboos on activity, when work and energetic recreation were forbidden and the purifying words of the Bible were read out, listened to, and meditated upon.

The period from the 1840s to the 1860s can be seen, in retrospect, as a high point of evangelical influence. The Public Worship Act (1855) allowed evangelicals to hold special services in theatres, music halls, and railway stations. Meanwhile, John Bird Sumner, the archbishop of Canterbury from 1848 to 1862, was an evangelical. And whilst Lord Palmerston, prime minister from 1855 to 1865, did not necessarily, as was once believed, follow the judgment of his stepson, the evangelical Earl of Shaftesbury, on Church policy, the latter was still a highly influential figure in public life. He, along with Lord Ebury, led opposition to the Anglo-Catholics in the Lords.[6] The picture presented by Boyd Hilton is of a Christian culture shifting from a focus on Atonement to Incarnation, but the Tractarian and subsequent Anglo-Catholic focus on the latter was widely regarded at this time as novel and extreme.[7]

In 1841, the then archbishop of Canterbury, William Howley (1766–1848), deprecated liturgical novelties in his annual charge to the clergy of his diocese.

The next year Charles James Blomfield (1786–1857), bishop of London from 1828 to 1856, did something rather different in his charge. Blomfield was trying to hold his diocese together in the face of increasing divergence of opinion amongst his clergy.[8] He said that one should not move toward Rome, but should look to Anglican tradition in relation to such issues as the appointing of bishops, Sabbath observance, and infant baptism. Crucially, he continued by contending that, although some revivers of ritual had gone a little too far, their efforts had still contributed to progress toward an 'exact observance of the Church's rubrical injunctions...If we are not to go *beyond* her ritual, at least we ought not to *fall short* of it'. More ceremonies, notably regular communion, must be a good thing and the surplice, now used only in cathedrals and college chapels, might be preferable when preaching after morning service.[9] Blomfield was trying to compromise and aimed to please both conservatives and innovators.[10] He was taken by surprise by the opposition to any such 'restorations' and in the following year, 1843, could be represented, albeit somewhat implausibly, as being the leader of 'Puseyism' in London, and with bringing back things that were obsolete even though he 'professes to repudiate the Tractarian doctrines'.[11] Blomfield's defence was that this was simply a return to good order, to the thirty-nine articles, and to the Prayer Book after the lapse of certain customs.

In 1843 it was alleged that 'a large portion of the outcry against Puseyism arises from the jealousy of the leading evangelical clergy, the spouters at Exeter Hall, [and] the committee-men of certain Societies, who have long been accustomed to act in defiance of Church or Bishop'. Other opposition at the time supposedly came from the 'low, calculating utilitarians, the mere nineteenth-century men'. Some Anglicans were suspicious of any change, whilst many others—'the middle classes, the mercantile and professional, not before having turned their attention to church matters'—were puzzled, hostile, and confused.[12] Vestry meetings provided a focus for the expression of opposition. The people there, who elected one of the churchwardens, did not have to be Anglicans. Sometimes, as we shall see, they were Dissenters, in cahoots with Chartist campaigners for political and social reform, working to disrupt church finances because of their opposition to the Church rates. Since Anglican parish churches were supported financially by ratepayers in the parish regardless of their religious profession, those who advocated the use of Catholic ritual forms in the Church of England needed to beware of the financial and doctrinal prejudices of those outside their own denomination. However, as will become clear, ritualists were able to develop backing from an extraordinarily wide range social range, from the very poor to members of the House of Lords (and their wives). This was to prove crucial in the ultimate endurance of ritualism and its development into Anglo-Catholicism.

Bennett, 1843–51

William James Early Bennett (1804–86) was born in Halifax, Nova Scotia, on November 15, 1804 (figure 3.1). His father was a major in the Royal Engineers, and his mother was the daughter of another army officer. She was born Mary Early and was noted for her ability to speak Portuguese, Italian, and French. In 1816, Bennett entered Westminster School, and he was Kings Scholar in 1818. It was in that role that he was present at the coronation of George IV in 1821. From May 1822 for a year he was captain of the school. The next year the Dean of Christ Church placed him top of three picked from his school for college scholarships, and he studied there until 1826. To put all of this in the context of the Oxford Movement, John Keble had been a Fellow of Oriel College since 1811, although he left in 1823. John Henry Newman, meanwhile, was a curate at St. Clements in Oxford and, in 1823, Edward Pusey was elected a Fellow of Oriel. Although Bennett did not know these three leading lights of the Oxford Movement personally, he did know the Tractarian George Anthony Denison, who was also an undergraduate at Christ Church.

Bennett was ordained deacon in 1828 and priest two years later by Blomfield, bishop of London. He was present at the coronation of William IV in 1831 when he was curate of Holy Trinity, Marylebone. From there he moved to become curate of the Oxford Chapel (subsequently St Peter's, Vere St.) for three months. Then from 1830 to 1833 he was at Holy Trinity, Marylebone, and from 1833 to 1838, at All Souls, Langham Place, before becoming the minister at the Portman Chapel (now St. Paul's, Portman Square) from 1838 to 1843. He married Mary Concetta Franklin, had two daughters and a son, and, after the time in Knightsbridge, which is the subject of this section, moved to Frome in Somerset. He died on the August 17, 1886.

Like many clergy at the time, he published a considerable number of his sermons, of which several were reprinted. These were sold to the congregation or in bookshops in London. The occasion of Bennett's first published writings was the 1832 cholera outbreak, which seems to have inspired him to wonder about the issue of privilege versus suffering. The impression given by Frederick Bennett, his biographer, was that of the systematic neglect of religion before the Tractarian revival. This was not just a question of laxity in ritual, but also because preaching was supposedly very hit-and-miss. 'Any improvement on this was,' we are told, condemned as '"popery"'. This, at least, is the story as it appeared to the Anglo-Catholic victors sixty years after the events.

In 1840 Bennett was invited by Blomfield to take charge of the new parish and church of St. Paul's, Knightsbridge, which was being built to relieve the

FIGURE 3.1. F. Holl (1854) after G. Richmond (1851–52), *William Bennett*. Photograph by the author, by permission of the Vicar and Churchwardens of St. Paul's, Knightsbridge.

huge parish of St. George's, Hanover Square. Support was to be pew rents, which, since the northern area of the parish was a new and fashionable suburb, were likely to be substantial. In 1840 the parish had 12,000 inhabitants, made up of a mix of the very rich and the very poor. The latter were concentrated farther south in Pimlico near the area blighted by the development of the railways and by the marshiness of the ground nearer the Thames. By contrast, farther north, in Knightsbridge and Belgravia, there was an explosion of prestige building that resulted in this becoming arguably the wealthiest area in London (which it still is today).[13]

In 1851, Charles Westerton (1813–72), neighbour, bookseller, publisher, and antagonist of Robert Liddell, Bennett's successor as incumbent, published *Julian; Or Reminiscences of Affection*, a novel by Jane Kennedy that is revealing of contemporary snobberies. One of the characters, Sir Charles Mounthill, lived in 'a rather old-fashioned part of London; yet having placed himself very comfortably in May Fair, he had no idea of rising up to follow the crowd to Belgravia'.[14] Fortunes were beginning to be made in publishing and lending books. The most famous example was Charles Mudie (1818–1890), who started lending books in 1842 and built his business up until, in 1864, it became a limited liability company with a capitalisation of £100,000.[15] Westerton was by no means in this league, but he was clearly a man of middle-class substance. Not only were many local inhabitants wealthy, but some of them were also very influential. Lord John Russell, Prime Minister from 1846 to 1852, was a parishioner and a frequent communicant. Rumours, alarming to the enemies of the Oxford Movement, went the rounds suggesting that Russell wanted to make Bennett a bishop.

On May 30, 1843, the church of St. Paul's was consecrated. It was found by one writer to be 'deficient in many points of architectural propriety' but overall a great improvement on other recent churches in the metropolis: 'Let Dissenters and evangelicals run up their cheap preaching-houses, but let Churchmen offer to God the best they have'.[16] Bennett paid for the chancel. William Upton Richards (1811–1873), a close friend of Pusey who could be found working until 1849 in the manuscripts department of the British Museum, was perhaps at that point the most prominent Tractarian in London. He was assistant minister, and then minister at the Margaret Street Chapel (which became All Saints, Margaret St.) from 1837 until his death. However, Bennett was the first to make major ritual innovations and a wider cultural and political impact, so marking a move from Tractarian to ritualist enthusiasms.[17] In 1842, as has been mentioned, Blomfield had delivered the charge to his clergy which was meant to ensure a moderate path between the embrace and rejection of Tractarianism, but which was interpreted by both sides as being pro-Oxford. Amongst other things, Blomfield was understood to have advocated the wearing of the surplice for the sermon. In 1843 Bennett mocked the use of Roman 'toys' such as images with tapers set before saints' shrines.[18] However, things began to change.[19] In 1846, not only was there a choir at St. Paul's, Knightsbridge, but it was also dressed in surplices.

Although Bennett was slow to develop material innovations, he was clearly influenced by Tractarian ideas from an early date. He published, for example, a major work in praise of the Eucharist in 1837, which went through a series of revisions and new editions. In the second edition of 1846, Bennett is found rejoicing that 'things are better…we can kneel down before the Altar and do acts of reverence, and place lights thereon according to the demands of the Church, without minding any Puritanic cry raised by the evil and the ignorant: Praise be to God'.[20]

But we should be very careful of assuming, as did many of his opponents, that such sentiments meant that he was an apologist for Rome. In 1847 Alexander Chirol, a curate at St. Paul's, Knightsbridge, became a Roman Catholic. Bennett preached violently against him, although it was alleged in an anonymous pamphlet that this was because this 'perversion' (i.e., conversion) had ruined Bennett's chances of a bishopric, bearing in mind that Russell, the prime minister, was a member of the congregation.[21] However, Bennett was clearly enthusiastic for a much more sacramental view of religion, for instance, in the case of marriage, and was rapidly drawing forth anti-Catholic and xenophobic repudiations of his views such as this:

> In France, Spain, and Italy, the marriage tie is continually ruptured without a stigma being attached either by political or spiritual teachers. In Christian countries only, where the rite of marriage is *not* held to be a sacrament, nuptial pledges are maintained inviolably. We speak not of exceptions, as they only confirm the rule.[22]

It is important to point out the significance of the parish to many Tractarians and their followers because of their devotion to in-depth work with local communities.[23] Bennett's mind was fixed not just on general moral issues but also more specifically on the composition of his congregations. He said that when he arrived at St. Paul's he had never seen such a contrast of wealth and poverty.[24] His church, situated at the north of the parish, just off Hyde Park, attracted the well-to-do. The pew rent system that financed it meant that there were, in any case, relatively few seats available for the less wealthy. This was the age of the maturing industrial revolution and the explosion of city populations. It had been widely recognised for some time that poor areas were underprovided with churches and that their inhabitants were insufficiently evangelised as a result. A lawyer involved in the series of legal cases subsequent to Bennett's resignation in 1850 noted that 'serious dissensions and differences have existed in this parish, which I regret to say is a fact of great notoriety'.[25] Those divisions were not just between rich and poor, although those were real enough, but amongst the affluent as to the degree of their responsibility toward their poorer fellows and the nature of the appropriate mechanisms for state or charitable support.

Not to mince words, parts of Pimlico, at the south end of Knightsbridge, were a slum. An unpublished manuscript by a local resident, W. H. Husk (1814–87), a critic and historian of music, gives details of local residential development, which echoed the experience of, for instance, Euston and Camden in north London, as being a region of slums built up against areas of gentility and affluence.[26] Poverty was a major factor in the presence of crime and prostitution, although the case for connection between cause and effect was as much disputed then as now. It is therefore hardly surprising that Bennett, with substantial resources behind him, should, in that age of reform, be concerned about the twin perils of moral and physical corruption in the south of his parish. In the absence of state systems of support beyond the poor house, parishes developed their traditional role as carers for local unfortunates. In 1848–49, the years of the return of cholera, a parochial dispensary was established. It might be thought that this was simply Christian charity and, as such, uncontroversial, but at the time various Protestant writers were busy making the claim that the endowment of Maynooth and other concessions to Catholics were National Sins, and that cholera was England's justified punishment.[27] The only possible course, for such people, required a return to staunch anti-Catholicism. The victims were predestined to die.

Bennett and his successor Liddell established a wide range of services for the indigent, including an Industrial School for training girls as servants, a charity school, two night schools for boys, an orphan school for girls, Sunday schools, a burial guild, a Home for Gentlewomen, Home for Incurables, House of Refuge for Abandoned Women ('a subject which no respectable people talked about until these Saint Barnabas' Clergy and their friends began to stir it up'), Provident Society, a Poor Needlewoman's Aid Association, Blanket Lending Society, subsidised coal cellar, soup kitchen, and dispensary.[28] Such foundations—with perhaps the exception of the mission to fallen women—were widespread at this time. One might compare those in Pimlico with those administered by Richard Burgess (1815–81), rector of Upper Chelsea who, by 1848, was funding two schools, a Relief Association providing winter coals and bread, a Philanthropic Sick Society, District Visiting Society, Provident Fund, Blanket Loan Society, Religious Books and Tracts Lending Society, dispensary, Association for Promoting the Due Observance of the Lord's Day, and a Church Missionary Association.[29] Such activities were, however, often controversial due to the issue of their cost to the parish. An anonymous barrister wrote to the Bishop of London that 'the stern spirit of our Saxon ancestors is hereditary...No scheme for bringing the children of the poorer classes under clerical direction will succeed'. His point was that such people were inherently degraded and, therefore, any such spending would simply represent an 'enormous and unproductive outlay'.[30]

However, work with prostitutes, which was to lead, in 1852, to a House of Penitent Women being established in Commercial Road, Pimlico, provoked much more intense debate about the boundaries of Christian charity, duty, and propriety.[31] Part of the problem for opponents was that fallen women were aided not only via systems of district visiting inspired by the work of the leading early nineteenth-century Scottish evangelical Thomas Chalmers (1780–1847), but also by women formed into a quasi-monastic order.[32] Priscilla Lydia Sellon (1821–76), the pioneer of Anglican nunneries, was responsible for the establishment of a small community of Sisters of Mercy in Pimlico in 1850. Scandal was not long coming. Elizabeth Law, the daughter of the Recorder of London, came to Bennett requesting to join. He allowed this, having asked her specifically if she had her father's permission.[33] Slanders suggested that Bennett had stolen her away from her family. These allegations forced the woman to write in refutation and self-justification to the Bishop of London in November 1850.[34] At that point, however, the whirlwind of opposition to Bennett was unstoppable and was soon to sweep him from the parish. The Sisters themselves did not long outlast him. They were, it would appear, disbanded in 1854 after two of the original members had gone over to Rome.[35]

Bennett's plan was for the rich of Belgravia to pay for a church for the poor of Pimlico, which could thus be without rented pews. It would be named after Barnabas, an early disciple of Christ and companion of Paul, who was stoned to death on Salamis by the Jews of his native island.[36] This church would put into effect Tractarian principles with a focus on evangelisation through ritual. The Marquis of Westminster gave the land, and the foundation stone of the schoolhouse was laid on St. Barnabas' Day 1846; that of the church followed on the same day the following year. Until 1848, Bennett had been living at 39 Wilton Crescent, by St. Paul's, but he then moved to the new 'St. Barnabas' College', where he lived with his curates in imitation of the apostolic friendship and companionship of Paul and Barnabas. The former church was, under Bennett's successor Liddell, also provided with shared lodgings with the ideal of producing a community of priests (figure 3.2). The overall projected cost was in the region of £19,000.[37] Holy vessels, candlesticks, and illuminated and jewelled office books came in the form of gifts.[38] St. Barnabas', as a chapel-of-ease of St. Paul's, might have been expected to have the same rite as the mother church.[39] However, Bennett seems to have seen the opportunity for a fresh start. Certainly, Bennett was quite clear by this point that he was not willing to compromise his evolving ritualist principles. This would be no exercise in the via media.[40]

The architect of both St. Paul's and St. Barnabas' was Thomas Cundy II (1790–1867), most of whose work on the Grosvenor estate consisted of Italianate neoclassical terraces.[41] It has been suggested, although it is not proven, that A. W. N. Pugin was consulted in the case of St. Barnabas'.[42] The original decoration was much plainer than what we see today, which is largely the result of the work of George Frederick Bodley working under Rev. Alfred Gurney after 1890 (figures 3.3 and 3.4).[43] The original glass by William Wailes was replaced by Charles Kempe in the nave and by Sir Ninian Comper in the chancel

FIGURE 3.2. Priests' lodgings (from c. 1869), St. Paul's, Knightsbridge. Photograph by the author, by permission of the Vicar and Churchwardens of St. Paul's, Knightsbridge.

FIGURE 3.3. Nave in 1850, St. Barnabas', Pimlico, *Illustrated London News*, June 15, 1850, p. 428. Copyright British Library Board, all rights reserved, DSC 4367.150000, December 12, 2006.

FIGURE 3.4. Nave in 2006, St. Barnabas', Pimlico. Photograph by the author, by permission of the Vicar and Churchwardens, St. Barnabas', Pimlico.

after war damage. The current screen and reredos are by Bodley. However, we should not assume that the original plainness was the result of choice. It is likely, as at the Roman Catholic Westminster Cathedral, that decoration was expected to be added as and when further funds became available—which is essentially what happened.

The earliest surviving ornaments of the church have been examined by the National Association of Decorative and Fine Arts Societies: these include a Pugin chalice and paten of 1849; sanctuary gates; Latin texts painted on the walls of the nave over the arcade; Bible stand; and, most spectacularly, the pulpit, which is painted with images by an unknown artist of Christ and saints Ambrose, Augustine, Gregory, and Jerome, the last in a cope, white alb, and cardinal's red hat. The watercolour painting currently at the southwest end of the nave depicts the east end of the nave and chancel before the changes of 1890s.[44] Pugin chalice, Latin texts, and cardinal's red hat—these images and objects declared ambiguous and unapologetic Catholicity (figure 3.5).

The consecration took place on June 11, 1850. Blomfield was later to get into hot water for giving his tacit consent to some of the liturgical furnishings, such as a rood screen with a cross upon it, although he was adamant that he did not see the cross that had been placed on the altar because it had been covered by a silver vessel. Bennett invited William Gladstone to the consecration, saying that 'rich and poor dine together with the bishop and clergy' after the service. Although the archive does not preserve Gladstone's reply, we know that he was subsequently to aid Bennett in the Parliamentary campaign to prevent him gaining a new parish after he was forced out of Knightsbridge.[45] In the course of the ensuing week a galaxy of Tractarian stars preached: Henry Edward Manning, John Keble, and Edward Pusey amongst them. The 'big names' avoided major controversy in their sermons, but two of the lesser known figures openly pursued Bennett's point of uniting rich and poor. William Upton Richards spoke on the danger of riches and Charles Kennaway, vicar of Chipping Campden in Gloucestershire, went further by combining equality with a vision of aesthetic brightness, saying that

> the solemn sentence, 'they parted them to all men as every man had need' [Acts 2: 45], comes back to us with new power; it seems to remove the foul principles of a neglectful carelessness, as antiquarians would restore a palimpsest; and the old bright colours of holy devotedness come out in all the freshness of eternal truth.[46]

The press was, initially, enthusiastic. The *Illustrated London News* thought that it was 'one of the most remarkable churches erected in the metropolis...the decorations of the church are of the most superb description'.[47] The style was that which the trustees thought was 'best adapted to the poor man's church'. The gates and other furnishings were by Hardman's of Birmingham, which was the usual supplier of Pugin; the firm provided, for instance, the metalwork at the medieval court of the Great Exhibition of 1851 (about which *Illustrated London News* was also thoroughly approving).[48] The *Ecclesiologist*, whilst finding

FIGURE 3.5 St. Jerome, pulpit, unknown artist c. 1850. Photograph by the author, by permission of the Vicar and Churchwardens, St. Barnabas', Pimlico.

fault with various matters, as was its wont, stated that St. Barnabas' was the most 'complete, and with completeness, the most sumptuous church which has been dedicated to the use of the Anglican Communion since the revival'. And it added, 'the services are most satisfactory'.[49]

There was to be a short lull of a few months before the storm broke, although we should not assume that Bennett had the full backing of his parish for his innovations during this time. On September 24, Pope Pius the Ninth (frequently referred to in England, as in Italy, albeit sometimes with blasphemous variations, as Pio Nono) issued a Papal Bull that restored the Roman Catholic hierarchy in England. Bishops were henceforth to be appointed to sees, so replacing the interim form of administration by Vicars Apostolic. Nicholas Wiseman (1802–65) was to become a cardinal archbishop and his see Westminster, a fact that he expressed in triumphalist terms of rule and destiny. The story appeared in English newspapers in early October.

November 2, 1850, was the date of Blomfield's 'charge' to his clergy. His 1842 charge had gained him a reputation in some quarters as an advocate of ritual in general and the surplice in particular. Once again, Blomfield attempted to negotiate a middle way between contending factions.[50] He started by discussing the dispute over the licensing of the evangelical Henry Gorham (1787–1857) in which a nonsacramental understanding of baptism was asserted as legitimate by the Privy Council, which was the ultimate court of appeal in Anglican ecclesiastical law at this time. He then stated that people who went over to Rome as a result of this were really only using it as a pretext. Papal authority meant that all sorts of absurdities were doctrinally indisputable within the Roman Church. He continued by saying that there were those who had, albeit with 'devotedness and charity', led people to this point. The result was that 'a taste has been excited in them for forms and observances which has stimulated without satisfying their appetite…they have been led, step by step, to the very verge of the precipice, and then, to the surprise of their guides have fallen over'. He also warned against reason and latitudinarianism, but these were common platitudes that did not have the shock value of his previous assertions. He gave a strong warning about the condition of the Church, 'menaced by dangers of opposite kinds,—on this side superstition and spiritual tyranny; on that side rationalism, with infidelity and pantheism in its train', but it was the former that struck home amongst his audience.[51]

That still did not mean, whatever the excitement in the diocese, that the public in general were quite so exercised. According to John Wolffe, 'public reactions in Britain were initially somewhat muted' to the events in Rome. In his view, it was what the Prime Minister, Lord John Russell, did next that made the difference.[52] Russell was in a difficult position. In order to pacify Ireland, he had long embarked on concessions to Catholics, but he faced political flak on the home front for this very policy. He had also been involved in negotiations with the Papacy, although he certainly had not given his permission to go ahead with the restoration of the Roman Catholic hierarchy in England. However, if he attacked Pio Nono openly, he would simply appear a hypocrite in the light of his previous policies. He was 'caught between his past record and the demands of political survival'.[53] Russell opted for his future.

On November 4, the Prime Minister wrote to Edward Maltby (1770–1859), Low Church bishop of Durham, denouncing the Papacy but stressing that England faced a greater peril—an enemy within! 'There is a danger,' wrote the Prime Minister, 'which alarms me more than any aggression of a foreign sovereign. Clergymen of my own church…have been the most forward in leading their flocks step by step to the very verge of the precipice…and are now reprehended by the Bishop of London in his charge to the clergy of his diocese'.[54] Russell 'was a rationalist anticlerical prepared to tolerate monkish superstition so long as it kept a low profile and was properly grateful; he was also an Erastian' (in favour of the connection and dependency between Church and State).[55] Bennett, badly shaken by the Gorham case, was unusually vehement in stressing the idea of separation of Church and State.[56] Russell, by contrast, was trying effectively to build on Gorham to emphasise the subordination and obedience of the Church to the State.[57] In Frank Wallis's analysis, this was also part of a wider struggle for institutional prestige, in which what was outrageous was the Papacy's apparent attempt to assert a premier status in England.[58] The English could not control the Papacy, but many thought that they should at least retain the loyalty and conformity of their own Church.

An anonymous writer, who satirised both sides, referred to this as 'a feint on Rome to cover a raid on St. Barnabas'. We could find several epithets to characterise the operation, and all of one class—cunning, sagacious, clever, perhaps a little slippery, but very successful.'[59] It *was* successful in bringing down Bennett, but in terms of longer term aims it was, in the words of Russell's recent biographer, 'the greatest mistake of his political career'.[60] Russell's action, following on from Gorham, did indeed look like an exercise in Erastianism, and members of the High Church party in general, not just Tractarians, were deeply unhappy.[61] It was a short-term political fix that exacerbated long-term divisions and animosities, and ultimately further undermined that stability of Ireland, to which Russell had diverted so much energy.

Thus, the Prime Minister had made his denunciation, drawing on Blomfield's charge, and had duly retained the confidence of the House of Commons. He probably hoped that the issue would slowly die away. It was not to be. The restoration of the Catholic hierarchy was to swiftly become the 'Papal Aggression' as the national media, led by *The Times*, 'engineered the uproar'.[62] *The Times* was the most influential paper in London in the 1850s.[63] Its proprietor, John Walter III (1818–94), fiercely anti-Roman, overruled the more moderate editor John Delane (1817–79). But even the latter had long been concerned about Puseyites. A list of the 'principal clergy of London' had been drawn up for him in 1844 that ranged from the very High to those 'on the verge of dissent'. Bennett, despite his own testimony of moderation at this date, was placed at the number one spot, the only one described as 'as near Romanism as possible'. Chanting, genuflecting, bowing to the high altar, and the use of surplices were all commented upon. The report concluded that 'Mr. Bennett is an active clergyman, but as is the case with all the High Church clergy, by no means generally popular'.[64]

On November 4, *The Times* editorial led with the Bishop of London's charge to his clergy and the Papal Aggression. The significance of the next day, November 5, was noted. The papal actions were understood to be an 'attempt to place the metropolis under the jurisdiction of a priest of the Church of Rome'. Blomfield's language was described as 'vigorous' and 'terse', whilst that of Wiseman was notable for its 'gross assumptions, rhetorical artifices, and corrupt jargon'. The editorial continued by saying that 'the Romish priests have yet to learn to speak to Englishmen in the freedom of our vernacular tongue, and there is a taint of impurity in the very expressions they employ to emit the decrees of their outlandish authority'. It was this article, rather than the charge, or the letter to Maltby (commonly referred to as the 'Durham letter'), that explicitly linked these events with Bennett as follows:

> The Bishop of LONDON may not have called to mind the ceremonies in which he himself consented to take part at the consecration of St. Barnabas', Pimlico; but it is a matter of general regret that he did not avail himself of that occasion to restore that and other churches of his diocese to the simplicity which their character and purpose seemed peculiarly to command.[65]

As the anonymous writer of *The Parish Priest and the Prime Minister* put it the following year, 'the affairs of the fashionable church of St. Barnabas' were brought to a crisis under the strange auspices of the Pope, Cardinal Wiseman, an unruly mob, a hundred constables outside the doors, and detective police within'.[66] The disturbances, which the passion of all parties contrived to refer to as 'riots', began on November 10. Not everyone who came to hear Bennett preach was bent on catcalling and jostling. Others were there to defend, and others simply attended out of curiosity. The main unrest took place outside St. Barnabas', where a crowd, which consisted 'mainly of boys and persons of the lower class' who were 'roughs', was contained by special constables.[67]

The rowdy scenes were repeated, with Sunday services as particular flash points. *Punch* dwelt upon this with undisguised glee and, in the words of Bennett's biographer, 'filled its pages *ad nauseam* with what were supposed to be jokes, all more or less profane' (figure 3.6).[68] One such item, pretending to be a sensational theatre bill at St. Barnabas', Pimlico, included 'monks in masquerade' and 'ecclesiastical poses plastiques', finishing off with '*Vivat Pontifex*

FIGURE 3.6. 'Master Punch. "Please Mr Bishop, which is popery, and which is Pusey-ism?" Bishop. "Whichever you like my little dear"'. The church steeple is in the shape of the hats that the Puseyites are shown as wearing in other Punch cartoons. *Punch* 20 (1851), p. 15. Photograph by the author, with permission, from the edition held at the library of Birkbeck College, London.

Romanus! No money returned!'[69] In fact, Tractarians were noted for their aversion to the theatre such that it was possible to suggest that numbers of them converted to Roman Catholicism in order to attend![70] But such abuse focussed on the widely held jibe that elaborate liturgy was nothing more than profane theatre. However, in terms of stirring up the mob, Punch was 'left in the background by the theological inscriptions which were chalked up in every street— "No Virgin Mary", "No Wafer Gods", "No Bishops", "No Creed Worship", "No forgiveness of Sins"'.[71] Bennett called for Blomfield to preach to the mob, but, as a critical commentator was later to note, 'London might have been in flames; Belgravia sacked, and Mr. Bennett tied to the stake by the "unruly mob," ere Charles James [Blomfield] would "have gone to preach to his people".[72] Bennett was the chosen sacrifice.

Bennett was not simply involved in defending himself; he joined the rest of Protestant England in hammering away at the presumption of the Papacy. But his voice was, quite literally, shouted down. One way to look at this wave of fear and its results is to follow René Girard's analysis of the scapegoat mechanism, whereby the marginal is purged by the mob: 'Those who make up the crowd are always potential persecutors, for they dream of purging the community of the impure elements that corrupt it, the traitors that undermine it'.[73] Nevertheless, to say that Bennett was a victim is not to say that he was, thereby totally, disempowered. He was still able to sermonise and publish. On December 4, Bennett resigned rather than give up ritual uses. He had in fact offered to resign when Blomfield asked him to change his ways prior to his denunciation of November 2, but had stuck to his guns. The resignation, when it came, was accepted a few days later, and Blomfield's affirmative reply appeared immediately in *The Times* on November 12. Bennett appears to have seen himself as something of a potential martyr, ready to give all for his beliefs. He was, in this way, participating in the contemporary enthusiasm for melodrama, whilst believing that he was engaged with reanimating the fervency and devotion of the early Church. The delicate bitterness of the situation between Bennett and Blomfield is suggested by the fact that either the bishop or his son (who memorialised his father and edited the correspondence) appears to have torn out many of the letters from the summer and autumn of 1850 that had passed between the two parties from the bound correspondence books now in Lambeth Palace Library.[74]

Bennett was, in fact, a victim of those with anti-Catholic prejudice, who regarded him as a Romanist on the evidence of a reading of the material and liturgical culture that he employed. He therefore became identified with standard Protestant slurs that he was the tool of a power that was plotting to subvert the English throne, adhered to idolatry, lacked respect for the Bible, and was obsessed with transferring power to priests. He was identified with the feared and hated French and Irish as well as with the superstition of the Middle Ages, and the excesses of the Renaissance and Counter-Reformation.[75] He was seen as far worse than a Catholic priest, because he and his associates represented the 'enemy within'. This was the pollution that threatened the English and their established Church.

The national allergic reaction to the Papal Aggression was so fierce partly because, from 1800 to 1850, the number of Roman Catholics in Britain had increased from approximately 100,000 to 750,000, much of this being due to Irish immigration and the Potato Famine.[76] Moreover, the sense of security that, for many people, derived from the alliance of Church and State had been under threat since the 1830s and so seemed doubly imperilled by this date.[77] The English Protestantism confronting Bennett and Wiseman was described by the Roman Catholic periodical *The Tablet* as a 'ferocious beast of brutish instincts, ungovernable passions, and a nature unamenable to the higher laws of morality'.[78] Wiseman's defiant, rather than mollifying, tract appealing to the 'reason and good feeling' of the English people on the issue of the hierarchy did not help to soothe the wounded lion.[79] His sermons, such as those given in December 1850 in St. George's, Southwark, appealed most to the members of his own denomination.[80] Roman Catholics had to weather several months of steady denunciation and obloquy before the immediate alarm abated. The link between Romans and Anglo-Catholics was often made, although, according to D. G. Paz, Russell's attempts to focus animosities most strongly on Puseyites were most effective where local conditions were right.[81] A typical example of a sermon that bought the Prime Minister's line was that of Rev. W. Spencer, delivered on November 25, 1850, in Princess Street Chapel, Devonport, where there was a campaign in progress against the nearby Anglo-Catholic nunnery of Miss Sellon.[82] The controversy also inspired a fair number of dubious novels and plays. One such was written by Joseph Turnley, resident of Eaton Square, Belgravia, who published a history and drama centred on the Thomas Becket controversy (the last time that the Papacy had supposedly exerted itself to the utmost against the English government). The work was addressed to the Tractarians and urged them to stand by their queen.[83]

The press, meanwhile, was mulling over the controversy. *The Tablet*, which was by no means always the best friend of Puseyites, was very sympathetic to them on this occasion, and to Bennett, in relation to the actions of Russell who was seen as a thoroughgoing hypocrite.[84] 'Lord John Russell is a more dangerous enemy than the Pope': that was the extraordinary conclusion of the High Church *The English Churchman*, which dedicated the majority of its edition of December 19 to a regretful account of the resignation of Bennett, who it strongly supported, even if it did not agree with all of his tactics or every one of this views.[85] The other extreme comes from *John Bull* (whose masthead shows a crown atop a Holy Bible, with the slogan, 'for God, the sovereign, and the people!'), which placed all the blame on Bennett.[86]

Bennett himself set out his defiant, self-justificatory stance in his 'First Letter' to Lord John Russell in which he emphasised that the Prime Minister had contributed to the building of Barnabas'. No wonder there had been disorder amongst the masses 'when the Prime Minister himself writes them a letter and tells them that we are more dangerous than even the Pope of Rome'. 'When the uncultivated, ignorant minds of the common people were so skilfully plied with incendiary matter by the Prime Minister of England, backed by the Lord Chancellor and an unscrupulous public Press' it did not matter that he only mentioned a certain party in the Church, because it was well known that St. Paul's was his parish church. Along with this widely circulated screed, Bennett reprinted the text of the sermon he preached on November 17, 1850, in which he denounced 'these great ones (specially one) joining the common multitude in their cry'.[87]

By the end of the year, the Protestant media was able to reflect with satisfaction on the outcome of the last few weeks. A famous victory had been secured against 'that fashionable place of public amusement' and the 'cumbrous ceremonial of a barbarous age'.[88] Blomfield, meanwhile, was shaken by the ferocity and rapidity of events and yet felt vindicated, commenting on December 16, 1850, that Bennett 'thought but to be his own bishop'.[89] On January 2, 1851, the bishop wrote to Rev. Edward Stuart, saying that churches with rich decoration did not, in fact, attract people in. The poor were excluded by services they could not follow, as with the case of Bennett, who had carried things so far as to 'destroy the characteristic features of the parish church'.[90]

Meanwhile, opinion elsewhere depended on the Church grouping to which the commentator belonged. For instance, Henry Phillpotts (1778–1869), High Church bishop of Exeter, complained of 'the late exhibition of rampant puritanism'.[91] More moderate opinion can be represented by the anonymous 'Simple Protestant' who, whilst regretting the 'mummeries', emphasised that the 'teaching and preaching has never been Roman'. The services were more silly than dangerous. Bennett had communion every day, so that those who went all the time thought themselves holy. Bennett's true source of support had been the 'tears and nonsense of the silly women', wives who carp against the breadwinners of their households, for 'at St. Barnabas' these unhappy devotees seem to live in the Church'![92]

From the side for the defence comes a paternalist Tory poem, perhaps a *slightly* silly and emotional one, which depicted the opposition to Bennett as being composed of worshippers of Mammon who did not care about the poor.

For the poet, Bennett's regime had represented an attempt to recover the spirituality and purity of the Middle Ages, when

There was a strong and holy band
Between the rich and poor;
Although the Castle owned the Land,
The Cottage was secure.
That same indifference to their woes
Could scarcely then be felt,
For men, perforce, would succour those
With whom they daily knelt.[93]

Whilst some of the rich disliked the cost of architectural and ritual ostentation (much of which was admittedly being met by the incumbent in this case), others shared the dreams of the early Victorian Tory clique 'Young England' for a new alliance between the rich and poor. Whilst aristocrats certainly did not want to empower the masses, it is notable that members of the latter group did feel affection for Bennett. Blomfield refused to hear a deputation from the poor of the parish against Bennett's removal, the members of which wanted to talk of the services 'so liked by us', and of his charitable works.[94] In March 1851, Liddell took over as incumbent, and on March 23 Bennett preached the 'Farewell Sermon' with discussion of which I end this monograph. Special constables had to be kept on until the summer of 1851.

Bennett went to the quiet country parish of Frome in Somerset. This was despite a parliamentary campaign to prevent him getting the position—and to remove him once he was there—led by Edward Horsman, then member for Cockermouth. This attempt sparked off Bennett's 'Second Letter' to Lord John Russell in 1852.[95] Bennett also had to fight against his own urge to give up and become a layman, from which he was dissuaded by Pusey.[96] In 1852 Bennett wrote a pastoral letter of greetings to the parishioners of Frome in which he acknowledged that 'we are not comfortable together', but that what he did was still going on in many churches in London. Moreover, 'you would not, no, you do not, tear down the Church and deface its walls; desecrate the altar, and carry havoc and ruin into the midst of the holy edifice; merely because once it was Roman Catholic'.[97] Meanwhile, the Tractarian James Skinner (1818–81) was put in place as curate along with Charles Fuge Lowder (1820–80), the ardent ritualist who, inspired by seventeenth-century Roman Catholic models of community service, was to found the Society of the Holy Cross in 1855 and the English Church Union four years later.[98] The battle for externals was, in other words, far from over.

Liddell, 1851–57

The Hon. Robert Liddell (1808–88) had been promoted to the vacant incumbency in the parish by Blomfield, who said he wanted a plain High Churchman and nothing more. Liddell was born in 1808, the fifth son of the future Lord Ravensworth of Durham (he was to be created a peer in 1821).[99] In 1836 Liddell gave up his fellowship at All Souls to become vicar of Barking. He appears to have been a much more gentle personality than Bennett, although he was still no pushover. James Skinner, as has been mentioned, was in place as the curate in charge of St. Barnabas' by the middle of Lent 1851, and it appears to have been Skinner who was instrumental in urging Liddell into maintaining or restoring Bennett's liturgical practices.[100] In 1853, for instance, choral services on Sundays were restored. He also started to turn his hand to fundraising and in the same year could be found insisting that Church rates should be paid by all regardless of whether they worshipped elsewhere.[101] The work of the parish intensified. He developed Bennett's practice of having several services per day so as to serve more people.[102] On a Sunday at St. Barnabas', for instance, Holy Communion was held at 7.30 A.M., there was a sermon for children at 9.30, matins at 10, litany 11, Communion and sermon at 11.30, evensong and catechising class for 'Children of the Upper Classes' at 3 P.M., and evening sermon at 7.[103] It is important to note, however, that Liddell was keen to prevent ritualistic changes proceeding too far. For example, when members of the congregation began prostrating themselves at Communion, Liddell sent a printed flyer around to reprove the practice.[104]

Such actions notwithstanding, opposition was not long coming, and unsurprisingly, it came from many of the same people who had been active against Bennett. For example, the butler of the local notable Henry Drummond (banker, Member of Parliament, and Apostle in the Irvingite Church), who had been a leading figure among the rioters, was arraigned for trying to break into the church, but the charges were dismissed by a sympathetic magistrate.[105] Meanwhile, Drummond himself denounced the 'sacerdotal coxcombry displayed at St. Paul's, St. Barnabas', and other places'.[106] However, the champion of opposition to ritualism came in the form of Charles Westerton (figure 3.7). He had been the second secretary of the 'London Members of the National Association' formed by supporters of William Lovett (1800–77), who was one of the leading figures of the Charter movement and a strong moralist.[107] According to the biographer of Lowder, who was a curate at St. Barnabas' from 1851 to 1856, Westerton, repeatedly elected as churchwarden, 'hovered like a malignant genius'.[108] Chartism drew great strength from elements of nonconformism and tended to sharp critique of Erastianism.[109] It should be clear, therefore, that neither Westerton nor Bennett represented viewpoints that enjoyed full support from the Establishment. Skinner was subsequently to downplay the level of elite backing enjoyed by Liddell and to conclude that Westerton was 'but the unhappy tool of men who ought to have known their duty better...no gentle-

FIGURE 3.7. Charles Westerton, *Illustrated Times*, December 27, 1856. Copyright Manchester Central Library.

man of rank and standing was found, in that wealthy and aristocratic parish, with enough chivalry to stand by him [Liddell], and put down the inflammatory abuse and vulgarity of the vestry meetings which were packed with Westerton's friends'.[110]

Westerton maintained a large lending bookshop and library from 1840 at 15 Parkside, Knightsbridge, and from 1849 at 20 St. George's Place nearby, where one could also buy stationery, writing desks, books, and pens. He was clearly a better businessman than his fellow bookshop owner, Lovett, who was to die in poverty. By the late 1850s, Westerton's lending stock exceeded 125,000 volumes accessible via an annual subscription of one guinea.[111] The catalogue shows a very wide range of authors in English, French, and German. Although there was nothing by Bennett, Pusey, and their like, one could pick up an explanatory (and presumably hostile) text on 'Puseyism'. The Lending Library also sold or lent newspapers, and one could purchase Bibles, prayer books, and '*Ten Thousand Valentines, from a Penny to a Pound* each' (figure 3.8). Westerton had a habit of publishing tracts and letters hostile to Liddell. He was reasonably learned and could discuss legal sources and doctrines. He was not very respectful to Blomfield and had a habit of ticking him off in letters (written in particularly bad handwriting) as when he alleged that the bishop was guilty of 'evading my charges by a stale trick of logomarchy'.[112] He was not much more respectful to Blomfield's successor, Archibald Campbell Tait (1811–82, bishop of London from 1856 and archbishop of Canterbury from 1868), who, according to his biography, understandably regarded the controversy as a quarrel not of his making that he had inherited from his predecessor.[113]

Tait had been picked as a man of stronger political instincts than Blomfield, one who would know how to deal with extremist nonsense from both Low and High Church ends of the spectrum of opinion.[114] Whether or not Westerton thought of Tait as insufficiently rigorous in holding the line against Catholicism, clearly the churchwarden regarded Bennett and Liddell as forces opposed to progress. A feeling for his characteristic mode of slightly incoherent bluster can be gained from his comments that 'the darkness which brooded over the Middle Ages casts again its lengthened shadow, as it approaches step by step' and that 'while the great body of the English people are sleeping, as they believe, out of the reach of danger' there is an enemy in the citadel who never rests. Not only was he given to (literary) Gothic allusions, but the boundaries of the physical and the material were at the core of his concerns. He thought there was great danger 'when once the wholesome balance separating the real and substantial essence from the ritual and symbolical shadow, is disturbed and made to oscillate between the substance and its shade'. From this it can be seen that he was not arguing against that which was substantial but that ritualism

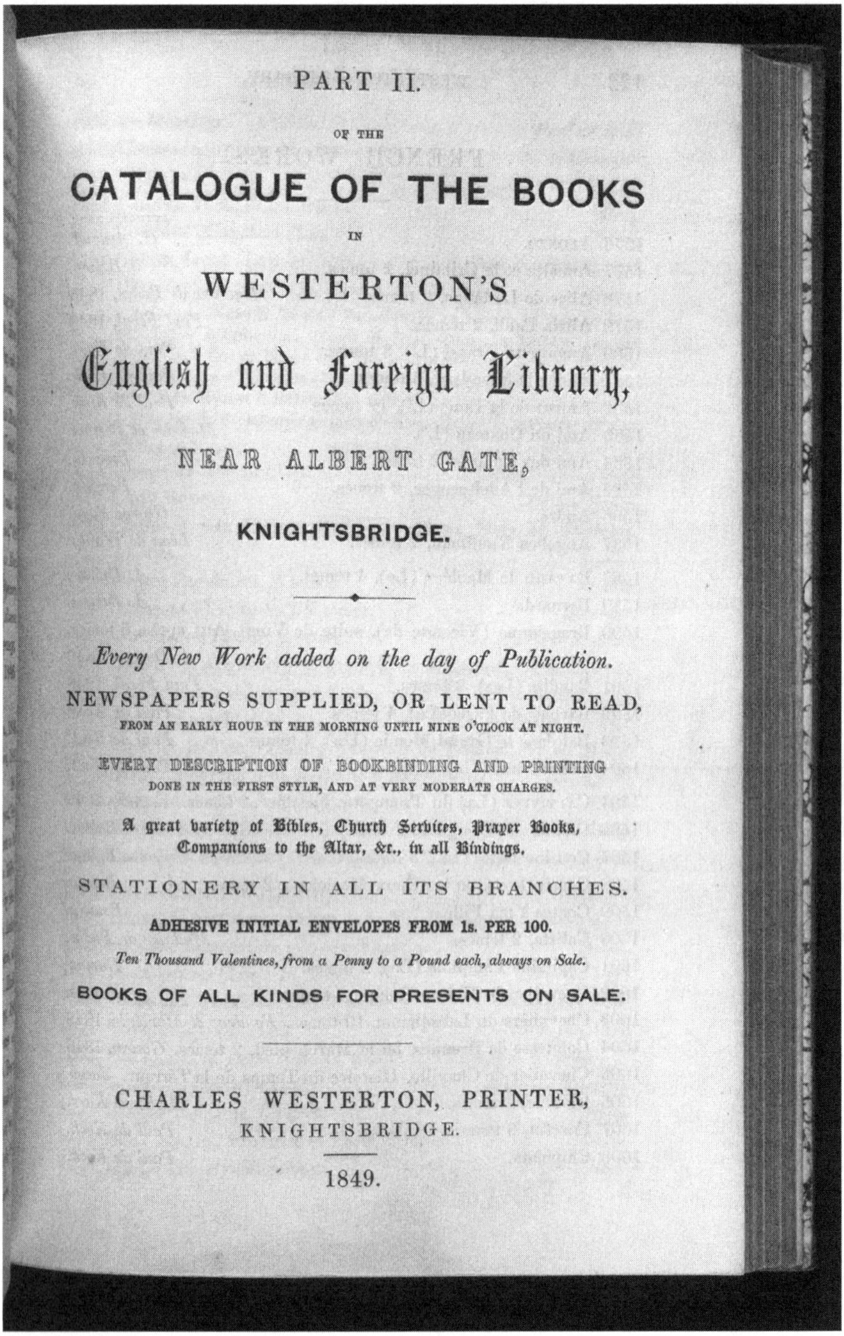

PART II.

OF THE

CATALOGUE OF THE BOOKS

IN

WESTERTON'S

English and Foreign Library,

NEAR ALBERT GATE,

KNIGHTSBRIDGE.

———◆———

Every New Work added on the day of Publication.

NEWSPAPERS SUPPLIED, OR LENT TO READ,
FROM AN EARLY HOUR IN THE MORNING UNTIL NINE O'CLOCK AT NIGHT.

EVERY DESCRIPTION OF BOOKBINDING AND PRINTING
DONE IN THE FIRST STYLE, AND AT VERY MODERATE CHARGES.

A great variety of Bibles, Church Services, Prayer Books,
Companions to the Altar, &c., in all Bindings.

STATIONERY IN ALL ITS BRANCHES.

ADHESIVE INITIAL ENVELOPES FROM 1s. PER 100.

Ten Thousand Valentines, from a Penny to a Pound each, always on Sale.

BOOKS OF ALL KINDS FOR PRESENTS ON SALE.

———

CHARLES WESTERTON, PRINTER,
KNIGHTSBRIDGE.

———

1849.

FIGURE 3.8. Charles Westerton, *A Catalogue of the Books in Westerton's English and Foreign Library near Albert Gate, Knightsbridge* (1849), p. 121. Copyright British Library Board, all rights reserved, RB.23a.21487, December 12, 2006.

were false and in fact almost vaporously insubstantial. The Church of England, he believed, needed to be preserved in its 'purity', rather than slipping into 'degrading' conditions of serfdom under Rome.[115]

The position of churchwarden was open to any adult male of good standing residing in the parish, with the exception of some excluded categories such as Members of Parliament and alehouse keepers. Candidates could be of any denomination, but they had to swear the appropriate oaths; the incumbent nominated one and parish the other. The term of office was for one year. Their main duty was to repair the church outside the chancel (which was the responsibility of the incumbent) and raise the Church rate.[116] In 1853, Westerton was elected churchwarden at St. Paul's and duly complained to the bishop on December 20 about the activities of the curate George Nugée (1819–92), making the point that the churchwardens were meant to be the 'guardians of the public decency of the parish'.[117] According to Westerton, Liddell had originally been better than Bennett, but Nugée, a former curate under Bennett, having been retained in office and, egged on by Skinner, had 'obtained a dangerous influence over the mind of Mr Liddell' with the result that the old system was restored.[118] Before sending the letter, Westerton had two meetings with Liddell, who said he would remonstrate with the curate, but this was to no effect. The bishop then delayed; the archdeacon of Middlesex was contacted, and also demurred. At Easter 1854, Westerton's term expired. Liddell tried to prevent his reelection, but on June 15 Westerton was reelected by 651 votes to his rival's 328.

According to a later account, Liddell was placed in a difficult situation by the increasingly entrenched positions in the parish. One party said that they would make a case against him in the courts if he made changes. Then, what Liddell later referred to as the 'Anti-Church' party made the same threat if he did not remove the contested liturgical objects.[119] Despite 540 people signing a memorial of support, the case was brought, for Westerton said that he was 'perfectly indifferent' as to the number of people approving these 'popish spectacles', and that what mattered was whether they were lawful.[120] Good attendance at services, in his view, did not mean approval but simply a vulgar appetite for sensation. As an anonymous pamphleteer put it, 'In London there is no difficulty in obtaining crowded congregations to witness any sort of histrionic exhibitions'.[121] Westerton's tone had none of the search for compromise that can be found coming from the bishop. For example, on the matter of processions Westerton commented that 'the performance of Mr Liddell may be in good taste, and may be pronounced very decent on the boards of a theatre, but I insist that it is wholly unbecoming in the Service of the Protestant Church, and highly indecent in St. Paul's, Knightsbridge'. He declared the whole thing to be nothing more than an 'ostentatious display'.[122]

Going to court was by no means straightforward. Many people thought ecclesiastical law something of joke, because of its arcane nature and not infrequent lack of logic or clarity.[123] Jason Horne, who was Liddell's nominee, and Westerton were the two churchwardens of St. Paul's. At St. Barnabas' both churchwardens, William Parke and George Evans, agreed with Liddell, but Jason Beal, a local resident, objected. Since the bishop declined to act, two cases were brought by Westerton against Liddell and Horne and by Beal against Liddell, Parke, and Evans.[124] The cases, being essentially similar, were heard together. They went first to the Consistory Court of the Diocese of London, where they were heard before Stephen Lushington, from whence they went to the Court of Arches, which was the court of appeal of the province of Canterbury, where they were heard by John Dodson. Blomfield's previous failure to make the bishops the final court of appeal in doctrinal matters meant that the final decision rested with the judicial committee of the Privy Council.[125] Arguing the cases in the first instance were Drs. Phillimore and Swabey for Liddell and Horne, Parke, and Evans, and Dr. Bayford for Westerton and Beal.[126] The key objects of contention were, first, at St. Paul's, a heavy wooden altar, a cross, gilded candlesticks and candles, a credence table (a small table where bread and wine are placed before consecration), and various coloured altar cloths; and, at St. Barnabas', a stone altar, a jewelled cross on the altar, a wooden screen with a cross on it separating nave from chancel, and a linen cloth with lace and embroidery for the altar.

Prior to the commencement of the case, Westerton received a detailed discussion of the issues from the bishop on March 28, 1854. Liddell, it was argued, had simply maintained what was done before, apart from a few things that the bishop had asked to cease, although 'for the sake of avoiding fresh disturbances in the district I may possibly have erred on the side of indulgence, not forbidding that which was not clearly "popish and superstitious"'. Processions, according to the bishop, were fine, unless they involved bearing sacred vessels, in which case they should be abandoned. Liddell had denied the accusation of bowings and genuflections. An anonymous observer was sent by the bishop and did not see any. The bishop said that it was hard to lay down rules for outward displays but 'the rule to be followed in this and similar cases is, not to use outward markers of reverence in an ostentatious or singular manner, so as to awaken suspicion and call forth observation'.[127] Westerton's objections to a 'high altar' were unwarranted, for this would only be correct where there were several altars. The problem was that 'altars' were associated with transubstantiation, so the term 'communion table' was preferred. As was commented a few years earlier, the Church of England had 'discovered a desire to "avoid even the appearance of evil", by a *silent* abandonment of a name which has a legitimate meaning, but which is liable to be abused to superstition and idolatry'.[128] The altar in St. Paul's was wooden and movable. Therefore, it 'cannot be termed an "altar" in any but a figurative sense' and was a table and so legitimate. As for candlesticks, he did not like them in parish churches, but was not willing to order their removal. He had wanted the cross to be removed from the communion table of St. Barnabas', but did not order it taken away since the congregation liked it. Moreover, it had been there at the consecration although 'not seen by me, a large offertory dish being in front of it'![129] As for the multicoloured altar cloths, he preferred plain linen but he thought there was nothing against this in any rubric or canon. Moreover, Westerton had gone into print on these issues before writing to the bishop, and his tone was disrespectful. Although Blomfield concluded by asking Westerton to desist, the churchwarden did not: the two suits were brought at the same time and were argued together between July 24 and 27, 1855. The judgment was delivered by the judge of the Consistorial Court, the Right Hon. Dr. Lushington on December 5.

Stephen Lushington (1782–1873), in political terms, bore some resemblance to Lord John Russell, being a Whig who supported parliamentary reform, the end of slavery, and rights for Catholics, Jews, and Dissenters and was in favour of Church reform and modernisation. He was not a romantic of neo-medieval tastes, and in this legal case, he followed the detailed doctrinal line taken by William Goode (1801–1868), dean of Ripon, one of the few to attempt to refute the ritualists' position systematically.[130] For instance, Peter Toon has identified Goode's *The Divine Rule of Faith and Practice* of 1842 as the 'most learned and elaborate' reply to Tractarian ideas. His key point was that our focus must be on Scripture, not on divine revelations that had supposedly happened since then. He provided key discussions of the Eucharist and baptism.[131] Crucially, Lushington's views were a mirror of Goode's arguments that the existence of practices since the Reformation, especially during the Laudian period, was no proof of their legality.[132] It was pointed out by the defence that two hundred churches currently had stone communion tables, seventy used candlesticks, fifty credence tables, and thirteen had crosses near the communion table, but this was dismissed as irrelevant.

The next major issue was that of congregational support. Westerton and Beal argued that the congregation was substantial, but much of it was not from the local area. In response, Liddell submitted a petition of support from five hundred of his parishioners. Lushington said that this was a parish church and its attached chapel, and he had to consider only those who lived in the locality. But he did recognise that there were very significant divisions of opinion even within the parish:

One party may apprehend that the things complained of may lead
to superstitious uses, and the other that they conduce to the more
decorous and effectual performance of divine worship. We must feel
that these things in themselves are utterly immaterial, and derive
their importance only from the ideas, connected, or supposed to be
connected, with them; by some considered as indicia of the ancient
and decorous worship of our Christian faith; by others as denoting
a disposition to return to those abuses from which our Reformed
church has been happily purified. [133]

In coming to his judgment, he announced that he would consult Acts of Parliament, the canons in force, ecclesiastical 'common law', judicial decisions of
superior courts which were binding, and finally 'usage and custom that has
prevailed'. He was quick to dispose of the argument that the presence of items
in church when consecrated renders them legitimate. He then referred to the
key case of *Faulkner v. Litchfield and Stearn* (1845).[134] This concerned St. Sepulchre's in Cambridge and had determined that the stone altar installed there was
not legal because it was, in the words of the presiding judge, Sir Herbert Jenner
Fust, 'connected with the doctrine of transubstantiation.' The associated negative publicity badly damaged the reputation of the Camden Society, which had
been restoring the Church after the tower had collapsed. St. Paul's communion
table was massive, but was wooden and, therefore, was legal. That of St. Barnabas' was of stone, and this was unlawful under *Faulkner*. As a side issue, that
case also ruled out the use of credence tables.

At St. Paul's there was a two-foot-high wooden cross (figure 3.9), whilst at
Barnabas' there was a rood screen with a cross on it, and a jewelled cross on the
altar. The Act of Unity of 1662 gave the Ornaments Rubric of the Book of Common Prayer the force of statute: it said that 'such ornaments of the Church and
of the ministers thereof, at all times in their ministration, shall be retained and
be in use, as were in this Church of England, by the authority of Parliament in
the second year of the reign of Edward the Sixth' (i.e., 1549). Lushington ruled
that he could not admit practice between 1549 and 1662 as a guide, but the key
problem was that it was hard to say what was the practice had been in 1549. It
was Lushington's opinion that the key authorities were the third and fourth enactments of Edward VI. These judgments defined the acceptable use of 'ornaments', although this did not determine whether, for instance, crosses were, in
fact, ornaments and so covered by the Ornaments Rubric attached to the Prayer
Book. Crucially, Lushington placed the burden of proof on the defendant; in
other words, Liddell had the difficult task of proving that the disputed objects
were in use and legal in 1549.

FIGURE 3.9. Altar cross, St. Paul's, Knightsbridge, 2006. Photograph by the author, by permission of the Vicar and Churchwardens of St. Paul's, Knightsbridge.

Lushington nailed his colours to the mast, saying that 'I agree that the Established Church is not the negative of the Church of Rome. [But] I think that the Established Church was intended to be comfortable to the primitive church, and consequently purified from the abuses of the Church of Rome'. Moreover, 'I must assume that what was done at the Reformation was right'. Should we not hesitate, he asks, before admitting practices that have the 're-motest leaning to the Church of Rome and her usages, which our Reformed faith holds in just abhorrence?' He did recognise that there had always been two parties in the Church of England. However, the ordinances of 1549 only legitimised practices done 'by the authority of Parliament'. Therefore, the practices which had been maintained by minority elements of the Church did not have the force of legal precedent.

He affected a dismissive attitude, saying that 'what can be more indifferent' than such issues as the shape or material of the altar, but concluded that ultimately they did matter because of the ideas that underlay them. The key issue, for him, was what objects might be 'perverted' by wrong practices. Crosses were not simply ornamental designs, but should be considered as idolatrous, along with crucifixes since 'they have been equally perverted to superstitious practices'. In relation to the other disputed objects, he found it hard to tell functional from ornamental candles but thought it best if the ambiguity was ended through their removal. The Eighty-Second Canon required that 'the communion table . . . be covered in times of divine service, with a carpet of silk or other decent stuff', rather than coloured cloths. He did not approve of the rood screen at St. Barnabas', but there was not the legal authority to remove it.

Lushington had a very clear view of material propriety in worship, declaring that 'a decorous simplicity is the characteristic of the Church of England. What is lace and embroidery but a meretricious display of fantastic and unnecessary ornaments?' This is but a 'servile imitation' of Rome, for 'chastity and simplicity are not at variance with grandeur and beauty; but they are not reconcilable with jewels, lace, variegated cloths, and embroidery which are better fitted for the gorgeous pageantry of the Church of Rome than the pure and severe dignity of the Church of England.' Lushington summed up by saying that 'by setting the heart too much on external appearances, the purity of God's worship is gradually corrupted, and an undue reverence attached to the things made by the hand of man'.[135] He decreed that the altar cross and credence table be removed from St. Paul's, whilst at St. Barnabas' the altar should be changed from stone to wood, the credence table, altar cloths, and crosses be removed, and the text of the ten commandments be placed on the east end of church. Ritualism was soundly defeated.

Responses were not long coming. Henry Phillpotts, High Church bishop of Exeter, suggested that the decision had been taken because these practices were unpopular and because of the fear of public opinion: the judgment was political rather than theological.[136] A particularly interesting response came from a 'parish priest who has not in use the articles complained of'. He agreed with Lushington that what was done between 1549 and 1662 was irrelevant, but drew the very different conclusion that widespread earlier use gave legitimacy to any practice that was not expressly forbidden by the ornaments rubric: 'The use of the Cross upon the Altar, then, being admitted prior to 1549, and not the slightest evidence being adduced of its being prohibited or censured', should be allowed. The third and fourth statutes of Edward VI, 1549, forbad the crucifix but not the cross, 'for the plain reason that the Cross is not an image'. To lump cross and crucifix together as idols was absurd since 'anyone who has seen in some of the Roman Catholic churches the painted crucifixes, seven or eight feet in height, representing our Lord to life, can readily perceive the grounds for this distinction between the Crucifix and the simple cross'. A 1547 injunction of Edward VI stated that 'all ecclesiastical persons shall suffer from henceforth no torches, nor candles, tapers or images of wax to be set afore any image or pic-ture, but only two lights, upon the high altar, before the sacrament, which for the signification that Christ is the very true Light of the World, they shall suffer to remain still'. Lushington had said that the high altar is abolished as being the adjunct of transubstantiation, and therefore, lights on the communion table are not lawful. The anonymous writer thought that the communion table, be it of wood or stone, was the high altar and, therefore, the use of candles, and their lighting, was legitimate. Lushington did not find against coloured altar cloths by reference to the practice of 1549, but merely on the basis that they were 'mer-etricious'. The Eighty-Second Canon simply said that altar clothes should be of 'decent stuff'. Should decency rule out the use of coloured fabrics? Lushington was inconsistent: large altar candles were found to be popish although this was not good grounds for excluding them. 'Decent', for the anonymous writer, did not mean those 'disgraceful coverings, which are far too commonly used on the Holy Table of the Lord, e.g. green baize with yellow worsted borders and fringes, or the like, vulgar, cheap and coarse; such that they who use them with complacency would not—no, not for an hour—suffer them to remain on their own table'. In comparison, fine coloured silk would do honour to the Lord. Lushington had read lack of endorsement in the Tudor enactments as indicating displeasure, but there was no mention therein of such decorative medieval 'outrages' as ornamental floor tiles and sarcophagi. Finally, this writer commented that Lushington's judgment was supposedly against the 'servile imitations of the church of Rome', but countered by saying that Dissenters say that about all the aspects of the Church of England![137]

In the following months, life in the parish continued to be rancorous, particularly as Liddell and his curates proceeded to expand their missionary activities and calls for funds. Charles Lowder, curate at St. Barnabas', was a focus for particular animosity. He had come to wider notice in 1854 after he was found guilty of inciting the choristers of St. Barnabas' to throw stones and eggs at a placard bearer for Westerton's reelection as churchwarden.[138] On May 2, Lowder was duly fined £2 in damages.[139] Meanwhile, financial accusations continued to fly. In 1854 'a Belgravian' wrote a letter to *The Times* pointing out that St. Barnabas' was intended for the poor but appeared to be attended by the rich.[140] A much reprinted (I saw it in its sixth edition) muckraking pamphlet alleged that Bennett had forced his church on a poor area that did not want him and argued that he should go back to his rich friends. The Protestant way to aid the poor was to subscribe to societies, such as those of which Lord Shaftesbury was chairman. But in contrast, Bennett 'confessed that he *vowed to revenge* himself for this mud-pelting [that he had supposedly received by hostile locals], by building a church. As if *revenge* was a proper spirit for a clergyman eating Protestant bread'. Another anonymous writer thought that this was all a conspiracy to get the loyalty of the poor. Protestants should replicate such missionary efforts 'if no other means can be found of counteracting their [the Ritualists'] effect'. 'Even beggars' are to be seen going to Barnabas', the writer continued, not with approval.[141]

Liddell was careful to emphasise that money was not, in fact, being wasted on the 'undeserving'. For example, in relation to the Provident Society, in order 'to prevent any portion of the money from being squandered in needless finery', each bundle of clothes saved for by the 'industrious Poor' was checked by the manager.[142] Yet his efforts were not appreciated by many of the petty bourgeoisie, one of whom exclaimed, in relation to the burial guild, that 'the friends of the deceased never pay a farthing to the undertaker!!! Such a manifest injustice to that respectable class of tradesmen is clearly worth the attention of the legislature'.[143] It was not simply the financial aspect of the burials that caused dismay, but their style.[144] In a nice Gothic Revival touch, Liddell employed what one writer described as 'obsolete medieval-shaped coffins'.[145] Such coffins with 'cruciform furniture' were advertised at one pound and five shillings, and a model was available for clergy who wished to introduce their use elsewhere.[146]

It was widely recognised that the missions to the poor had, in fact, brought Liddell and his curates a substantial degree of local support. As one hostile commentator admitted,

> Most other people in the parish are on his side, or he could not
> get on as he does. If it were not for such patriotic tradesmen as
> Mr. Westerton, and his friends the Licensed Victuallers (for the public
> houses are dead against St. Barnabas', and would not mind how
> liberal they were to put it down), if it were not for these we do not
> believe there would have been the least opposition in the parish.
> As even it is, Mr. Westerton is obliged to beat about in other
> neighbourhoods for people to come and help him.[147]

Such support must have stiffened the resolution to stand for God over Mammon and to oppose the 'patriotic tradesmen' whose stand had been vindicated by Lushington's condemnation. Liddell's appeal was therefore duly pleaded before the Court of Arches. The judgment was delivered by the Rt. Hon. Sir John Dodson (1780–1858) on December 20, 1856. He argued that the aim of Edward VI's injunctions was to prevent idolatrous worship of objects and images and, in addition, to remove all ornaments that had been or could be abused. Dodson found that crosses would 'naturally…be included under the head of images'; for even if it was not an image, devotions could be made to it and that would certainly make it a 'monument of idolatry'.[148] He supported Lushington's line that a bishop could not give permission for an illegal practice, either deliberately or as a result of an accident. That there were some crosses in churches in Edward's time was simply evidence that there were illegal acts taking place! Therefore, there was no authority for the use of the cross in church. In St. Paul's, he ordered the removal of the cross, credence table, and cloths. The wooden 'table' (i.e., altar) and candles could stay. In St. Barnabas', the order was for the removal of the stone table, replacing it with one made of wood, the removal of the credence table and all crosses, and replacement of the coloured cloths with plain ones. And the Ten Commandments must be written at the east end. In most aspects, therefore, Dodson upheld the decisions of the lower court. Moreover, unlike Lushington, he awarded costs against Liddell.

On the Fourth Sunday in Advent, Liddell preached a sermon justifying his desire once again to appeal the decision.[149] The legal battle had driven the two parties into ever more entrenched positions. On January 5, 1857, Frederick Baring, who worked with Westerton on the case, protested in a letter to Tait that 'we ask for nothing unreasonable but simply that the nursery for Bastard Popery should be removed from Belgravia'.[150] He was quite clear that the ritualists were leading the people to Rome. Liddell, by contrast, swore that the removal of such things as the cross would be what would drive people to convert in desperation.[151]

The ultimate court of appeal was the judicial committee of the Privy Council. Its judgment was the occasion of considerable tension, and it was remarked that 'as several points of the case were disposed of there was an attempt to cheer, but it was instantly suppressed by the officers of the court'.[152] The appeal was heard February 9–16, 1857, in front of the Lord Chancellor, Lord Cranworth, Lord Wensleydale, the Right Hon. T. Pemberton Leigh, Sir John Patteson, and Sir William H. Maule. The archbishop of Canterbury and the new bishop of London, Tait, were summoned to advise. Sir Fitz-Roy Kelly, Q.C., and Dr. Phillimore acted for the appellants, and Dr. Bayford and Mr. Stephens for the respondents.

Kelly argued that crosses were in use in the time of Edward VI and were therefore legal. Crosses and crucifixes were not distinguished in the legislation; only 'images' were forbidden, and he noted that even Elizabeth had a crucifix in her own chapel. Phillimore, meanwhile, contended that 'the cross was a Christian ornament, and used in the Primitive Church'. There was no specific definition of altar or table in the authorities, and nor was anything said of the colour of cloths in the canons. Moreover, an 'altar' was required for the coronation service, as for instance that used in Westminster Abbey for the coronation of Queen Victoria, which was made of stone and was the gift of George IV. For Westerton, Bayford argued that *Faulkner* must be upheld, saying that altars were abolished along with the doctrine of transubstantiation. Credence tables and altar cloths were borrowed from Roman Catholics. Crosses were indistinguishable from crucifixes in Catholic worship and both were images rather than ornaments. Stephens contended that the intention of the Reformation was the 'abolition of books, images and ornaments, not essentially necessary'.

The judgment was delivered on March 21, 1857. The Privy Council found that Lushington had relied on the enactments of year two of Edward VI. Dodson had also relied on various royal acts on images. It was found that the Ornaments Rubric did not cover items that were simply decorative rather than necessary for services. So, then, the question was whether objects such as crosses were covered by Acts of Parliament that talked not about ornaments but about images, as Dodson had argued. The Privy Council contended that saints' cults were based on lies but that was not the case with the worship of Christ. Moreover, the cross had been used as an early Christian symbol and employed as an ensign of honour 'without any relation to superstitious or even religious uses'. The royal decrees had only said to remove images that were used for worship, yet the Privy Council argued that greed had led silver objects that were not so employed to be made away with at the Reformation. The decision was that crosses, as opposed to crucifixes, were legal, but only if they were 'architectural ornaments' rather than objects that were in danger of idolatrous employment.

On this basis, the cross on the rood screen of Barnabas' could stay, but the portable crosses could not.

Faulkner meant that the stone table had to be replaced by a wooden one. However, it was found that the credence table was not, in fact, a Roman Catholic object. It was an adjunct, not to the altar, but to the communion table and could, on that basis, be retained, because 'nothing seems less objectionable than a small side table'. The Privy Council reversed the judgment of Dodson on the altar cloths, because the canons proposed 'to secure a cloth of sufficiently handsome description, not to guard against too much splendour.' Having said which, lace would be going too far, since the canon simply specified a fair linen cloth. The archbishop of Canterbury and the bishop of London concurred, and costs were to be shared by the parties.[153]

This was a substantial victory for Liddell and was crucial in allowing the legal expansion of ritualist practice within the Church of England, so arguably ensuring that Disraeli's Public Worship Regulation Act of 1874 was to be an example of too little too late. Thomas Perry of All Saint's, Margaret Street, promptly published a very detailed six hundred page defence of the 'Ritual and Ceremonial movement which has been gradually developing itself during the last twenty years (whether always judicious or not) [and which] was, in the main, consistent with the Ecclesiastical law'.[154] After the court victory, Liddell appealed to those of his flock who had left to come back now that the remaining ritual practices were clearly legal.[155] But there was a defiant Protestant reaction to their party's defeat.[156] It was argued that 'as the judges travelled beyond the simple question, *the law of the case,* it is evident that their unconfirmed opinion or recommendation can have no legal efficacy. It is a fearful record of the extent to which learned and well-meaning men can be misled.' It was a repeated Protestant accusation that this would lead to worse violence and disorder. One such apocalyptic claim was that the judgment is a 'firebrand which will probably be extinguished in blood'! Elaborate ritual would not be allowed to remain for 'the people can and will crush the serpent'.[157]

Pimlico remained more or less at peace now that Westerton had reached the end of his opportunities for legal appeal, but it is interesting to compare what happened to Bennett at Knightsbridge with what occurred in the next famous case of ritualism and riot in London.[158] Despite the judgment in *Westerton v. Liddell*, the incumbent of St. George's, Bryan King (1811–95), while lasting longer than Bennett, was forced out in very similar circumstances. Whilst at Oxford, he had listened to the sermons of Pusey. Shortly after, in the summer of 1842, he was presented to the Rectory of St. George's-in-the-East by Brasenose College. Married on September 28 of that year, he was to spend the best part of the next two decades in the very much earthier surroundings of Stepney.

As early as 1844, it was reported to Delane, editor of *The Times*, that he was one of the most strongly Tractarian ministers in London, that his church was badly attended, that he was possessed of an unfortunate 'hauteur', and that he was attempting to force his views on an unwilling populace.[159]

King himself had complaints. On his arrival, he found that his church was 'blocked up with huge and high boxes [box pews], which the poor with their timid delicacy ever shrink from entering'.[160] It was no wonder there was a small congregation, for in this slum parish, few could afford seatings. In King's view, the previous rector had been negligent. No one, by contrast, could accuse him of lacking energy. He 'established two mission chapels, five or six schools, affording religious instruction to upwards of 600 children, a penitentiary for the reclaiming of fallen women with whom the neighbourhood abounds, an establishment of ladies actively involved in the evangelisation of the parish, and an energetic system of parochial visitation'.[161] From 1857, he used vestments presented by parishioners in the aftermath of the Knightsbridge judgment.

Just like at St. Paul's, Knightsbridge, the incumbent and his curates were arrayed against the elected churchwarden. But, to make things more complex, there was also a lecturer appointed to the parish. The trigger for riot was perhaps set by Tait when he licensed Hugh Allen to this post, a man who was as antiritual as was the vestry that had selected him.[162] Allen was a friend of the barnstorming Baptist Charles Spurgeon and was 'almost alone amongst the clergy in this district of London for the extravagance of his tenets in the direction of puritanism'.[163] His invective inflamed the parish, and disturbances began on a regular basis. At one point, the mob became so threatening that the ritualist Alexander Mackonochie, who was giving a sermon, had to be rescued with the help of five policemen. A group of men were formed to act as a defence force for King. Furthermore, 'a respectable inhabitant of the parish, as respectability is reckoned on Ratcliff Highway [a street notorious for crime], was seized in the act of exciting a small mob of boys and idle ruffians to assault the Rector, and was taken before the magistrate at Thames Police Court'.[164] There were accusations of stone throwing from both sides.

On August 14, 1859, elements of the crowd seized the choir stalls and cried out that they wanted to attack the choirboys. King himself refers to all this as sacrilege and wrote uncompromisingly to the bishop about it.[165] As was commented at the time, 'if there be such a sin as sacrilege, it has certainly been committed at St George's. I refrain from direct allusion to the filthy obscenity of certain acts which have taken place within the very sanctuary of the church'. It was alleged that if such things had happened at St. James', Piccadilly or St. George's, Hanover Square, they would never have been allowed to continue. Apologists for King argued that the services were no different from those of

St. Paul's Cathedral, let alone those of St. Paul's, Knightsbridge! As for the lurid stories in the press, it was alleged that they were written by those ignorant of theology and that the many stories which 'invariably (as some people have observed) contain so many glowing allusions to the "praiseworthy attempts of Mr. Churchwarden Thompson to preserve order," are carefully prepared on Sunday evening in the bar-parlour of that respectable official's public house'.[166]

It was, in fact, alleged to be the result of a selfish conspiracy of the mercantile and the ungodly:

> The passion that provoked them was not Protestantism, but Black-guardism. They were organised by the alien sweaters, who perceived that the gospel of Christ, if practically applied, must tend to emancipate those slaves of labour on whose toil they lived; and by the local brothel keepers, who, like Demetrius the Silversmith, were alarmed for the gains of their occupation. They were fomented by rich men of evil character at the West End of London, who, at least in some notorious instances, combined an ostentatious pietism in public with systematic profligacy in private life. The rioters were the very dregs of Wapping.[167]

Tait did not calm things down. In a letter sent to the vestry on September 5, 1859, he talked of 'this childish mummery of antiquated garments'.[168] 'If he had acted with that manliness about which he talked so glibly', King's biographer and son-in-law asserted, then disaster could have been avoided. Instead, Tait was led, according to the same, if clearly partial, source 'to sacrifice Bryan King to the mob' because 'popularity is too frequently the test of methods, and leads to the profanation of holy things'.[169] In other words, it was a deliberate political decision, as had been widely hinted at that time. For instance, 'Alpha' said that there are 'those, and there are many, who maintain that it is the policy of the Home Office to permit these riots, in the hope of suppressing altogether the "Puseyites"'.[170] King was forced into a leave of absence, having become ill. He went first to rest at Bruges, before moving to Avebury in Wiltshire. Like Bennett, he had been found a quiet parish in the countryside west of London.

It is notable that neither Bennett nor King converted to Rome or became members of an exotic new Anglo-Catholic monastic order. In this they make a contrast to the Anglo-Catholic vicar of Charles Kingsley's novel *Yeast* (1848–51), who ended up 'under the name of Father Stylites, of the order of St. Philumena... preaching impassioned sermons to crowded congregations at St. George's, Bedlam'.[171] The parish of St. Paul's ceased to be a site of national controversy. Financial supporters in 1858 included the Marquis of Londonderry and the Rt. Hon Sidney Herbert, who each gave £100; Earl Clanwilliam, who gave £50; and Earl Jermyn, who gave £25.[172] Rich gifts enabled building works to recommence. From 1859 onward, stained glass, tiles, statues, and new furniture were installed at Paul's, all placed there with the knowledge of the bishop. In 1866, St. Barnabas' became independent and was, over time, to gain the complex decoration scheme that it bears today. The reredos was erected 1893. The present chancel screen was installed in 1906 by Bodley but retains the old brass gates of the original. The original high altar was placed in the side chapel of the Holy Sepulchre. Its stone top was reused as a base so that it could be substituted at will if the law changed.[173]

By the end of the nineteenth century, the use of many previously controversial elements of ornamentation and liturgical elaboration had come to be accepted. As Nigel Yates has commented, 'an Anglican worshipper of 1660 would have noticed few liturgical changes in his parish church if he had returned there in 1840. Sixty years later he would have found it hard to believe that the services in his parish church were those authorized by the Book of Common Prayer'.[174] What is revealing for the present study is the intensity of the fascination and opposition during the early Victorian age. As we have seen, the commercial classes, led by Westerton, but also including publicans, led the campaigns in Pimlico, whilst brothel-keepers were alleged to have stirred up opposition against Bryan King because of his missionary work with fallen women and drunkards, work that was also carried out by Liddell in Knightsbridge. Clearly Anglo-Catholicism, because of its missionary work, was seen as bad for business. It will be important, therefore, to think how it can be understood in its economic, as well as in its cultural and theological context.

One anonymous critic of Lushington's judgment seized upon the judge's use of the word 'meretricious', as in his comment that 'what is lace and embroidery but a meretricious display of fantastic and unnecessary ornament?' The critic's counterclaim was that this equated pleasing decoration with defilement and prostitution. 'Hear it, ye ultra-Protestants of Pimlico', thundered the writer, 'revilers and despoilers of that beautiful Temple, raised, by the piety of priest and people, amid a dense and long neglected population, only becoming the most depraved of outcasts—a common HARLOT'.[175] This imagery was repeated by the spokesmen for the opposition in a piece of the following year that appeared in *Lloyd's Weekly Newspaper* and was reprinted by Westerton. This described the ritualist practices as being worse than those of Papists, since they were 'at best a wretched, mincing, harlotry imitation of the Church of Rome'.[176]

How might an altar cloth suggest a prostitute's bodice? How was that sexually fetishistic gaze inspired? Why did liturgical objects and images that evoked Catholicism have such power to provoke sexualised anxieties? Sigmund Freud suggested of his notion of the fetish as a boy's replacement for the idea of his mother's penis that 'in later life a grown man may perhaps experience a similar panic when the cry goes up that Throne and Altar are in danger'.[177] Nationalistic English Anti-Catholicism serves as a label but not as an explanation for such a combination of anger and excitement. Why was such a fuss being generated about material culture when Lushington was able to conclude that 'what can be more indifferent' than material forms in religion?[178] And why did the local opposition feature prominently lawyers, publishers, brewers and, if one can believe the proritualist propaganda sheets, the patrons of the local whores? In the following chapters, I show that the answer lies partly in the interrelations between commerce and theology.

It is important to think of these battles not simply in terms of theological parties, but also in relation to social groups. There is evidence that both sides attempted to mobilise working-class support, in terms of both mob action and more peaceful purposes. A certain Mr. Buxton, saying that he was working on behalf of Westerton, spoke in return for thanks offered up by the Wigan Working Men's Protestant Association, by denouncing 'the crafty operations of men who eat the bread of Protestants, but do the work of Rome'.[179] This reference to Protestant bread recalls the title that William Lovett, the Chartist leader who inspired Westerton, gave to his autobiography: *The Life and Struggles of William Lovett in His Pursuit of Bread, Knowledge and Freedom* (1876). In this book, Lovett describes how a group of forty or so supporters of the National Association got together to set up the 'London Members of the National Association' in 1841, the main action of which was to publish the *National Association Gazette*. In this autobiography, Lovett recalls Westerton as the second secretary of this group and notes his attendance as representative at the Complete Suffrage Conference, held in April 1842 in Birmingham. He also notes that Westerton later 'rendered great service to the liberal cause by his opposition to Puseyism'.[180]

On June 15, 1846, and so before the battle with Bennett and Liddell had blown up, Westerton gave a talk at the City of London Mechanics Institute in Gould Square in which he highlighted some of the radically anticlerical aspects of English romanticism:

> If Byron, from his close acquaintance with and disgust for a number
> of would-be priests, poured out a stream of invective against the
> unholy and time-serving men of the Church, he still pressed on Man
> that he should not forsake the worship of Great Nature's God, but it
> should be done in the great places he himself has made, the moun-
> tain and the desert, or the still sanctuary of the human heart, instead
> of doing so in buildings made of human hands.[181]

Dreams of perfection that lead Ecclesiologists and Ritualists to attempt the visual resurrection of the Middle Ages were not shared by Westerton. He would reject artifice, but if there had to be building work, it should be Classical rather than Gothic, as he recounted in another essay:

> What strikes the eye when looking a Gothic building more than
> the variety of its details?—its ornaments, its fretted work, its pillars
> springing to the roof?
>
> But with what feeling do we look on a Grecian Temple? There,
> all thoughts of details are banished; there is nothing in the unpre-
> tending simplicity of its columns to court our attention—no glaring
> ornament to attract—no variety to confuse.[182]

The glaring, meretricious, surface attractions of Gothic distracted the eye and the mind from the truth. To Westerton, a Grecian temple was the symbol of democracy; a Gothic church, that of despotism. He told his audience of mechanics in 1846 that a new ethical and aesthetical regime was close, for 'the time is at hand for a new class of Poets to arise—Poets whose sympathies are with the people'. For while

> the extremes of wealth and poverty swarm around us as they do
> now—while Institutions, worn out with age, are tottering to their
> fall—while superstition and idolatry have ceased to dazzle and to be-
> guile—while the worm eats through the bishop's staff, and the moth
> is busy with the ermine robe, and dust is on the plume—our poets
> need not fear a want of themes.[183]

The threat or dream of revolution may have faded along with Chartism after 1848, but Westerton was not the only person in the ensuing years for whom the discourse of idolatry was not just a tool in a struggle against Popery. He and others like him were fighting against clericalism in general and patronage by the elite in particular, for what they saw as progress, and for cash.

4

Satan Transformed: Comparative Religion

The paradox of the church of St. Barnabas', Pimlico, like many another Gothic Revival buildings, was that it was a brand-new structure attempting to project the venerability of great age. It was therefore an attempt to provide a secure connection between a supposedly stable past and the chaotic present of the Victorian metropolis. Whilst the Ecclesiologists thought they had located a brief moment of architectural perfection in the later Middle Ages, others dismissed any such attempts as appropriations of primitive barbarism into a dynamic modern age. Opponents and proponents of ritualism were engaged in attempts to understand the past and to learn how to make use of it in contemporary society. That past was littered not simply with the astonishing mystery of the early Church and the flamboyant growth of Roman Catholicism but also with the remains of other religions. The heritage of classical paganism and its supposed relationship with Catholicism and Hinduism provided a key battleground in the disputes over the alleged impurity of Roman practices in the Church of England. It also gave rise to a sort of ecclesiastical equivalent of the eighteenth-century grand tour in which clergymen visited Italy to make up their own minds on such questions.

Rome was an interesting choice of destination for an evangelically minded Irish Protestant to take his bride on a kind of extended honeymoon. Yet for a man who was intent on never being morally off duty, it made a certain kind of sense. Ritualism was attacked for its supposed embrace of Catholicism. The latter was understood as representing a superstitious system of moral tyranny that had grown up in the passage of the centuries through the corruption of the practices of early Christianity. To engage at any level beyond the merely polemical with Roman Catholicism required, therefore, a consideration of historical change. If Catholicism was a monster, it was a monster from the past uncannily alive in the present. And where better to confront that monster than in Rome itself?

The happy newlywed was Michael Hobart Seymour (1800–1874), the ardent Irish Protestant who appeared in the introduction to this book. He took his B.A. in 1823 and M.A. in 1832 at Trinity College, Dublin, and was ordained deacon in 1823 and priest in 1824. From 1827 he was the travelling secretary of the Irish Protestant Reformation Society and lived in five Irish counties until 1834, when he migrated to England. Ten years later he moved from Guildford to Bath, which was to become his permanent home.

Seymour learned Gaelic and made great and, it would appear, disappointing missionary efforts in his Irish youth.[1] He was to look back on the country of his birth toward the end of its life and condemn it for its centuries of bloodshed and 'disloyalty'.[2] He thought that the Irish, being an 'excitable, imaginative and dreamy race', were easy targets for superstition.[3] He was to become something of an English nationalist, perhaps because he thought himself descended from the Tudors, who had brought the blessings of the Reformation to their kingdom. He praised that land's ancient traditions, even defending such palpably Catholic documents as the Anglo-Saxon penitentials (codes of penances as adjuncts to confession) for their freedom from Roman models.[4] The bitterness of his frustration in early life can be felt in his comments when a curate at Ballinrobe, Mayo, just before he left for England. Why, he asked, was the self-evident truth of Protestantism being ignored? The answer lay in the power of the Catholic priests and their 'bitter and malignant spirit'.[5] He, like many another Irish Protestant in England, brought his rancour with him. Late in the same year, he was addressing the Society for Promoting the Religious Principles of the Reformation at Exeter Hall, expressing his alarm at finding Romanism spreading in England and not just due to the arrival of Irish immigrants.[6] In 1838, he could be found disputing—with no sense of compromise at all—with the Catholic Priest Joseph Sidden in Guildford.[7] He was, in the ensuing decades, to pitch into most of the anti-Catholic controversies of the day, notably, the panic over women (supposedly) trapped in nunneries in the course of which controversy he took on Nicholas Wiseman himself.[8] He can even be found, in the last year of his life, putting the boot into William Bennett as one of those who 'have long laboured to galvanise into life the mouldy relics, the foul skeleton and ill-flavoured carcase of Romanism, now three long centuries buried in this land'.[9]

But Seymour's fame rested substantially on two volumes he wrote based on time spent in Rome in the 1840s: *A Pilgrimage to Rome: Containing Some Account of the High Ceremonies, the Monastic Institutions, the Religious Services, the Sacred Relics, the Miraculous Pictures and the General State of Religion in That City* (1848) and *Mornings among the Jesuits at Rome* (3rd ed. 'considerably enlarged', 1850). Critical responses were entirely sectarian. The Roman Catholic *Rambler* found *Pilgrimage* 'pre-eminently bad', whilst *Mornings* was very enthusiastically lauded by the *English Review*. The High Church periodical, the *Church of England Quarterly Review*, was tart: '[H]e is so utterly unable to take any but the coarsest and most sensual view of every thing which is presented to him'.[10]

Seymour says that he went to Rome trying to put to one side his previous prejudices. *Pilgrimage* was based on his observations, *Mornings*, on his conversations. His observations repeated time-honoured anti-Catholic tropes: no one can read the Bible and the city is given over to the worship of Mary; the Pope and cardinals spend much of their time kissing the toe of the statue of St. Peter, and so forth.[11] Yet there is more to his work than cliché. Not only was he a lively writer, but he was, perhaps unexpectedly, also a listener. He admitted that he became friendly with a number of Jesuits and grasped that great achievements and intellect could be possessed in combination with belief in gross superstition. And he made it his business to let his reader know how enthusiastic the Jesuits were about the Tractarians.[12] He seemed, at times, to be in awe of their missionary success, for example, in Central and Southern America, although he suspected that the quantity of the converts was greater than their depth of understanding.[13] Such success, he thought, was based on the missionaries' obedience and (excessive) moral flexibility. Like good members of the workforce today, they would move and reskill so as to achieve their ends. As 'A. M.', a member of the Church of England put it, in his review of the book: '[Jesuits] will shift stations, rank, employment, professions, callings, and with equal pliancy, wear the livery of the court or the kitchen. Hence this virtue sinks into abjectness'.[14]

'A. M.', although he thought that Seymour's researches into the reality of monasticism were salutary, had certain strong reservations. He disliked Seymour's conclusion that Catholicism was simply Paganism in modern dress. For Seymour, when he gazed at the modern city of Rome, saw that it was physically built on top of the classical city and then leapt to the conclusion that the same thing applied to its morality. He declared that 'the very shrines dedicated to the excesses of the licentious Venus became consecrated as the shrine of the tears of the repentant Magdalene'.[15] Using the same logic as the protestors at Walsingham that we met in the introduction, he regarded the crowned Virgin Mary as the goddess of fertility returned to power.[16] Meanwhile, the ascetic aspects of Roman Catholic life were denounced as being 'oriental'.[17]

'A. M.' also questioned whether Seymour had 'not filled this chamber of horrors with spectres and phantoms conjured up by a lively imagination'?[18] In other words, was he, in some ways, relishing what he should abhor? To see what 'A. M.' meant, let us journey with Seymour from the parlour into the basement, so to speak, into the catacombs and relic chambers of Rome where Catholics had, for centuries, buried the 'poorer classes and their [household] slaves'.[19] Here he is addressing a meeting in Bath in 1866 on the subject of Mary:

> I hope the ladies present will forgive me, I won't say anything very
> indelicate, but I was myself shown and I have handled a bottle of
> milk from her breasts as she suckled the child Jesus…and I did
> handle with my own hands—I hope the ladies will again forgive me
> for explaining myself in plain English—what seemed to be a red rag,
> but which was shown to me as a piece of—what shall I call it?—the
> chemise of the Virgin Mary [which was used in former times to re-
> enact the birth of Jesus].[20]

Why should the ladies be warned about the basic facts of the female body with which they must have been familiar? The reason is that the transgressive element here is Seymour himself. His argument is that this infernal system encouraged men to engage in such perverse (in this case, necrophiliac) bodily encounters with women in the name of Jesus Christ. What was not quite so clear was whether disbelief rendered such activities morally safe for the Protestant tourist. This is why he needed to express disgust so vehemently.

There are two other interesting points to be made about Seymour's anti-Catholicism. One is that he was very keen to use facts and figures; for instance, he can be found informing us of the 'social evil' (i.e., prostitution) that 'despite the action of the [Roman Catholic] confessional' there were twice as many harlots per 10,000 population in Paris than London.[21] He was also keen to sound the alarm that Catholic populations were growing more rapidly that Protestant ones.[22] The other point is that this man combined a desire to see and handle lurid expressions of Catholicism with an intense focus on purification. He was quite clear that the Reformation represented the 'restoration of ancient truth in all its primitive purity'. He spent his life loudly denouncing 'those doctrines which ulcerate her system [i.e., the body of the Whore of Rome], and which have compelled us to separate from that Church, lest we partake of her sins and receive of her plagues'.[23] He was so driven to the urge to purge that he provided tender Protestant parents with a 'family version' of John

Foxe's 'Book of Martyrs', which was designed to remove 'coarseness of expression'.[24] Seymour's engagement with Roman Catholicism combined, as 'A. M.' was aware, a decidedly ambiguous combination of a drive to textual purity, an embrace of comparative religion and sensual oriental horror, and a desire to classify and tabulate. In this, as this chapter will show, he was representative of his times.

'Primitive' Religion from Rome to Home

Anglo-Catholic ritual was inspired by the English Catholic medieval past and, to a lesser extent, by the Roman present. The ensuing focus on the symbolic and sacramental material expression of religion was condemned by its opponents as being an idolatrous profanation and pollution of spiritual worship. This corruption was understood to extend far beyond the simple worship of images, although idolatry was, first and foremost, 'heathen' adoration of spiritual beings who were depicted, particularly, though not always, through sculpture. This understanding was extremely widespread, representing a popular awareness of a variety of religious traditions outside Christianity. However, the iconoclastic traditions of the Reformation were still alive and well: '[E]ven worshipping *the true God*, through the medium of an image representation', for some, was idolatry, since to do so represents 'a bold overturning of the Divine economy; and a substitution in its place of the vain imaginations and wild conceits of men!'[25] In fact, so potent was idolatry as a pathological sin that it could be conceived very broadly indeed so as to involve anything evil and monstrous, as in the following example: let there be an 'attempt but to touch any of the forms of idolatry, or of superstitious worship, in any part of the world, and what a power is instantly aroused in its defence. What efforts were made, and continue to be made, to support Negro slavery and the slave trade!'[26] Idols were used as a metaphor for sins such as that represented by the idol of uncleanness and impurity whose worship was the product of seduction outside marriage.[27] Money and power could be idols, as in the concept of the worship of Mammon.[28] Idols were impure material things that tainted humans by appealing to their base desires, so distracting and deluding them from their struggle toward purity and salvation. Idolatry, for one polemicist, was a 'pestilence that walks in the Church of Christ'.[29]

For Alexander Pollock, chaplain of the Church of Ireland Leeson Street Magdalen Chapel in Dublin, speaking before the YMCA, an idol did not have to be something material; it simply had to be 'anything or any being that takes the place of God…if any one thing be loved more than God, that one thing is an idol.'[30] For an intelligent 'Brahmin', the image is not the God, but is a channel of communication, and 'bears something of the same relationship to the deity it portrays, that one of our gas-pipes does to the gasometer of the manufactory'. However, 'when dealing with an illiterate people [such as these things were supposedly designed to teach], it is, and it must be, almost impossible to prevent the use of images from degenerating into positive and direct Idolatry'.[31] Like sex, image worship was all too alluring: 'Idolatry is all natural, down-hill,—easy, like the broad way', because 'there is a natural proneness and tendency in us all to give God a sensual, carnal worship, and not that which is commanded in his Word'.[32] Hard-line opinion excoriated not just images, but also ritual objects of the liturgy. It was claimed that 'all nature is invoked, enlisted and laid under contribution...[Allegedly] there is holy virtue in water and bread; there is sanctifying power in cotton or wool; and iron and wood are terrible in their spiritual influence'.[33] It could thus be alleged that the objects themselves were not just worshipped as representations, but were thought of as somehow potent in themselves. In these ways fetishism and idolatry sapped the individual as it sapped the nation. It had been very different in Israel where 'a strong monotheism grew...out of intense nationalism, the religious patriotism, which bound the whole people together'.[34] Yet anti-Semitic discourse claimed that oriental decadence had claimed the Jews after they had rejected Christ through pride, leaving their modern representatives trapped in ritual and mummery.

Those who defended religious statues and other images were keen to stress their improving rather than idolatrous qualities. The Irish Roman Catholic priest Thomas Maguire argued that we should consider,

> if a scandalous, wanton and lewd picture was placed before them,
> whether its effect at first sight would be to bring lewd thoughts into
> the mind; and hence it was that these pictures were forbidden by
> the Church. If these pictures had such an effect, did it not stand to
> reason that pious and holy pictures or images would bring on similar
> grounds, corresponding feelings in the imagination?[35]

Some Roman Catholics seemed not to have the decency even to be appropriately defensive. John England, the Roman Catholic bishop of Charleston, for instance, was quite happy to confess that 'the altar is a consecrated stone'. And he had no problem with ecclesiastical dress being descended from that of the ancient Romans; this made it venerable not impure.[36] However, the Jewish and hence Biblical prohibition of sacred images was used by many Protestants to argue that it was simply too dangerous to have these ambiguous objects around. People might simply start to worship them by mistake. Once it was within the citadel, the pollution of superstition would inevitably spread. Ultra-Protestantism was having none of it:

> Unblushing monster! Thy infectious breath
> Spreads, where it goes, contagion linked with death,

is how 'Papistry' as 'Satan transformed! Though in Christian dress' is described by one writer.[37] There had been a time when there had been 'no wooden cross adored, nor penance known', but then came the 'satanic phalanx' that 'filled with pollution the Christian air'.[38] This view of Roman Catholicism meant that the physical objects of their liturgy, such as holy water, were seen as contagious, rather than as purifying.[39] A chapter titled 'Papists are not Christians' in a book by Robert Taylor (1784–1844), sometime Anglican priest turned deist and freethinker, alleged that Roman Catholicism was ancient paganism, and that as paganism fell, the Devil was reborn from the ashes like the phoenix.[40] 'Paganism and Christianity are mixed up in Popery, and consequently in stating that Popery is Christianity corrupted would only be stating the truth', adds another writer.[41] Consequently, the Roman Catholic Church was 'Satan's masterpiece'.[42] The alliance of Church and State was heathen, seen in its highest form in Rome, both imperial and Papal.[43]

From such a viewpoint, the splendours of the Church of late antiquity and the Middle Ages were so much dross. The iconoclasm of the Reformation found stout defenders, as when the Macclesfield Congregationalist George Kidd deplored Wiseman's attack on those who burnt effigies at the Reformation.[44] Yet not everyone was quite so uncompromising. John Ruskin, moving somewhat away by 1853 from the evangelical opinions of his youth, agreed that Romanists were idolaters, and yet, he asks, might there not be spiritual feeling there too? Conversely, Protestants may be spiritual, yet is there not some idolatry that comes between God and us?[45] Nevertheless, the ultimate fear for Protestants was that Rome was trifling with people's chances of salvation and cynically exploiting the ignorant. The danger was that once the masses saw how idiotic idolatry was, as supposedly they had begun to in ancient times, then this would lead to infidelity and so would come the end of morals, particularly among the working classes.[46] One writer thought that this process was well under way, because Catholic children were often models of piety, but adults, understanding the rituals as nonsense, tended to become cynical nonbelievers.[47]

The identity of the fallen city of the Apocalypse was a key battleground. Was it Papal Rome? And could an answer be found by comparing Catholic practices with those supposed to have existed in ancient Babylon? John Cumming (1807–81), minister of the National Scottish Church in Covent Garden, and a virulent anti-Papist, thought they could: 'In Pugin's *Glossary of Ecclesiastical*

Ornaments are...accounts of Babylonish robes and splendour and precious stones, the very reading of which is a commentary on the Apocalypse'.[48] Babylon, it was argued even by the classical scholar and generally moderate Anglican Christopher Wordsworth (1807–85, future bishop of Lincoln), was not so much a type of pagan Rome as Christian Rome: a seductress, 'putting forth her claims and veiling her corruptions, under the most specious, seductive and alluring colours'.[49]

Hard-line Protestant opinion tended to draw on fear of the last times in order to lash into the Pope as the 'man of sin' and 'priestcraft' as a 'corruption of the Devil'.[50] This normally extremist stuff was rife in 1850–51, as when Wordsworth, preaching in Westminster Abbey, condemned 'the self-called successors of St. Peter [who] *sit in the Temple of God as Gods* [original emphasis]'.[51] Yet things calmed down, and by 1856, a tract appeared that was the result of favourable press reviews of a series of lectures that denied that the fallen city at the end of time was Rome pagan or Papal. The beast with seven heads was Rome, and it carried the fallen city of Jerusalem. The message was that we all needed to put our houses in order.[52]

Progressive opinion was indeed painfully aware that all was not well at home. Whilst money flowed into foreign missionary activities, it was clear that the burgeoning conurbations of England simply did not have the religious personnel in place to ensure the spiritual welfare of the poor. There were rallying cries for the evangelisation of the 'home heathen'.[53] The key point was that their unbelief and superstition were understood to go hand in hand with vice and crime.[54] The level of hysteria that could be reached on this subject can be seen from tracts such as John Knox's, *The Masses Without! A Pamphlet for the Times, on the Sanitary, Social, Moral, and Heathen Condition of the Masses Who Inhabit the Alleys, Courts, Wynds, Garrets, Cellars, Lodging-Houses, Dens and Hovels of Great Britain, with an Appeal for Open-Air Preaching, and Other Extraordinary Efforts to Reach the Perishing Masses of Society* (1857). To go into a pub in a poor district was to feel the force of the terrifying, out-of-control, pullulating, reproducing masses. He tells us with horror that 'young females are seen in light dresses whirling round in a silly dance, uttering obscene language, and half-intoxicated with the draughts of beer which have been profusely lavished on them'. 'We talk of savagism, idolatry, and cannibalism in heathen lands,' he thundered, 'but what are we to say of such low grovelling, sensual, debased practices at home?'[55]

The peoples of the Bible were thus joined by their latter-day counterparts in understandings of comparative religion and morality. The fear of idolatry was associated with thinking that, as we have seen in the case of Seymour, opposed antiquity with modernity, national with foreign and western with oriental. Thinking about comparative religion was a useful tool for ministers who wished to expatiate on evil and salvation. It was of particular relevance when money was to be raised for missionary activity, or, as we have seen, to combat Catholicism. Much of this 'wisdom' was in the popular domain and circulated as truisms, but beyond relying on general prejudice, preachers were able to draw on books of antiquarian research, some of them indeed written by clerics, but others by gentlemen of leisure, or by professional men, such as soldiers who had served in India.

One of the most influential respectable texts of comparative religion was produced by Sir William Jones (1746–94) in 1784 (published in revised form in 1801). This argued for strong similarities between classical and contemporary Indian pagan deities. 'The Gothick system', Jones argued, 'which prevailed in the northern regions of Europe, was not merely similar to those of Greece and Italy, but almost the same in another dress, with an embroidering of images apparently Asiatick'.[56] However, since this area of research was not regulated through university or Church structures, it was something that attracted all manner of writers of greater or lesser intelligence, fairness, and probity. These people in their turn carried their prejudices to their studies, of which pro- and anticlericalism were important strains. On the one hand, comparative religion could be used to denounce particular forms of religion, but on the other it could be employed, by radicals and freethinkers, to mock religion in general as so many shades of primitive absurdity. It is notable how many Protestant preachers were willing engage with comparative analysis bearing in mind its subversive potential even in relation to their own traditions. From their point of view, however, it was not that religions were more or less misguided, but that they were more or less perfect. From that perspective, contemplating the imperfections of heathen spirituality acted, through comparison, to validate their own.

In addition to moral pontification, a further feature of antiquarian scholarship was its tendency to attempt to create classificatory systems in uneasy juxtaposition with lurid sensationalism. It was from such antiquarian books that preachers and the congregations learned, for instance, of the supposed druidic practice of making a wicker man and filling it with human victims to appease their gods.[57] Pagan antiquity, particularly classical pagan antiquity, did have its defenders. There had long been a minor industry in trying to provide some sort of get-into-heaven-free card for the literary heroes of Greece and Republican Rome who had had the misfortune to have been born prior to the spread of truth. This led to such improbable special pleading as the argument that Seneca's writings were 'often almost purely Christian' and 'plainly in imitation of the *language* of inspired teachers respecting the "Spirit of God"'.[58] Yet, in the hands of most enthusiasts for comparative religion, classical paganism evoked a striking combination of ignorance and hedonism.

If heathenism had flourished in ancient Europe and was, by analogy, persisting in archaic institutions there to the present day, what of it in its native lands, notably India? The British imperial encounter appears to have been a crucial element in the development of traditions of comparative religion. It is important to keep in mind the complex circumstances of that encounter, including its variations in time and space which led to a great diversity of moral approaches to the oriental Other. I do not address this vast topic as a whole here; rather, I focus on those aspects of sensationalised images of eastern religions, particularly Hinduism, that played an important role in the interpretation of the activities of the ritualists through the creation of an orientalised image of Rome.

'Exotic' places were an open invitation to the imagination, and led to what might be termed 'tropical Gothic'. For was it not 'in the climes where flowers are fairest, and fruits are sweetest, and fullest sunshine warms the air and lights a cloudless sky, that nature prepares her deadliest poisons [?]. There the snake sounds its ominous rattle, and the venomous cobra lifts her hood'.[59] Orientalism, that notorious Western creation of the Orient, was itself, in a sense, created by Edward Said and other scholars through their celebrated revelation of despotism, splendour, cruelty, and sensuality as elements of stereotype.[60] This has been seen not simply as an interpretative mechanism, but also as one that has shaped Asian realities, as in the assertion that 'it is the European orientalism of the eighteenth century that gradually systematizes knowledge about the people of India and the various beliefs and practices into an integrated, coherent religion called Hinduism'.[61] In the following account, I use the words 'Hindu', 'pagan', and 'heathen' in the essentialising manner with which they were employed in the nineteenth century.

There are myriad specialist studies of European attitudes to religion in India.[62] Naturally, there are far more studies of Hinduism, which we, unlike many Victorians, might wish to see less as a unified 'religion' but more as a complex of cultic practices related, amongst other things, to the 'sacralisation of a social order'.[63] Detailed nineteenth-century studies of Indian religion tended to be labours of love or eccentricity. One such was E. A. Rodriguez, *The Hindoo Pantheon* (1841–45), printed for the author in Madras, at the Christian Knowledge Society's Press. The author was sufficiently fascinated to spend a great deal of time and money on his work. Yet he also moralized. In an interesting parallel with criticism elsewhere of Roman Catholicism, he condemned Hindus for the production of grotesque 'unnatural' statuary and for self-indulgence and self-torture (in other words, for delight in extremes of bodily sensation):

We find immortal beings foregoing celestial happiness for the gratification of temporal and sensual pleasures, and the supreme being, Siva, countenancing and abetting them. What a pattern of morality!... Penance and self-torture are regarded as essential to the attainment of a character for holiness. Not only do devotees boast of renouncing all the decencies and pleasures of life, and all the charms of social intercourse, but they rack their inventions to contrive the most intense sufferings. [64]

But orientalism, it can be argued, was not just the construction of an Other by westerners, but part of a dialogue of mutual influence.[65] Thus, David Cannadine argues that the British empire was also about domesticating the exotic and creating a common culture based on class rather than racial superiority. In his analysis, 'ornamentalism', theatricality, and ceremonial were ways of blending the elites together and so distracting people from the politically inconvenient spectacle of bodily differences.[66] The prominence of racialised discourse in the later nineteenth and twentieth centuries is the main obstacle to the acceptance of Cannadine's arguments, but ideas such as his do seem more persuasive when considered in the context of the eighteenth and early nineteenth centuries. The East India Company, for example, had a policy of caution in relation to missionaries since their views of native religious practices tended, perhaps not surprisingly, to be 'decidedly unfavourable'.[67] Utilitarian pragmatism suggested that disruption and unrest were more likely outcomes of missionary activity than the mass conversion of the natives. The Indian mutiny of 1857 is often thought of as a crucial event in the intensification of stereotyping. Indians assaulting and raping British women were constructed as oriental polluters desecrating pure British womanhood.[68] In a paper published by Charles Westerton, one J. J. Macintyre advocated seizing Mecca as 'a defensive and offensive measure for the war in Asia'. This was called for because Britain had been attacked by 'idolaters and heathen people, whose inhuman temple practices and obscene rites partake of the nature of the demon worship of the ancient Canaanites, and of the crimes of the cities of the plain' [i.e., they were sodomites].[69] Nevertheless, both before and after the mutiny, many westerners were genuinely interested in exploring native art and religion, although even such people, as has been pointed out in a recent study on Buddhism, and as we have seen with Rodriguez on Hinduism, tended to analyse India through the distorting lens of western superiority.[70]

An intellectual tradition from the late eighteenth century had identified a common classical ancestry of Europe and India, in terms both of heathen cults and of Indo-European language origins.[71] This was accommodated into racist processes of Othering through the notion of cultural and moral evolution by which the native peoples of the empire were seen as natives stuck at a primitive stage of development. However, this also generated considerable controversy about the boundaries and location of the east and the degree to which the founding cultures of Europe, Greece, and Israel had come under 'Asiatic' influence.

An interesting work to consider in this context is *A Few Remarks on the Sculpture of the Nations Referred to in the Old Testament, Deduced from an Examination of Some of Their Idols* (1845) by James Legrew (1803–57). This was dedicated to Prince Albert by the author, a sculptor who lived in St. Alban's Road, Kensington, not too far from Pimlico. He defended the notion of a qualitative difference between classical Greece and the Orient. His view was that Greeks differed through their appreciation of pure form. He compared this with an 'Asiatic' enthusiasm for precious materials. Orientals had

> the habit too of covering or ornamenting their statues with gold...[and this] does not convey to us a very exalted idea of the purity of their taste. The objection does not lie in the substance itself; for it need scarcely be repeated that gold is as capable of exhibiting the finer lines as bronze or any other metal. But the use of it is almost always connected with that deficiency of taste, which would substitute a splendid and costly material for beauty of form, and which is so common in the sculpture of the barbarous nations. [72]

Whilst he admitted that the Greeks had gilt statues, this was because they 'most probably received their religion from the Phoenicians and the Egyptians'. Here 'feeling overcame their otherwise pure taste and independent genius'. It was a 'remnant of barbarism' that was 'perpetuated by superstition'. Similarly, the mysterious graven images and objects of the Jewish Temple were all the product of 'Asiatic' influence, representing a focus on gold rather than beauty. If God told them to ornament the Temple thus, it was because that was all the Israelites could have understood at the time. This moral and aesthetic impoverishment had occurred because they had been living amongst the Egyptians.[73] Therefore, in sum, Roman Catholicism inherited a classical art in late antiquity that was debased by Asiatic influences. Such ideas had a fairly widespread circulation; they surface, for instance, in John Taylor's lectures on early Christian history (1857). Taylor believed that Hellenic religion was concerned with physicality, but it was aesthetic and shot through with moral wisdom, since 'the character of the *national faith*...was not darkened by one shadow of gloom or mystery; it shone forth brilliantly in the light of day' [my italics].[74] A key aspect of this anachronistically nationalistic and anti-Gothic brilliance was, supposedly, 'entire exemption from the control of a priestly corporation'. In 'Asiatic' religion, by contrast, 'gross symbolism acted with the most injurious effect. Such higher meaning as might be hidden under it, the multitude never reached. It debased and sensualised their most familiar conceptions of deity.... To the priesthood it acted as a convenient hiding-place for their most recondite thoughts'.[75]

A crucial issue was that approaches that stressed cultural evolution implied that all religions represented particular stages of progress, as in Auguste Comte's (1798–1857) view of the evolution from fetishism to idolatry to modernity (discussed in the introduction).[76] In this analysis India represented a land that had got stuck in the middle stages of religious development, or had decadently regressed to it, as was described in Edward Robertson's poem, *Idolatry*, of 1849.[77] In similar vein, William Laurie, an officer in the Madras Artillery, attested that the original Indian belief was in the Creator Brahm, and he wondered at how such a 'sublime belief as this, the revered of a great antiquity, should have degenerated into the present brutal, licentious, and obstinate idolatry'. His explanation was to blame the priests. This caste, the 'Brahmans', thinking monotheism insufficiently comprehensible to the masses, changed their ritual practices and 'what might now have been, through wise and liberal management, a pure and spiritual worship, has become a system of external abominations. There can be no doubt whatsoever that the Hindus are the most corrupt people on earth'.[78] By corruption, he undoubtedly included sexual corruption since prostitutes were allegedly being used to worship the 'lingam' (i.e., phallus), a word that, as one normally fearless writer, from which we will hear more, says, 'I do not choose to translate'.[79]

Just as fear of Catholic priestcraft read across into the discovery of the same phenomenon in India, so there were repeated attempts to find similar despotic processes taking place in both cultural contexts. The observation of pilgrimage provided an excellent opportunity for the 'discovery' of comparable atrocities. The Jagannath temple (referred to by the British as 'Juggernaut') at Puri became notorious in this context. According to the ardent supporter of Baptist missionary activities William Gurney (1777–1855), Juggernaut was represented by 'an ugly wooden figure, with a black face, and large red mouth' as he tells us in his little book of Hindu idolatry for the young (figure 4.1).[80] The priests allegedly said that the deity liked human sacrifices, and it was claimed that people threw themselves under the wheels of the cart on which the statue was drawn. The East India Company continued the practice of previous native rulers by levying a tax on pilgrims and providing a subsidy for the temple's upkeep from the receipts. The Pilgrim Tax was employed by the British in Orissa from 1806 to 1840, but subsidies continued to be paid until 1863. This was,

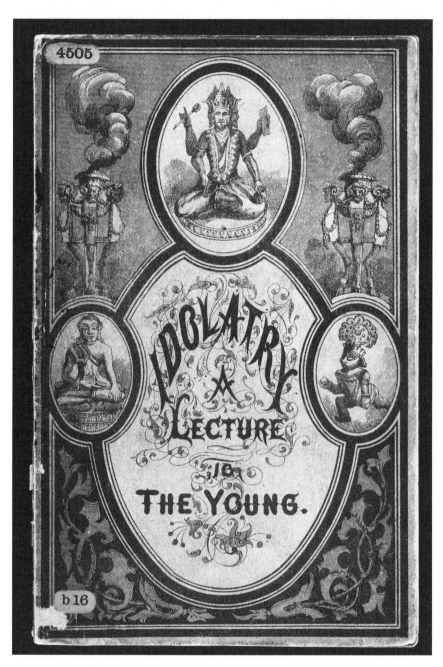

FIGURE 4.1. William Brodie Gurney, *A Lecture to Children and Youth on the History and Character of Heathen Idolatry* (1848), front cover.

arguably, the result of the wish of Richard Wellesley, Governor General from 1797 to 1805, 'not to hurt the religious sentiments of the people', as an aspect of the Company's belief in religious neutrality.[81] There were many missionaries and evangelicals who campaigned against the tax and who also opposed a wide range of government arrangements with temples and festivals across India.[82] Stuart Piggin, in his detailed study of the topic, has commented that 'one vainly searches the writings of evangelical ministers for any favourable reflection on non-Christian religions', but even less hostile observers were critical, seeing Company policy as a mark of Christian endorsement of heathenism.[83] One Methodist referred to the Catholic pilgrimage centre at Lough Dearg in County Donegal as the 'Juggernaut of Popery', since he alleged it was a money-making exercise that cynically exploited superstitious ignorance.[84] Puri become so notorious that the temple became a synonym for idolatry in its broad sense of general vice, hence 'The English Juggernaut', a temperance engraving showing alcohol as the idol rolling forward and leading to disease, misery, and death (figure 4.2).[85]

A further similarity between the Tiber and the Indus was pointed out in a children's book from the Religious Tract Society. The Vedas were in a dead language, and 'this is as though our Bible were only printed in Latin...but, then, the heathen priests do not wish the people to read their sacred books'.[86] One might compare this with the championing of John Wycliffe (c. 1325–84), 'first who gave to the English, in their own fine Saxon English, those "Gospel Truths", till then hidden from them in learned languages, known only to the Priesthood, and some few of the educated of the descendants of the Norman barons'.[87] One can even find occasional examples of the linking of the European past and the Indian present in modern scholarship, as in the suggestion from 1991 that 'the art of mediaeval Christendom is closer to the art of Hinduism than it is to the art of the modern world'.[88]

It is interesting to compare the Protestant reception of Roman Catholicism and Hinduism with that of Buddhism. This philosophical system was abhorred by Europeans in the first half of the nineteenth century as a cult of nothingness (which feeling Roger-Pol Droit sees, in a recent study, as a reflection of their own personal fears of losing their faith in God).[89] But, interestingly, the antimaterialism of the tenets of Buddha was often seemingly contradicted by a lively material culture focused on the rich corporate possessions of temples, which could then be read as a mirror of medieval Catholic practice. In both cultures, the ideals of personal privation and corporate splendour were complementary rather than contradictory.[90] This made it worse rather than better in the eyes of the missionaries. Buddhism was referred to as the 'devil-worship' of Ceylon (present-day Sri Lanka), being supposedly composed of both atheism and idolatry and thus

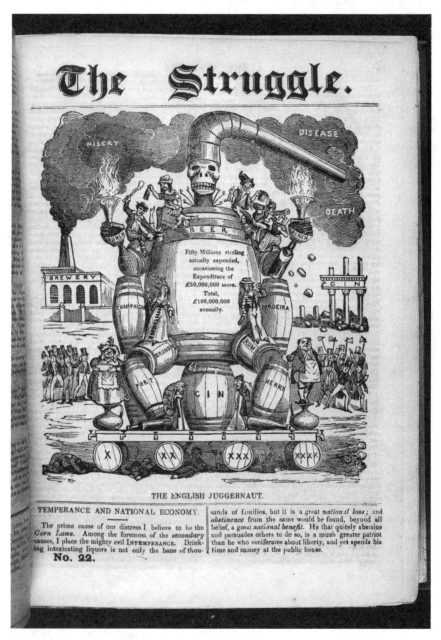

The Struggle.

THE ENGLISH JUGGERNAUT.

TEMPERANCE AND NATIONAL ECONOMY.

The prime cause of our distress I believe to be the *Corn Laws*. Among the foremost of the *secondary* causes, I place the mighty evil INTEMPERANCE. Drinking intoxicating liquors is not only the bane of thousands of families, but it is a great *national loss*; and *abstinence* from the same would be found, beyond all belief, a great *national benefit*. He that quietly abstains and persuades others to do so, is a much greater patriot than he who vociferates about liberty, and yet spends his time and money at the public house.

No. 22.

FIGURE 4.2. 'The English Juggernaut', *The Struggle* 22 (1842), p. 1. Copyright British Library Board, all rights reserved, pp. 1424 c, October 3, 2008.

being as nonsensical and as bad as things could get.[91] Conversion to Catholicism on the island was thought by Protestants to be fairly straightforward due to the alleged similarities of heathenism and Roman Catholicism in their devotion to external show, ritual, superstition, and the celibacy of priests.[92] Moreover, according to Baptist missionaries, Singhalese Roman Catholics were 'of all classes of the natives, the most superstitious, and sunk in ignorance even below the heathen who surround them'.[93]

The link between India and Rome was made repeatedly, for instance, in a tract written in 1851 in response to the building of large Roman Catholic churches in Sheffield and to the announcement that there were seven thousand Roman Catholics in the town:

> If one morning when waking from the slumbers of the night we discovered that 7,000 of our fellow-subjects were transported from the plains of India to the town of Sheffield; carrying with them a devoted attachment to the worship of Vishnoo—that by some magic touch a beautiful temple, for their use, rose in the heart of the town...that some persons were beginning to think that Idolatry had been greatly wronged and misrepresented, being after all but a matter of opinion; that it is illiberal and narrow-minded to speak hard of it...if it was stated that more than 600 of these temples stud the length and breadth of England; served by nearly 900 sacrificing priests...[would there not have been an outcry? Therefore,] have those to whom reference is made a weaker claim [on our consciences] because their faces are not black, and that they worship, not Vishnoo, Sciva or Budha [sic], but a little flour-and-water wafer, not having even the shape of an intelligent being?[94]

John Poynder (1779–1849) was an evangelical lawyer who had never visited India; but then, most of the writers who discussed Indian religions had not been there either. His *Popery in Alliance with Heathenism: Letters Proving That Where the Bible Is Wholly Unknown as in the Heathen World, or only Partially Known as in the Romish Church, Idolatry and Superstition Are Inevitable* (1835) was a sustained attempt to find connections between these religious systems. He identified, on a host of levels, a 'remarkable agreement between Pagan India, and Papal Ireland'. For example, he drew analogies between Christian and Hindu shrines and linked canonization directly with heathen deification.[95]

However, comparisons between Rome and India need not have involved mutual denigration. Wiseman fought back against Poynder, suggesting that the latter was writing to deflect criticism that he was ignoring the sufferings of Britons at home. As for similarity between Catholics and Hindus, might that, the future Cardinal had asked in 1836, reflect not borrowing, but a common impulse to kneel in prayer and gaze up to heaven?[96] In a similar vein, for William Bennett, the fact that the setting of a place apart for a holy shrine was universal showed that it was true, rather than that it was pagan.[97] This line of argument did not as much reject similarities as seek to excuse or even to rejoice in them. As another anonymous writer argued, should we not rather marvel at the fact that there were Christian things even amidst the heathen: 'No one, who has not considered the subject, can contemplate the wonderful agreement of Heathen mythology with the sacred scriptures, without a surprise nearly allied to awe'. Moreover, 'Brahma of Asia', was, for this writer, the same as Bacchus, who was the same as Jesus, just 'disfigured by sin and superstition'.[98] Thus, comparative religion could be used in different ways. Typology could be a way of identifying Christian truths behind pagan beliefs. Such work was potentially ambiguous in that it could be use to damn the heathen for corruption or praise them for their similarity to Christians. This is one reason why comparative religion was of interest to a wide spectrum of people. It could be used to prove pretty much what you wanted.

Exegetical, antiquarian, and ethnographic research was used both to attack and to defend Christianity in general and its Protestant and Catholic variants in particular. There was general belief in England in the superiority of British over European and of European over eastern cultures, albeit with some disagreement over the status of ancient Greece and Rome. However, many people seem to have viewed this superiority with trepidation as being a fragile achievement. Idolatry and its attendant immorality were, from certain perspectives, satanic impulses that still ruled in India and on much of the continent of Europe and that were threatening to pollute Great Britain. The more evangelical Protestants knew of the world, the more seeped with sin it appeared to be. Many of them believed that purity was only possible in heaven. Yet when Victorians looked up at the stars, some of them can be found having the different thought of embracing the physical complexity of Creation. Perhaps the solution to the diversity of beliefs on earth was a Supreme Being who showed 'Himself' in different places in different ways. One writer, Richard Hawley, thus, wondered 'whether the benefits of the Christian revelation were confined to the human race, or whether they extended to the inhabitants of other worlds?' He suggested that 'the doctrine of the blessed Trinity may in every world be the same, with this single exception, that the Christ of each world may consist of the union...of an emanation of himself united with the highest intellectual being that inhabits that world'.[99] If memorials were put up to the deaths of these alien Christs then perhaps future evangelicals would even have to denounce idolatry on Mars.

Bodies of Christ[100]

Shoring up the boundaries of Protestant purity required lessons drawn from abroad to be applied at home. As we have seen, in the case of Pimlico, the material culture of ritualism was scrutinised for signs of idolatry and superstitious fetishism. Whilst there was anxiety about the animation of the material world in general, it is clear that human bodies were a focus of tension in relation to the boundaries of the physical and the divine. The role of statues in classical paganism and Hinduism was clearly important in this, as was, of course, the inherent tension within the Trinitarian theology of Christ as both spirit and flesh. All that notwithstanding, it is hard for us to grasp the intensity of concern with which many in England reacted to any visible reminders of Christ's physicality. Consider an illustration from *Punch* in 1850 showing William Bennett as a moth fluttering before the Roman candle and, we may assume, about to expire on the flame. This was a satirical comment on Bennett's concern to light candles on the altar during the mass in defiance of Protestant norms. But it is important to note that the wick is in the form of a cross. As a word, the cross was the symbol of resurrection, but in this image it was the vehicle of death (figure 4.3).

Items of the liturgical and sacramental culture of Catholicism, such as the host, were regarded by opponents as being neither sacred nor even wholesomely symbolic, but as being both idols and also the equivalent of the magical fetish objects of primitive peoples. Other 'Catholic' ornaments such as altar cloths and vestments were also denounced as adjuncts of idolatry. Ritualists were, as we saw in chapter 3, accused of bringing a very particular idol into Anglican churches, which, in its simplest form, consisted of two pieces of wood laid across each other at right angles. In Brighton in 1852, the prominent ritualist Arthur Wagner (1824–1902) got himself into trouble by distributing prints of the crucifixion.[101] The local Protestant Defence Association criticized the bishop for allowing this. An anonymous priest of the diocese noted that this was 'however, scarcely sufficient to excite public feeling… but call these simple prints by the extraordinary and mysterious name of Pictorial Crucifixes [as the bishop had done], and a certain amount of odium' would immediately be generated. The anonymous writer assured the reader that the poor needed pictures in order to learn and the fishermen were getting such prints from the French Catholics in any case![102]

We have seen in chapter 3 that the issue of the cross on the altar was one of the major points of dispute in the Knightsbridge cases and that the evidence of the Reformation was equivocal. Queen Elizabeth had, it seems, had a crucifix, but whether for private devotion or for the furthering of diplomacy was

FIGURE 4.3. 'Fly away silly moth', *Punch* 19 (1850), p. 217. William Bennett as moth flutters round the Roman candle. Photograph by the author, with permission, from the edition held at the library of Birkbeck College, London.

disputed by the sources. In any case, this use ended in 1567 and was, suppos-edly, unique at this date and regarded by all in the Church of England as scan-dalous.[103] Crosses and crucifixes appear to have been completely and officially banned only in the 1640s on the grounds of idolatry.[104] The crucifix was seen as more dangerous than the cross because of the bodily form upon it. It is in this light that one should regard the allegations aired in the press that there was a crucifix in the room used for confession at St. Barnabas'.[105] The legal distinc-tion between a physical cross and the image of a cross on the wall, as reached by the John Dodson in *Liddell v. Westerton*, was condemned by one attentive barrister as 'miserable sophistry and rank intolerance'. Where would it end? Was the cross to be struck from the crown and sceptre?[106] After the judgement of the Privy Council the altar cross was, much to the complainants' dismay, not disposed of but was merely transferred from the altar to the 'sill of the east window'.[107]

The sort of attitudes that would have horrified early Victorian Protestants can be found in full force in Allard Montpincon, *My Crucifix, Or, Thoughts at a Prie-Dieu* (1895). This Roman Catholic priest assures us that 'the crucifix is a great gift from God'. It is 'to the eye of man what the Word is to the ear of man, both are means of enlightening the mind and kindling the affections'. We must feel inner anguish as we gaze upon 'that wounded Side through which we can almost see the wounded heart within'. The crucifix was not simply to be stared at, it must be held: 'we must stand there and hold those pierced feet...We must wash His feet with our tears of penitence'.[108] This intensely emotional response can be found in much earlier narratives such as Elizabeth Charles, *Rest in Christ, Or, The Crucifix and the Cross* (1848). Published anonymously, this small book gave an account of one who grew up believing in the ideal of a universal Church, but thinking that the Roman and Greek Churches were in error. She now understood that the Anglican Church was but a branch of the universal Church and that the Reformation was not so much a 'necessary puri-fication', as a 'presumptuous schism'. She tells us that, before her conversion, she had longed to confess her sins and spent her nights weeping and reciting penitential litanies. She became worried that her yearnings might be the result of a 'diseased imagination'. But finally she travelled to France, where she found that religion was not 'banished, as with us, to the corner of the week or of the city'. 'By the wayside stood the Cross with the emblems of the Sacred Passion, the nails, the sponge, the spear': weeping, she threw herself prostrate before the crucifix.[109]

The sufferings of Christ on the cross, for an anonymous ritualist London curate writing in 1850, were salutary for us: 'Let us love the Cross, let us rejoice in humiliation. Let us, however contradictory it may appear to flesh and blood,

be assured that there is ground for thanksgiving in all cases, more ground, perhaps, where the matter is distasteful, as medicine not luxury is best suited to
disease'.[110] George Nugée (1819–92), briefly one of Bennett's curates at St. Paul's
in 1845, believed that people should imagine the sufferings of Christ when on
their deathbeds. The spur to this should be material contemplation, for it should
happen 'while the cross-bearer stands at its [the bed's] foot, overshadowing the
dying man with that most blessed emblem of the Redeemer'.[111] It could be argued
that the sickness of the recent cholera (of 1848) was sent as a message from God,
though it be 'bitter medicine'.[112] This agenda of embracing illness and suffering
as God's will was resisted by those who looked to scientific medicine rather than
to what appeared to them to be superstitious masochism. The crucifix's extreme
visual evocation of torment and self-sacrifice remained largely Roman Catholic
territory in the early Victorian period, but many Anglo-Catholics did wish to adore
the cross. As one anonymous 'Puseyite' put it, 'How sad that that which was the
pride of every Christian in the earlier and purer days of the Church, should now
be trampled under foot, and despised as a thing abhorred'.[113]

We should not assume that evangelicals and Dissenters were uninterested
in the cross; far from it! The power of notions of atonement meant that the sufferings of Jesus were intensely present in the imaginations of Low Churchmen.
This was why opponents cared so much about the presence of crosses that
they saw as wooden idols distracting the faithful from the true message of the
crucifixion. The cross was, thus, denounced as 'that original cause of idolatrous
observances in the Church of Christ'.[114] In Rome, Hobart Seymour saw the ceremony of the Adoration of the Cross, 'idolatrous' adoration, he says, of the *wood*
of the cross. The Pope disrobed, the chapel was bare, and he was made to kneel
and rise several times. 'I felt a fearfulness', says Seymour, 'a solemn dread, and
could not refrain from weeping, seeing that aged man, so near eternity, led like
a victim, and apparently an unwilling one, to an act of IDOLATRY, the most
clear and perfect my imagination could conceive'.[115]

Part of the problem was an unwillingness to understand material culture as
a system of signs, in other words, as a form of the word and of the 'Word'. The
Pre-Raphaelite Holman Hunt (1827–1910) was interested in just such a use of
paint for devotional subjects and wanted to persuade his fellow Protestants of
the contribution that art could make to Christian understanding. He countered
the predictable opposition by partially concealing his crucifixion imagery. His
Shadow of Death (1869–73) presents a prime example of such suggestion and
evasion (figure 4.4). Christ's shadow, at which Mary looks, forms a cruciform
on a wall, the crosspiece of which is formed of a set of carpenter's tools. This all
seems pretty unsubtle, but this was not quite how the pamphlet produced for
the exhibition of the painting described it:

The setting sun tells him the hour for cessation from his toil has
arrived, that his day's labour is over. He has just risen from the
plank on which he has been working, and is portrayed as throwing
up his arm to release that pleasant sensation of repose and relax-
ation...and in perfect harmony with this physical act, so natural

FIGURE 4.4. William Holman Hunt, *Shadow of Death* (1869–73). By permission of
Manchester City Art Gallery.

and graceful to everyone, the Divine Labourer, pours forth his soul in fervent gratitude to his father that the welcome hour of rest has come.[116]

This focus on life rather than death may have helped the acceptance of the image. A more subtle and important example of the same method can be seen in Hunt's *The Light of the World* (first version 1851–53), as is discussed by Maas:

> Perhaps the most brilliant compositional device, no hint of which appears in the preliminary sketches, is the prefiguration of Christ on the cross. The distant landscape, with the trees and their trunks to the right, exactly mirrors the upraised right arm to the left. If we add the slight tilt to the head, the gentle bending of the left knee, the foot below the robe and the pose of the hands as tradition- ally adopted in all Renaissance crucifixion iconography, we have a form of symbolism in its most perfect symmetry. If we add, too, the crown woven with thorns and the stigmata on the hands [now more easily discerned in the engraving] we now see not only, as Ruskin put it 'Christ in his everlasting offices of prophet, priest and king', but also Christ the holy martyr who suffered for mankind.[117]

Those who regarded the cross and crucifix as idolatrous looked to the historical record to provide vindication for their opinions. Behind the actions of Protes- tant iconoclasts of the Reformation lay a precise vision of Apostolic purity and simplicity of worship. Such thinking regarded the cross as the product of the fourth century A.D. rather than of three hundred years earlier: 'The gloomy patristic doctrine of the crucifix arose amid the darkness of a drear pagan age, [for] among the several emblems of Christianity down on the tombs of the earliest Christians, in the catacombs of Rome, no crucifix is to be seen'. For this author, 'Constantine's [the first Christian Roman Emperor, c. 274–337] law- made Patristic Christianity was Paganism with but a veneer of Christianity, and [it] took over all the unspirituality it found in the Jews, mistook God for its pagan gods and feared him'.[118]

This comes from an Edwardian text by 'Didymus'. But the idea of the cross as being heathen in origin had been a focus for intense interest in cer- tain quarters of moralising, Protestant scholarship several decades earlier. Two examples are the American Episcopalian priest Henry Dana Ward's, *His- tory of the Cross: The Pagan Origin, and Idolatrous Adoption and Worship of the Image* (1871), and the English Anglican Mourant Brock's, *The Cross: Heathen* and Christian. A Fragmentary Notice of Its Early Pagan Existence, and Subsequent Christian Adoption (1879). Brock (1825–80), who was vicar of Christ Church, Clifton, from 1856 to 1871 before becoming Chaplain of the East Bay, Mentone, until 1880, noted that crosses could be seen on many of the Egyptian and Etruscan exhibits in the British Museum: 'All nations of antiquity, civilised or uncivilised, our own druids included, delighted in the Cross. It seems to have been a sign connected with the *natural religion* which everywhere more or less underlies our humanity'. According to him, when the Chi-Rho seen by Constantine (i.e., the first two letters of Christ's name in Greek which supposedly appeared to the emperor in a celestial vision) fell out of use, it was the 'heathen emblem' of the cross that replaced it. The cross, for Brock, as for 'Didymus', came into use from the time of Constantine when 'superstition abounded'. It was only in the eighth century when this imagery had sufficiently 'perverted' the Church that we find the development of the crucifix. Both were adopted by 'nominally converted' heathens.

Such studies as these equated pagan influence with evil. Brock saw a man cross himself before leaping off a high rock near Monaco: the lesson, 'the sign of the Cross and—death! Superstition and—self-murder!'[119] There were, of course, Roman Catholic attempts to refute such accusations. In 1833 Daniel Rock (1799–1871), Catholic priest and antiquarian, published in defence of Roman Catholic ritual and material culture. A second edition appeared in 1851. His motive for publishing was, he tells us, because 'the more intelligent and inquiring amongst our Protestant fellow-countrymen' have been desirous of such a survey. We are assured that the 'the primitive Christians were exemplary in the reverence which they manifested toward the Cross' and that the Chi-Rho was itself a cross. And in sharp contrast to many Protestant authors, he was adamant that the 'cross was regarded by the Pagans with the greatest horror'. This was why the crucifix was absent from the early Church, not because it was a later pagan import, but lest it be off-putting to converts.[120]

The cross, however, raised bodily fears and excitements that went well beyond the basic taint of paganism, as can be seen by reading an extraordinary tract published in 1858 by the firm Effingham Wilson at the Royal Exchange in London, a firm with a large output and, although a little past its prime, still an important firm. This was written by 'Investigator Abhorrens', and was titled *Idolomania; Or, The Legalised Cross Not the Instrument of Crucifixion, Being an Inquiry into the Difference between the Cross Proper and the Symbol of Heathen Processions.*[121]

The preface begins by telling us that the final decision in *Liddell v. Westerton* had spurred the author to put pen to paper, and he wrote in a situation of emergency to strengthen the resolve of the bishop of London. For 'if it be culpable to tell the simple truth of indecent symbols [what] is not the guilt of those who not only display them to the unsuspecting as objects of love or adoration, but...compose hymns to the cross to be sung by Christian ladies, and not only that, fill them with smutty ideas?' He refers to the 'daring pollution' committed in such verses from Rev. R. Roper's *Hymnal Noted* as

> Faithful Cross! Above all other,
> One and only noble tree!
> None in foliage, none in blossom,
> None in fruit thy peers may be;
> Sweetest wood and sweetest iron!
> Sweetest weight is hung on thee.[122]

This, for our author, is deeply obscene; for his tract is dedicated to proving that the cross represents 'the phallus of universal antiquity'. Words will not be minced, for 'he that would avert the destruction of evangelical purity in morals, and holiness in religion, must not be prudish in language, when morality is menaced by the foulest image that ever sanctimonious imposters placed before Christian eyes'.

The argument is based on a considerable discussion of ancient evidence. The writer was clearly a learned antiquarian. His view, however, is not likely to be upheld today. It was that Jesus was crucified on a single stake, and the horizontal was a pagan symbolic interpolation derived from the phallic worship that was supposedly universal in the pagan world. The cross became so widespread because 'it prevailed among the first Christians soon after the crucifixion'. Catholicism was then taken over by phallus worship, which our author illustrates by reference to such scenes as witnessed by Seymour when on Good Friday 'the pope and cardinals crawl on all fours along the aisles of St. Peter's, to a cross which they glorify, embrace and kiss'. A parallel is drawn with the 'lingga' that Hindus place upright in their temples (which are, in another interesting parallel, described as being of 'Gothic architecture').

The 'candle and its stand is the upright lingga...obscene representations of that which may not be described'. Meanwhile, the chalice, as used for Communion is interpreted as being the vagina and womb, since 'whatever has the property of receiving, containing, and producing...is symbolical, throughout Asia, of the female nature'. This was also true in Greece and Rome, and thus, 'it is probably perceived why the popish priests jealously guard the chalice from the touch of the laity. What it denotes is reserved for their own use'! The crossed-keys of Peter are particularly lewd since 'the key itself is a complex phallus, with its circle of Venus'. It is all a devilish plot, since it is not for nothing that we find this 'foul image...lewdly exhibited upon the backs of Puseyite theurgists'. Ritualism does nothing other than 'bring the animal organization and sensations into undue prominence' and 'the Tractarian churches are but temples of Bacchus and Venus'.[123]

Moreover, viewing the phallus leads to sex and violence. Based on statistics largely derived from the previously mentioned champion of 'no popery' and recent visitor to Rome, M. Hobart Seymour, we 'know' that the more the cross is revered, the higher the number of murders and of children born out of wedlock. The number of yearly murders per million of population was supposedly 4.1 in England and Wales, 30.7 in France, and 113.1 in the Papal States. The table of 'comparative bastardy' gives the number of 'illegitimate' births as being 4.2% of the number of legitimate ones in London in 1851, 49% in Paris in the same year, and 260.6% for Rome in 1836.[124]

The author of *Idolomania* tells us that, apparently unlike himself, the evangelists 'had anything but a phallus on their minds'. The aim of his paper was intended to dissociate Christ from the pollution of sexuality, although the effect may have been quite the opposite. In fact, there was clearly a complex dance of desire and repulsion taking place in which the author could not avoid being implicated (which is why he remained anonymous). There appears to have been a particular fear (and, perhaps, excitement) of thinking about Christ in passive terms as being penetrated, for 'how else have we learnt that Jesus suffered on the disgusting image of a phallus'?[125] Moreover, since impalement was, as Brock put it, an 'oriental punishment'; Christ, who was typically depicted as being white, was being male-raped by the sinful east.[126]

The study of phallic worship was a subset of antiquarian analysis of comparative religion and one that had enjoyed a minor vogue in libertine and libertarian circles in the later eighteenth century. Publications on the topic were frequently published by radicals and dealers in pornography and were either anonymous or produced by people whom one might term eccentric in their willingness to ignore popular opprobrium.[127] One such was George Witt (1804–1869), whose studies focussed on phallic worship and who gave the British Museum's *Secretum* (secret collection) 434 'symbols of the early worship of mankind' in 1865.[128] The taboo on such material meant that many works on the subject were privately printed and circulated and were not collected by public libraries. Nevertheless, from the surviving material, we can see that *Idolomania* is not alone in its phallic interpretation of Catholic traditions.

Priapic imagery had long been used to discredit Catholics (e.g., *Priapus Periclitans*, 1690) and Dissenters (*Priapeia Persbyteriana, or the Presbyterian Peezle*, 1720).[129] A lively tradition of anticlerical erotica in France crested at the Revolution.[130] Such erotic visions denied elite status to priests, who were seen as equally, if not more, bestial than anyone else (the same radical effect was achieved by erotic cartoons of the French royal family).[131] Pornography as a genre that is intended simply for erotic stimulation of the viewer is widely understood to be a product of the nineteenth century.[132] During the early modern period, many erotic materials were part of a culture of burlesque in which inappropriate arousal on the part of the subjects of the texts was part of a critique of current power relations. Personal sexual pleasure was often mingled with anti-Catholic and, more or less covertly, anti-Christian messages. There was no clear boundary between religious, scientific, and erotic works: 'The readers were the same as those of the clandestine or semi-clandestine erotic book trade, since scientific documentation [of fertility cults] required the collaboration of collectors of erotica.'[133]

Some of the more respectable early studies of comparative religion tended to posit a general belief in fertility as a key aspect of 'primitive' worship, but the impetus to a specifically phallic interpretation of paganism and Catholicism occurred in the 1780s. William Hamilton (1731–1803), diplomat and collector, heard of a surviving 'phallic cult' north of Naples in which wax images were offered at a local church by women in the hope of ensuring their fertility. He was interested in the cult because it 'offers a fresh proof of the similitude of the Popish and Pagan religion'.[134] In May 1785 he travelled to the location, and examples of the ex-votos were sent to British Museum.[135] Hamilton described the cult to Richard Payne Knight (1751–1824), who published on the subject. Payne Knight was the eldest son of the Rector of Bewdley and from 1780 to 1806 he was a Member of Parliament, sponsored by Charles James Fox. In 1781 he was elected a member of the Society of Dilettanti, which in 1786 issued his publication, *An Account of the Remains of the Worship of Priapus*.[136] A trustee of the British Museum from 1814, he left his huge collections to the museum.[137] Other men associated with these figures were Pierre Hugues, the self-created Baron d'Hancarville (1719–1805), scholar and publisher of erotic prints, who addressed the Society of Dilettanti in 1781, and Charles Townley (1737–1805), the first European known to have acquired an erotic Indian sculpture group.[138] It has been commented of Payne Knight's book that 'lurking on almost every page is some form of scepticism about Christianity' and this, implicitly, if not explicitly, was not just about abusing Catholicism. It is arguable that Payne Knight desired an enlightened paganism that would give more scope for homosocial expression. His 'libertine' work was read by most critics as erotic, depraving, and seditious.[139]

A vital element in the intellectual world of these gentlemen and rogues was enlightenment deism. The word 'deist' made its appearance first in France when it is described as referring to a novel threat in 1563.[140] There was no such thing as a deist religion or movement; rather, deism was a rethinking of the relations between mankind, nature, and the divine. The advocates of 'reason' over superstition looked to nature and its laws as a source of answers.[141] God, it was thought, could be understood by his evidences, but not influenced. Organised worship, for the more radical thinkers, was thus potentially a diversion from true understanding. Such concerns, in an age of revolution, were of direct political importance. Thomas Paine's *The Age of Reason* (3 vols., published 1793, 1795, and 1807) was original not as much in its ideas as in its strident tone.[142] The immaculate conception was, for Paine, 'blasphemously obscene', since it saw Mary 'debauched by a ghost'.[143] The English publisher was himself duly prosecuted for blasphemy in 1797.[144]

The erotic elements of comparative religion could be, and were, employed in the service of radical politics. Perhaps the most influential study in this vein was written by Charles Dupuis (1742–1809) in the second year of the French republic (1794). This startling work was strongly anti-Catholic, presenting an unambiguous picture of Christianity as being directly related to solar worship in which the phallus was the emblem of the sun.[145] Dupuis was offered the Chair of Literature in Berlin by Frederick the Great, had become the French Commissioner of Public Instruction in 1790, and was a founding member of the French Institute.[146] Meanwhile, in Britain his 'atheism' was blamed on his Catholic upbringing, since it is not surprising that 'disgusted by whatever had appeared to him under the form of religion, he should have rejected it altogether'.[147]

But numbers of the pious, notably missionaries, were also drawn to write on the subject of heathens and sexuality, partly because of their desire to bring natives into line with their own ideas of morality and also because of the presence of explicitly sexual themes in Indian art. John Smith of the evangelical London Missionary Society tells us that the '*licentiousness* of the Hindoos is too notorious to render it necessary to enlarge on its evidences ... yet the wonder is that their external deportment is usually so decent, considering that the history of those whom they are accustomed to look up to as divinities is not fit to meet the eye of decency'.[148] This testimony suggests that the impurity was discovered, perhaps one might say produced, by the moralising gaze of the British. The missionaries in India, like Seymour in Rome, were, in other words, implicated in the production of pornographic readings of religious cults.

In nineteenth-century Britain, meanwhile, the authorities were to make an intense effort to separate the radical from the erotic and in due course would develop separate legal strategies for containing each. One result was an increasingly narrowly defined genre of 'pornography', which was to become legally distinguished from scientific, judicial, or medical discourses on sexual acts and 'offences'. This resulted in the marginalisation of radical views on sexuality, such as those expressed on birth control by the radical journalist and freethinker Richard Carlile (1790–1843) in his *Every Woman's Book* of 1826. In this volume, he asserted that 'the Greeks and Romans had their temples of Venus, where young people could appease their passions under the form of worship, and well it would be if such were the religion of every country'.[149] But, as time went by, serious work on sexuality needed to be provided with increasing doses of moral or scholarly authority in order to avoid being categorised as pornography. Thus, when Payne Knight's work of 1786 was republished in 1865, it was in an expensive privately printed edition that says in its preface that it is intended for serious scholars. This edition included a new essay (by 'Thomas Wright and others') on the worship of the 'generative powers' in the Middle Ages. However, the difference between this and *Idolomania* was that the essay accuses neither the medieval nor the modern Church, saying that such worship happened when pagan elements were incorporated into the practices of heretical sects. Moreover, the essay contends that the sole example of phallic worship in the British Isles today was to be found in the far west of Ireland, on a remote island where there was not even a Catholic priest.[150]

All this did not mean that research on the subject ground to a halt, but it was marginalised. Gentlemen with resources could gather their materials from such sources as the back issues of the journal *Archaeologia*, as in the article of 1800 that argued that standing stones were linked, via Popes consecrating columns, to the modern-day setting up of crucifixes as phallic symbols.[151] The same idea could be gleaned from the aforementioned *Every Woman's Book*, which appears to have had a substantial, if semiclandestine circulation.[152] The resulting Victorian scholarship on 'phallic cults' may be exemplified by the work of Thomas Inman (1820–76), a Liverpool surgeon who appears to have devoted his last years to research in comparative religion. He took a specifically visual approach, arguing, in relation to iconography, that 'anything upright, longer than broad, became symbolic of the father' (figure 4.5). Typical of his analysis is his discussion of a decorative motif by A. W. N. Pugin: 'In the two forms of the Maltese cross, the position of the lingam is reversed, and the egg-shaped bodies, with their cover, are at the free end of each limb, whilst the natural end of the organ is left unchanged'. Another detail was described as 'an unmistakable bi-sexual cross'. Unlike the author of *Idolomania*, he did not adopt a stance of staunch disapproval, arguing that 'England will be as upright, and as civilised, when she has abandoned the heathen elements in her religion, as when she hugs them as if necessary for her spiritual welfare'.[153]

Where *Idolomania* differs markedly from such 'secular' study is in its use of comparative religion in the cause of Protestantism. Its evangelical tone shows the desire of its author to spread ideas, rather than to contain them within a coterie of cognoscenti. Closer to *Idolomania* in its mixture of antiquarianism and

Figure 15 is from D'Hancarville, *Op. Cit.*, vol. i., plate xxiii. It resembles Figure 11. *supra*, and enables us by the introduction of the sun and moon to verify the deduction drawn from the arrangement of the serpent's coils. If the snake's body, instead of being curved above the 8 like tail, were straight, it would simply indicate the linga and the sun; the bend in its neck, however, indicates the yoni and the moon.

Figure 16 is copied from plate xvi, fig. 2, of *Recueil de Pierres Antiques Graces*, folio, by J. M. Raponi (Rome, 1786). The gem represents a sacrifice to Priapus, indicated by the rock, pillar, figure, and branches given in our plate. A nude male sacrifices a goat; a draped female holds a kid ready for immolation; a second man, nude, plays the double pipe, and a second woman, draped, bears a vessel on her head, probably containing wine for a libation.

Figure 17 is from vol. i. *Recherches*, etc., plate xxii. In this medal the triad is formed by a man and two coiled serpents on the one side of the medal, whilst on the reverse are seen a tree, surrounded by a snake, situated between two rounded stones, with a dog and a conch shell below. See *supra*, Plate iv., Fig. 6.

PLATE XI.

—With two exceptions, Figs. 4 and 9,—exhibits Christian emblems of the trinity or linga, and the unity or yoni, alone or combined; the whole being copied from Pugin's *Glossary of Ecclesiastical Ornament* (London, 1869).

Fig. 1 is copied from Pugin, plate xvii., and indicates a double union of the trinity with the unity, here represented as a ring. *Vesica.*

Figs. 2, 3, are from Pugin, plate xiv. In figure 2, the two covered balls at the base of each limb of the cross are extremely significant, and if the artist had not mystified the free end, the most obtuse worshipper must have recognised the symbol. We may add here that in the two forms of the Maltese cross, the position of the lingam is reversed, and the egg-shaped bodies, with their cover, are at the free end of each limb, whilst the natural end of the organ is left unchanged. See figs. 35, 36. This form of cross is Etruscan. Fig. 3 is essentially the same as the preceding, and both may be compared with Fig. 4. The balls in this cross are uncovered, and the free end of each limb of the cross is but slightly modified.

Fig. 4 is copied in a conventional form from plate xxxv., fig. 4,

PLATE XI.

FIGURE 4.5.   Thomas Inman, *Ancient Pagan and Modern Christian Symbolism Exposed and Explained* (1869). p. 9 and plate XI. Reproduced with the permission of the Cambridge University Library.

moralizing is a freemasonry pamphlet that appeared in 1873. This American text inveighed against one Colonel Bland who had had the temerity to suggest that Baal was the same as Jah, who was the same as Jehovah—in other words, that all sorts of ancient peoples worshipped the one true God but under other names. Better 'put the name *Priapus*, or the symbol by which certain nations represented the generative power of Baal, Osiris, Mithras, Vishnu, and Khem...as well put *that* on the Ark', the writer exclaims, before denouncing the 'statue of Baal, priapic, between the great phallic columns of the magnificent Temple at Hieropolis.' Would you be with them, he asks, as they 'kneel at the feet of the colossal Phalli and make their offerings to the Syrian Baal, or as the Egyptian worshipped the obscene Khem, or the Hindu adored the Lingam as the symbol of Brahm' and argue that they were worshipping the supreme God?[154]

Overt attempts to garner the most potentially explosive element of the antiquarian study of comparative religion, the worship of Priapus, to the cause of Protestant purity were, not surprisingly, few and far between. But it is my contention that there was a widespread understanding of alternative religious traditions as carnal. This meant that contemporary anxieties concerning the body, sexuality, and gender roles influenced, when they did not determine, the interpretation of the religious Other. *Idolomania*, in other words, was unusual not in its ideas but in its explicit presentation of what was often implicit.

The ultimate problem with bodily depiction of Christ was not just that it was idolatrous, but that it threatened His status as a figure of power and authority. For instance, the most troubling aspect of the cross and crucifixion for 'Investigator Abhorrens' was that they appeared to present the weakness of the body in such a way that this, rather than spiritual triumph, appeared to be emphasised. Since 'normal' sexuality and gender roles were equated with dominant/submissive positioning in which the man was meant to be in control, Christ's passivity in the face of physical abuse was read as problematic for His manliness. Moreover, the seminudity in which Christ was normally depicted in the crucifixion was seen as adding to the ambivalence of the image and increasing his humiliation.[155] The weak, effeminised, abject shame of the Pope on his knees before the cross as envisioned by Seymour can be further understood though Ward's description of the cross as an instrument of active violence: 'Suppose we take up reverently in honour, and glory in, and even kiss a weapon which, in cruel hands, has, without the slightest provocation, slain our best friend and benefactor—our elder brother—and brought him to an untimely, shameful, and agonising death! No mortal in his senses is capable of such perverseness'.[156] The problem with the phallus and, by extension, the cross was not just that it was sexual, but that it was regarded as a weapon of male aggression.

Similar unease about the connections among religion, sex, and violence can be found reflected in modern commentary such as the *New Yorker* review of Mel Gibson's *The Passion of the Christ*:

> For two hours, with only an occasional pause or gentle flashback, we watch, stupefied, as a handsome, strapping, at times half-naked young man (James Caviezel) is slowly tortured to death. Gibson is so thoroughly fixated on the scourging and crushing of Christ, and so meagrely involved in the spiritual meanings of the final hours, that he falls in danger of altering Jesus' message of love into one of hate.[157]

We are looking here at two starkly different interpretative traditions. The first revels in the morally educative power of ascetic suffering, whilst the other, popularised during the Reformation, denied the value of such a spiritual redemption through self-abasement and found a place for such displays only by relegating them to the realms of aberration, sensuality, and sensation. Thus, the instruments of martyrdom that appeared to the Roman Catholic apologist Rock as the holy evidences of saintly heroism were rejected by opponents as the hideous evidence of sadomasochistic excitements (this idea was perfectly thinkable even if the formalised theories of sadism and masochism had yet to be formulated) (figure 4.6). However, in the process of the discovery of bodily horror, there is, as the film review reveals, a danger of the return of pleasure through the mechanism of voyeurism. Sensitivity to such issues provides much of the reason why the early ritualists, though stoutly defending the use of the cross, did not attempt to introduce the crucifix, with its explicit dramatisation of suffering.

However, in relation to the sacraments, they were dealing with matters concerning which their beliefs did not allow compromise. In Anglo-Catholic ritual, the body of Christ was also present in the form of the Communion wafer. Of all Christian ritual, the mass, Eucharist, Holy Communion, was perhaps the most important, at least for Catholics. The sacramental and sacrificial aspects of the priestly role were as vital for them, as the didactic and sermonising role was for the Protestant minister. For Rock, priesthood was about sacrifice and 'nature herself invariably inspired man with the idea that *sacrifice* was the first—the most essential act of exterior religion'. The Roman Catholic position was to go beyond the Real Presence, where the divine spirit is held to be present, to Transubstantiation, in which wafer and wine become body and blood by the words of consecration.

It was the opinion of the Roman Catholic apologist Rock that, countering Protestant accusations that the wafer and cup tasted of bread and wine,

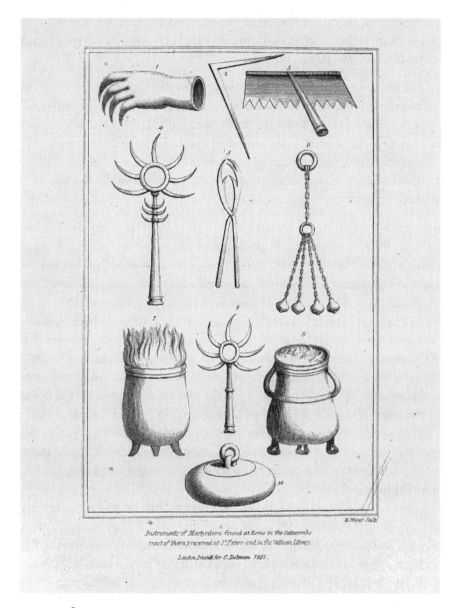

FIGURE 4.6. Daniel Rock, *'Hierurgia', or Transubstantiation, Invocation of Saints, Relics and Purgatory* (1851), plate facing p. 263. Reproduced with permission of the Cambridge University Library.

one should not taste with one's tongue but with one's faith.[158] For Dissenters this was anathema. For them, the bread of the Eucharist was but the image or representation of the Lord, so that in the Holy Communion priests were doing reverence to an image.[159] 'What possible difference can there be made between the idolatry of the man who bows down to a bit of wood he has fashioned into an image...and the idolatry of the man who pretends by the utterance of a few words to cause bread and wine to become the Body and Blood of Christ and so Christ Himself, and then pray to the idol that they have so made?' asked the Baptist minister Thomas Oyler Beeman. He objected, as evidence of such idolatry, to the *Eucharistic Manual* of the Anglo-Catholic George Prynne (1818–1903), vicar of St. Peter's, Plymouth, and particularly to phrases like these: '"Hail, Sweetest Jesus! *Prostrate in lowliest devotion*, I worship and adore thee"; "*most adorable Body, I adore Thee* with all the powers of my soul" and "*most adorable blood*, that washest away all our sins, *I adore thee*"' [emphasis original].[160]

An anonymous 'Churchman of the Reformation', taking Communion at Anglo-Catholic All Saints, Margaret Street, London, watched a priest upending the Communion vessel so high, as he drained it into his mouth, that he almost lost his balance. In such scenes we can gain a strong sense of hostile viewers finding the ritual overblown and ridiculous.[161] Taking this one stage further was the prominent Irish anti-Papist campaigner Robert James Macghee, Rector of Holywell, Huntingdonshire, who, in Exeter Hall in 1853, brought in a wafer-making machine and showed it to the audience but, to save the feelings of Catholics, did not have a display of wafer-making, as he was intending to do, for 'on reflection, I thought better it not to do so'.[162]

The Tractarian view was more emphatic than it was clear or straightforward. The difference between the Real Presence and Transubstantiation was not always easy to justify or explain. The key point was that the former was concerned with the spiritual presence of Christ in his transformed body, rather than in his 'carnal body' from before his Resurrection.[163] Even this was regarded in the 1830s and 1840s as going too far. In 1843, Edward Pusey preached a university sermon on 'the holy Eucharist as a comfort to the penitent', in which he advocated the Real Presence; as a result of this he was suspended for two years from preaching by Oxford University.[164]

Pre-Tractarian practice had generally been for rather infrequent Communion. This took place at a movable table, rather than at the Gothic Revival altar centrally placed in the chancel as advocated by the ecclesiologists. Charles James Blomfield, bishop of London, in his charge of 1842, advocated regular Communion, and Bennett refers to this in his two-volume work of the same year which was carefully printed and designed in a devotional manner so as to instruct on the meaning and practice of the mass.[165] Bennett had already published a more compact work on the Eucharist in 1837, and this work went through various revisions and new editions. In the second edition of 1846, Bennett is found rejoicing that 'we can kneel down before the Altar and do acts of reverence'. He was, however, quite clear about rejecting transubstantiation, seeing this as a 'peculiar doctrine' of the 'darkness and ignorance' of the ninth century, that 'by the word of prayer and the invocation of the Holy Ghost bread and wine were transformed into the actual and material body and blood of our Saviour'.[166] Bennett is later to be found defending his views in relation to the attacks made on Denison.[167] George Denison (1805–96), who was made archdeacon of Taunton in 1851, was prosecuted from 1854 to 1858 for advocating the Real Presence. The case was finally to be thrown out on the technicality that it had not commenced within the two years required by the legislation.[168] John Keble, hoping that the Denison case would not set a precedent, also advocated the Real Presence. He drew the parallel that, just as Christ 'is the name most expressive of his humiliation, *therefore*, His thoughtful servants would instinctively select it in preference to all His other names for especial honour and reverence': Christ's body is his inferior part and seat of humiliation and yet should, for just this reason, be specially honoured.[169]

It is perhaps hard for a nonbeliever to capture the intense emotions of this debate. For one side, if the host were in fact to be the immaculate body of Christ, was it not horrible to contemplate its joining with the imperfect body of the communicant? We are invited, by one sceptic, to imagine someone who 'swallows that immaculate God down his throat, reeking most frequently with the fumes of stinking tobacco and spirits, and food in the process of digestion'.[170] And, as another writer put it, 'If the body of Christ is literally eaten and digested, how can we reconcile this with the prediction that "his flesh shall not see corruption"'.[171] On the other hand, we can sense the awe in Bennett's cry concerning the Eucharist: 'He is there—He really is there'. The sense of power and glory associated with the ceremony is palpable. He warns that 'the Church sets a very solemn guard and warning against too promiscuous an approach'.[172] For Bennett, the host was of the resurrected perfect body of Christ; for opponents, it was a deceptive, carnal, and poisonous husk.

It is important to realise that the period from the 1840s to the 1870s represented a phase during which moralising discourse and knowledge of comparative religion were often combined. The British antiquarian reception of Roman Catholic antiquities began in eighteenth-century amusement and disdain and entered the period of moral histrionics that I am now describing, before fading back into a calmer mode. Outside hard-line circles, Catholics were being seen increasingly by the end of the nineteenth century as one of a series of 'peoples' with particular folk customs and associated material cultures, rather than being part of a demonic conspiracy that was bent on world domination. Yet it is important to emphasise that the attitude, even it was a pose, of disinterested inquiry, never entirely disappeared during the early Victorian period. This was the approach taken, for example, by Henry Wreford, correspondent of, amongst other publications, *The Times*, who went to Rome at the mid-century not as a

convert but saying that 'I am less interested in it as a theological or party question, than as an historical and antiquarian inquiry'. He was not disassociated
from contemporary prejudices for he believed that the cult of the saints 'closely
resembles the Pagan system of deities'. He was, however, pro-art: 'I have always
considered the connection between the good and beautiful and true to be most
intimate...so when surrounded by the more perfect forms of art we cannot
but have our religious sensibilities in a like manner awakened'. Like a modern
anthropologist he bemoaned vanishing customs: 'Alas! For these pious orgies,
civilisation is fast sweeping them away....So great is the pleasure with which
we linger about these traditionary customs connecting us with the past, that it
is difficult at times to suppress a feeling of regret, that improvement should
[not] hold on its silent and steady march'. Crucially, he thought that ancient
material things validated rather than defiled modernity. 'Never let us sneer at
these relics of the past', he says, 'for often they contain a deep philosophy we
know not of'.[173]

The widespread projection of intense hatreds and excitements onto objects
such as the cross, crucifix, and host needs to be seen as the product of specific
circumstances. Attitudes toward depiction as well as description were, by the
later nineteenth century, to moderate considerably as Wreford's position became more widely accepted. Bryan King, the former rector of St. George's in
the East, wrote in 1879 to his friend J. B. Knight, who was helping to install
a mosaic of the crucifixion in the church, saying that 'if I had proposed in
my time to have inserted a simple cross in the place of the proposed crucifix, I should have been burned alive'.[174] The gradual acceptance of Roman and
Anglo-Catholicism can be chronicled through a minor rash of publications that
chronicled the history of cross and crucifix in a spirit of archaeological inquiry
and mild regret. For example, James King Hewison, in *The Runic Roods of Ruthwell and Bewcastle with a Short History of the Cross and Crucifix in Scotland* (1914),
noted that 'with reverential awe the early Church [in Scotland] shrank from de-
lineating Christ as the sufferer' but did not draw the earlier nineteenth-century
opinion that moderns should do the same. With the Reformation crosses were
thrown down, but there was a change in the nineteenth century:

> In Roman Catholic and Episcopal churches in Scotland crosses and
> crucifixes are much in evidence, both within and upon these edi-
> fices. They now are also distinctive ornaments upon Presbyterian
> churches, and are often seen within these sacred buildings and their
> stained-glass windows as conventional ornaments.[175]

Thus, the aftermath of the successive and successful Gothic and Anglo-Catholic
revivals left the cross as a widely acceptable subject both for ornament and for

art-historical research. This is why it can be a challenge for us to appreciate, first, the scale of opposition in the earlier nineteenth century and, second, what all the fuss was about.

The Horror Is All Mine

In the wake of Catholic emancipation, many English Protestants had a nightmare vision of Romanism as a growing force that would overwhelm the country. They saw evidence for this not only in the form of the springing up of new Roman Catholic churches but also through the apparent resurgence of Roman Catholicism within Anglicanism itself. Moreover, the ritualist focus on the Body of Christ and the desire to visually suggest it through the display of the cross, if not the crucifix, violated powerful taboos concerning not simply what was acceptable to Protestant faith, but also what was regarded as decent in everyday society. Of course, ritualists and Roman Catholics were not alone in their belief in the sacraments, but only they stridently emphasised the literal presence of Christ in the host, so focussing the Eucharist on a physical as well as a spiritual bodily encounter.[176]

Taboos were originally studied in South Pacific contexts in which they referred to the emanations of power without reference to right and wrong. Westerners saw this as being inherently magical and primitive. Christianity was supposedly superior in that it did not simply highlight power, but classified it according to its position of good and evil. No longer was it sheer power that led to danger, but only the satanic elements of disorder (dissident, evil power). Mary Douglas, building on Edmund Leach and moving from the notion of taboo to that of pollution, argued that the latter is based on ambiguities of classification and that it is about preventing danger from anomalous situations. When Protestants, therefore, identified the presence of dangerous objects in churches, they were themselves constructing the boundaries of purity through acts of classification.

Valeri has recently criticised Douglas and other canonical anthropological writers on boundary transgression for not being sufficiently keen to 'think with the body', both physical and social, on the basis that 'it is quite likely that the unwanted invasion of the body by decay-inducing substances is the basic model of pollution everywhere'. The problem is that the body desires to consume things, to take them into itself, and the challenge is how to police this so as to prevent harm. Moreover, Valeri also expressed the idea that it is only at the theoretical level that there is maintained a full separation between physical pollution and sin in Christianity.[177] Attributions of sin to items of Christian material culture reflect, therefore, not just moral disagreement but contestations of power. That being so, it is notable that it was items associated with the body that formed the greatest focus for dispute. Julia Kristeva has provided a prominent discussion of the phenomenon of abjection in her book *Powers of Horror* (1982). She delved fearlessly into rejected materials and abased contexts, arguing that 'refuse and corpses *show me* what I permanently thrust aside in order to live'. There is a process of misrecognition here. It is 'not lack of cleanliness or health which causes abjection but what disturbs identity, system, order. What does not respect borders, positions, rules'.[178] The taboos being violated were, in other words, were not just about religion, but also about the body, society, and the self.

But we do not need to think with Kristeva, in a Freudian echo of Original Sin, that the abject is ever-present. The visual and textual presence of abjection can be read as evolving through processes of social contestation. In 1989 the American photographer Andres Serrano (b. 1950) challenged the conceptual boundaries of dirt and holiness (and, as it turned out, of criminality) by placing a crucifix in a container of his own urine.[179] The photograph of this construction is shining and radiant: disgust sets in only when one finds out how it was made. The challenge of this work, *Piss Christ* (1987), was to popular ascriptions of abjection: is piss worthless and polluting when it can be so beautiful (figure 4.7)? This work can be seen as an attempt to 'reclaim the properties of the dung-heap from over the borderline of that which has been discarded, and which therefore threatens social order.'[180] Since piss happens, the artist might argue, we should make the best of it rather than trying to exclude it from the gaze. This is a way of redeeming particular forms of the abject through art. The fascinating thing about opponents of this work is that they generated a vast amount of public discussion in the process of calling for it to be banned from public exhibition. The key battleground appears not to be over repression as much as over the forms of expression.

To transfer this thought back to the early nineteenth century, the deviant expressions of marginalized groups, such as ritualists, could be transformed into the sanctimonious satisfaction of the 'shocked' reader in the parlour via the production of moralising discourse. In turn, this moralising discourse legitimated those institutions, such as nonconformist chapels, which justified their existence substantially with reference to their attempt to control deviance from healthy norms. Such norms can be thought to be more threatened at certain times and in certain contexts, leading to pollution scares in which the fear is that the abject (it could be rubbish in the streets, communists, zombies, or vampires) is out of control and might take over; this was the case with the Papal Aggression in 1850–51. Studies of comparative religion implied that what might

FIGURE 4.7. Andres Serrano, *Piss Christ* (1987). Copyright A. Serrano, courtesy of the artist and the Paula Cooper Gallery, New York.

break out was a bodily irruption of violence and sex, and the discourses of Protestant disgust betray a powerful attraction to the fantasy that this was what was about to take place. But there is more to it than that: many Protestants were intimately and actively involved in constructing a sinful Catholicism in order to turn beliefs that they did not share into cultural expressions that effectively buttressed their own moral position and made for pleasurable viewing.

5

Gothic Novelties

In chapter 4, I distinguished a range of approaches to comparative religion, the extremes of which can be represented by two books that I have already quoted. The first is by the anonymous 'E. I. O.', *The Scarlet Book; Showing the Connection of the Roman Catholic Ceremonies with the Pagan Rites. With an Account of the Bishops, Patriarchs, and Popes of Rome, from A.D. 60. Also an Explanation of the Revelation of St. John the Divine, as It Applies to Modern Events* (1852) (figure 5.1). This represents the use of cultural comparisons as a stick with which to beat anything other than the certain brands of Protestantism. In the group of writings of which this is an example, the truth is found in Holy Scripture. The world, in comparison, presents a catalogue of error. 'E. I. O.' is locked into Biblical time, such that he actively interrogates the Apocalypse in order to understand current events. From this perspective, narratives of human progress are overshadowed by the looming of God's judgement.

The opposite extreme may be represented by Thomas Inman, *Ancient Pagan and Modern Christian Symbolism Exposed and Explained* (1870, 2nd edition 1875) (figure 5.2). From 1861, Inman was a member of the Royal College of physicians in London, physician of the Royal Infirmary in Liverpool, and president of the Liverpool Literary and Philosophical Society. He had interests ranging from phallic cults to spontaneous combustion.[1] He argued that the people should be the judge of whom they want to believe. He himself had had to reject the views of the 'most sensible' clergyman he had ever known

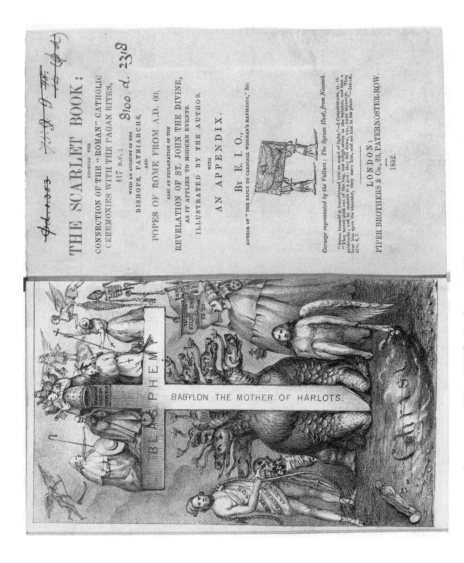

FIGURE 5.1. Anonymous, 'E. I. O.', *The Scarlet Book; Showing the Connection of the Roman Catholic Ceremonies with the Pagan Rites* (1852), frontispiece. Reproduced with permission of the Cambridge University Library.

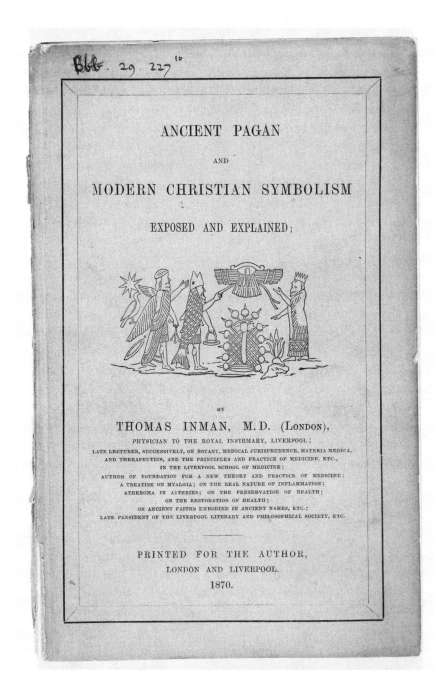

ANCIENT PAGAN

AND

MODERN CHRISTIAN SYMBOLISM

EXPOSED AND EXPLAINED;

BY

THOMAS INMAN, M.D. (London),

PHYSICIAN TO THE ROYAL INFIRMARY, LIVERPOOL;

LATE LECTURER, SUCCESSIVELY, ON BOTANY, MEDICAL JURISPRUDENCE, MATERIA MEDICA,
AND THERAPEUTICS, AND THE PRINCIPLES AND PRACTICE OF MEDICINE, ETC.,
IN THE LIVERPOOL SCHOOL OF MEDICINE;
AUTHOR OF FOUNDATION FOR A NEW THEORY AND PRACTICE OF MEDICINE;
A TREATISE ON MYALGIA; ON THE REAL NATURE OF INFLAMMATION;
ATHEROMA IN ARTERIES; ON THE PRESERVATION OF HEALTH;
ON THE RESTORATION OF HEALTH;
ON ANCIENT FAITHS EMBODIED IN ANCIENT NAMES, ETC.;
LATE PRESIDENT OF THE LIVERPOOL LITERARY AND PHILOSOPHICAL SOCIETY, ETC.

PRINTED FOR THE AUTHOR,

LONDON AND LIVERPOOL.

1870.

FIGURE 5.2. Thomas Inman, *Ancient Pagan and Modern Christian Symbolism Exposed and Explained* (1869), front cover. Reproduced with the permission of the Cambridge University Library.

because the man insisted on sticking to his creed rather than agreeing with what most people thought obvious.[2] He argued that he was not attempting to attack 'true Protestantism', but nevertheless he insisted that the Bible is the word of man rather than of God.[3] Furthermore, he was of the opinion that 'men made the devil, whom the pious fear, just as a negro dreads Mumbo Jumbo'.[4] Neither 'the childlike confidence of the Hindoo, [nor] the subtle reasoning of the Brahmin, [n]or the fierce orthodoxy of the Mahometan' will substitute for the exercise of reason.[5] Such works as these focussed their attention on the classification of cultures based on the tacit assumption that modern European understanding was superior to, and so could analyse, the practices of the past and of foreign nations. His agenda was the expanding of the domain of scientific classification as a way of understanding and controlling superstition.

Although one can identify publications that stand at various points between these two, it is clear that the former had greater popular cultural purchase. Antiquarian scholarship was restricted to learned journals and volumes with small circulations, whilst thousands of tracts carried the prejudices of clerics far beyond the ambit of their own congregations. Furthermore, the likes of Inman had to rely on their supposed 'scientific' objectivity to defend them against accusations of prurient immorality. Since such antiquarian study was carried out by gentlemen of leisure, and by the likes of lawyers and doctors in their spare time, it was hard to project the required aura of professional disinterest. It was all too obvious that such study was undertaken for pleasure. By contrast, it was much more difficult to accuse Protestant moralists of immorality for being interested in such issues in the first place. Ministers could claim a quite legitimate concern for rival faiths and their peculiarities since the souls of their flocks were held to be at stake.

Even bearing in mind their influence on the pronouncements of churchmen, it is possible to relegate these two books to the fringes of Victorian debate: on the one hand, to Millenarian extremism and, on the other, to eccentric antiquarian prurience. However, it is important to realise that these works, along with Tractarianism and ritualism, represented part of a significant and complex process of active engagement with the study of history and culture. The desire to map the world, to classify its forms both biological and cultural, was one of the major intellectual preoccupations of the nineteenth century and one from which religion certainly was not immune. The role of ministers in this process should not be underestimated. In the age through to the implementation of mass compulsory education, popular knowledge about other peoples and cultures derived most often from sermons delivered in church and chapel.[6] The growing apprehension of cultural difference was therefore, to a considerable extent, generated via the pulpit.

I have been keen to point out, however, the ambivalences inherent in moralising Protestant use of comparative religion. In order further to understand the resulting combination of pleasure and disgust it is instructive to compare the way in which a particular body of the Other was viewed in the early nineteenth century: the 'Hottentot Venus', Saarti Baartman (1789–1815), an African woman with unusually large buttocks and breasts. She became the object of mingled European curiosity, horror, and lust, first, when she was paraded around alive, and then, postdissection, as a Parisian museum exhibit.[7] The bodies of the idolatrous Other were, as we have seen, powerfully contested, exhibited, and textually dissected in early Victorian England. Moreover, the moral authority of those who were looking at these images and objects was a particularly important factor because so many of those individuals were clergymen. This contributed much of the energy to campaigns against the supposed carnality of Anglo- and Roman Catholic worship. Since the aim of such activity was to shore up the moral security of the viewers, it was imperative to engage in strident denunciation so as to disguise one's role and pleasure in constructing the Other as a sensational horror and delight.

One might assume that people would simply flee from what was grotesque and corrupt. However, Peter Stallybrass and Allon White argued in their classic study *The Politics and Poetics of Transgression* (1986) that 'disgust always bears the imprint of desire'.[8] Ultimately, it was fear and desire, over moral reform, personal advancement, and prurient experience, that drew people to write and read texts that advanced sexualised readings of religious corruption. The search was on for ways in which to approach these excitements in moral safety. In this chapter, I explore the urge to construct and experience abominations through discourse as the result of desires to engage with the forbidden.

Facing Corruption

In order to understand further the linkages between disgust and desire, it is important to explore the wider cultural role played by conceptions of corruption and pollution. If you believe the texts of the time, corruption was everywhere. Edward Bellasis (1800–73) was a leading parliamentary barrister who converted to Roman Catholicism on September 28, 1850. In February 1851, he published anonymously on the terminology used by Anglican Bishops in relation to the so-called Papal Aggression. He noted that the most frequently used descriptive term was 'corrupt'.[9] It was alleged that the Pope was out to set up a corrupt growth of Catholicism within the geographical boundaries of the kingdom of England and that the Puseyites were the active agents capable of taking that corruption within the boundaries of the Church of England and, so, into the moral heart of the nation. Perhaps the most frequent image that was used in relation to Anglo-Catholicism was that of pollution. It was feared that ritualists were sullying the purity of Protestant worship by the importation of material culture that was tainted, or out of place by virtue of its femininity, foreignness, Romanism, Judaism, or even (as in chapter 4) heathenism. Perceptions and descriptions of the Reformation were a key battleground. The relationship between England's past and present was very much at stake in a situation in which the Reformation was presented by many as a crucial step toward the recovery of pure religion. The notion was that by cleaning off the dross of centuries a renewed state of Grace could be reached to match the one that had been lost. This vision comes through strongly in our old friend Hobart Seymour's 'The English Communion Contrasted with the Roman Mass', preached (on November 5, predictably) at St George's Church, Southwark in 1843:

> Like those who would restore or renovate some ancient temple, removing the dust that defiled it, the mould that tainted it, the moss that covered it, and yet retaining all that was beautiful and useful; so the Reformers of the Church of England, longing to restore and renovate her in all her original purity, removed all the corruptions that had crept into her doctrines, and all the abuses that had crept into her practice, while they retained all that was scriptural in doctrine, and all that was holy in practice; all that was conducive to the beauty, and all that was essential to the order of her services.

Reformers, thus, 'restored the Church of England to her primitive objects and her primitive beauty, treading in the steps of our Lord'.[10] Speaking a few weeks later, Samuel Lee, professor of Hebrew in Cambridge, attacked Edward Pusey using similar invective in which terror of the tyranny of tainted flesh was intensely expressed. Shall we, he asks, again 'succumb to the rule of an hierarchy, at once the most usurping, tyrannical, oppressive and cruel; again to incrust itself as it were, in the unintelligible and useless jargon of the schools, the traditionary trash of useless religious fraternities; the dust and darkness of the monastery, the cell or the hermitage!' In this miasmic world of physical and spiritual dirt, pollution, and danger, we look round with Lee and see a horrid vision of 'the flesh mortified under the vain hope of thereby purifying the spirit; [with] the rotten and rotting bones of saints, pictures and images of the Virgin' lying strewn about.[11]

The very persons of the Anglo-Catholic clergy were also held to be tainted. Arthur Wagner of Brighton was described by one Protestant polemicist as 'as oily a piece of fluid tallow as ever mistook its way into a surplice, or a *sewer*! ... Puseyites will pole their smooth chins into all kinds of filth, so carefully avoided by honest men!'[12] It is important to emphasise, however, that ritualists and Tractarians felt that they, too, were on a mission to clean up Church and society. This even comes across in the anti-Tractarian skit *A Paper Lantern for Puseyites* (1843), in which the 'Puseyite' on arriving in a new parish opines that

> The surplice is covered with stains old and recent,
> and I am sure it looks neither 'comely' nor 'decent'
> ... every corner and cranny is smothered with dust,
> which shows how these 'questmen' have heeded their trust.[13]

Both sides were fascinated with purity, but had very different views on the role of (supposedly) sacred objects in the achievement of that aim. What for one side were expressions of symbolic and sacramental reverence were transformed by the other into an obsession with the dangerously seductive bodies of priests, worshippers, and their idols. This discovery of corruption provided moral justification for the activities and institutions of opponents. I therefore now examine the ways in which criticism expressed in such ways was harnessed in the production of money, power, and pleasure.

Warwick Anderson has published an interesting study of American doctors and scientists in the colonised Philippines of the early twentieth century. He talks of the 'medical production of colonial bodies and colonial space', in which the 'vulnerable, formalized bodies of the American colonists demanded sanitary quarantine' from the disease-ridden natives. In other words, the Americans defined the locals as unclean and, thereby, generated a sanitary justification for their own presence through bringing modern hygiene to the islands. Moreover, the ultimate imperative was not purification but self-glorification; within the 'ritual frame' of the laboratory 'American scientists ... obsessively collected any specimens of Filipino feces they could lay their gloved hands on', and such study of the faeces of the locals launched meteoric medical and scientific careers.[14] In essence, this is what opponents accused Catholics of doing. These men arrived from foreign parts, identified sin in the local population, required adherence to purificatory practices and rituals from regular confession to confession and penance, and in so doing acquired fame and authority.

We have seen in chapter 3 how the decorations of ritualist churches could be spoken of as meretricious (i.e. showy, deceptive, and suggestive of prostitution) and also the way in which objects and practices could be interpreted as evidence of the rebirth of fertility cults. Yet it should be emphasised that the evidence points to a high degree of sexual austerity amongst Anglo-Catholic clergy. Indeed, one of their key enthusiasms was the fostering of celibacy. How is it, then, that they became so intensely sexualised? I suggest that the mechanism that operated in the Philippines should rather be applied to the critics of ritualism, for the classificatory power that condemned ritualism as a pollution was that of Protestant opponents. Anglo-Catholics were thought to be morally dirty, or, to put it another way, Protestants discovered and analysed that dirt.

But the result was not an iconoclastic destruction of the Anglo-Catholics and their culture. Just as in the case of the Philippines, the objects of classification were necessary to the classifiers. However, the problem for the anti-Catholic position was that the classification of Catholicism placed it in a dangerous proximity to Protestantism and, moreover, that the spectre was raised that all religion was in fact primitive and superstitious. This is why the use of comparative religion by Protestants was highly selective and melodramatic, rather than lucidly reasoned. This, then, generated a specific set of fantasies of the supposed relations between ancient pagan Rome and its modern papal incarnation, that presented the opportunity for the voyeuristic objectification of Catholicism as a fantastic 'other'. The more fantastic the image of Catholicism was, in other words, the greater its potential to legitimate the accuser.

Protestants, therefore, thought Anglo-Catholicism (as a supposed extension of Roman Catholicism) into a site of pollution and sex. This was substantially a projection of exciting Gothic fantasies that drew attention away from the less spectacular moral transgressions of other Protestants. It was, in other words, an act of moral scapegoating, in which blame was fixed on a powerless minority so as to improve the cohesion of the majority. But it is important to realise that most of the participants were anything but callously cynical and disinterested. They thought of themselves as attempting to help and save by revealing and denouncing. I honestly believe that many of them tried their best to halt the spread of Catholicism in both its Roman and Anglican manifestations. Their campaigns were, however, remarkably ineffective. Why?

First, the Protestant belief in the necessity of self-reformation and the power of Grace meant that they were better equipped to denounce impurity than to cleanse it. Second, because their own purity shone in the context of the sins of others, the suppression, as opposed to the pillorying, of Catholics threatened the Protestants' own self-constructions of personal purity. Third, Catholic ideals did have strong elements of moral allure. The aim of the monastic life of poverty, chastity, and obedience was, of course, to approximate as closely as possible to the ideals expressed by Christ. What made Roman and Anglo-Catholic activity so dangerous was that it threatened to reveal the degree to which conventional society transgressed from the life of Jesus. The Catholic adulation of ascetic humility had great purchase, which was precisely why it had to be countered by variously plausible images of luxury, hypocrisy, and despotism.

In addition, reasoned discussion of the cultural life of the concept of asceticism threatened the standing of moral accusers because of its overlap with contemporary constructions of class, gender, and sexuality. For example, in 1856 the Pre-Raphaelite painter Ford Madox Brown completely reworked a section of a painting that had been exhibited with mediocre success four years earlier. He wrote in his diary on that 'to suit the public taste...it must be clothed! To suit my own, not' (figure 5.3).[15] The first seminude form of Brown's *Jesus Washing Peter's Feet* (1851–56, retouched 1857, 1858, 1876, and 1892) can be seen in a couple of preparatory studies as well as a watercolour of 1876 now in the Manchester City Art Gallery. The scene illustrated is that described in John 13: 1–17, when Jesus washes the feet of his disciples after the last supper. What exactly was the problem? One writer of the time complained of Catholic images of Christ that 'what adds not a little to the irreverence as regards our Lord is, that His body is generally represented as nearly naked. Those parts which are ordinarily clothed, and which in the case of an earthly friend or relative we would count it shame to expose to public gaze, are in His case so exposed'.[16] Yet it is

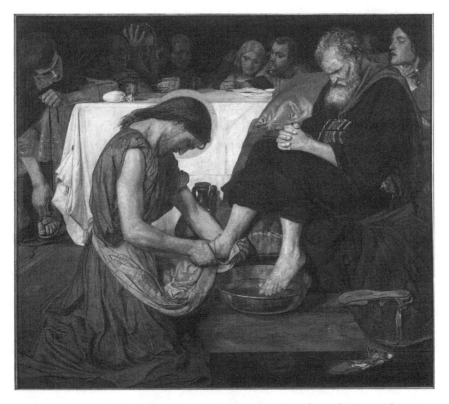

FIGURE 5.3. Ford Madox Brown, *Jesus Washing Peter's Feet* (1852–56). Copyright Tate, London, 2008.

clear that Jesus was originally shown with an ample loin cloth, much as he was in Holman Hunt's *The Shadow of Death* (1870–73) (see figure 4.4). It seems that those twenty years saw a shift in public taste concerning depictions of Christ. Gerard Curtis, through identifying *Jesus Washing Peter's Feet* with Christian socialism and the assertion of the value of humble labour as also seen in Madox Brown's *Work* (1852–66), has suggested political reaction as another reason for the critical response to this artist's paintings in the 1850s.[17] But what happens if the two themes, nakedness and social degradation, are analysed together?

On Holy Thursday in Rome, Hobart Seymour saw a cardinal washing the feet of pilgrims while the 'stench' ascended around him. Mrs. Seymour saw the same scene with female pilgrims, and the whole thing represented the 'most disgusting spectacle, as well as the most loathsome penances, I have ever witnessed'.[18] To return to Brown's painting, the artist noted that he made a special point of giving Judas, who is just about to have his feet washed, red hair, since this appeals 'out to the beholder'.[19] Red hair was powerfully associated in Pre-Raphaelite painting with sensuousness, and of course, Judas is the truly carnal figure in the painting.[20] Jesus, in other words, has just debased himself before carnality. The washing of dirt was, in Victorian England, the work of servants, the sexual implications of which became explicit in the life and practices of Arthur Munby (1828–1910), a middle-class man who met Hannah Cullwick (1833–1909), a servant, in 1854 and married her in 1873. Martin Danahay has argued that Munby and his partner's long years of sexual fetishism and role playing, centring around the notion of Munby as the effete master and Cullwick as the coarse servant, were culturally, but not conceptually, marginal; in other words, their lives reveal that which was implicit in mainstream contemporary values.[21] In a society in which power relations between men and women and between the classes were enormously unequal, it is hardly surprising if the inequality of those relationships became eroticised. The erotic economy also extended beyond this world. When Cullwick was photographed 'in her dirt' (unwashed) posing as the Magdalen, she was playing with the erotic potential of sacred narratives.[22]

But this was a society in which such explorations of the complexities of power and eroticism were normally relegated to private life. A taboo was laid over public discussion of erotic responses to Christ's body, for instance, not merely because of the boundary between sacred and profane, but also because of that between those who must be obeyed and those who must obey. We now understand that cultural taboos do not come out of nowhere, but are culturally produced. When Brown painted Christ washing the feet of Peter and exhibited the result at the Royal Academy, the conceptual boundaries of contemporary society were felt to be threatened. Christ performing the work of a servant could be accommodated with some discomfort. Christ in a potentially arousing state of seminudity could, with some disquiet, also be accommodated. But Christ as seminude servant threatened to highlight issues that not only questioned His moral authority, but also, crucially, that of the English middle and upper classes.

The great fear was the threatening of the boundaries of high and low. Such boundaries were a defence against social revolution, one that had been honed by centuries of engagement with the potentially revolutionary doctrines of Christianity on the moral superiority of the poor, such as Christ's dictum that it was 'easier for a camel to pass through the eye of a needle than for a rich man to enter the kingdom of God' (Luke 18: 25 and Matthew 19: 24). It was therefore a dangerous thing to 'wash' the poor because this threatened to erase social distinctions. *Punch* made the point quite clearly in 1844, when commenting on moves to build public baths. We, readers are told, are stood upon a soap pedestal, above those who on their filthy faces bore the 'lasting badge of serfdom'. The '"unwashed" were of a lower species—the mere negroes of poverty'![23]

The foot-washing on the part of the cardinal witnessed by Hobart Seymour in Rome was so threatening because it revealed the way in which Roman Catholicism had discovered how to control the believing poor by locking them into the position of mutual acclaim in which the spiritual authority of the high was balanced by the moral authority of the poor. By contrast, the moral position of the home heathen, the unbelieving masses of the Victorian metropolis, was dangerously unclear. On the one hand, they were possessed of fearful revolutionary potential, but on the other hand, the tenets of Christianity urged the need to grant them respect. As Christopher Herbert puts it, in these circumstances 'the holiness and purity of the poor would render them frightening and untouchable, and could only be felt, sentimentality aside, as a repugnant and dangerous form of dirt'.[24] So why would a respectable Protestant bourgeois *enjoy* abasing himself with the bodies of the poor? The fact is that 'respectable' men did so on a regular basis when they had sex with servants or prostitutes. Furthermore, because women were generally held to be inferior to men (morally and physically), even a married man was lowered by his passion for his wife. Therefore, the desire of the superior to touch the inferior was powerfully eroticised. Ascetic Catholicism, therefore, came to be read via the terms of a pornographic imagination that eroticised social transgression. This meant that the subject had to be approached with heavy doses of hypocrisy.

On the north side of St. Barnabas', Pimlico, over the arcading of the central arch of the nave is written 'elegi abiectus esse in domo Dei mei magis oram habitare in tabernaculis peccatorum' (I have chosen to be abject in the House of my God, rather than to dwell in the tabernacles of sin) (Vulgate Psalm 83: 11).[25] In the King James Bible, this is Psalm 84: 10, 'I had rather be a doorkeeper in the house of my God, than to dwell in the tents of wickedness'. The standard Latin dictionary, Lewis and Short, indicates that the Vulgate text is definitely about throwing oneself down with the sense of degradation and abjection, because 'abiectus' implies 'downcast, disheartened, desponding; low, mean, abject, worthless, unprincipled'. The Ecclesiologist and Anglo-Catholic John Mason Neal commented of this passage that this should not be read to mean I am happy to be abject, but that I am happy to be the humblest in a place of glory. He notes that the Vulgate, 'looking rather to the spirit than the letter' of the Hebrew, which read 'I had rather be cast down in the house of the Lord,' referred to 'suffering in the Church militant on earth' since there will be no such pain in Heaven.[26] He therefore was keen to skirt defensively away from the notion of the courting of pain and abasement. It has recently been commented that 'Munby's philosophy was that "nothing is low or disgusting if it be done for love"'.[27] The mainstream of Victorian society could simply not accept publicly such a view that threatened so many social boundaries. The ritualist programme, from the adulation of the host, to the abasement of the penitent, did not advocate such an uncompromising moral reformulation, but it polluted Victorian public discourse by highlighting for its opponents the question that preoccupied so many Victorians with painful intensity: how far, in safety, can I follow my low physical desires?

These moral ambivalences meant that the attack was not made on the reality of ritualist practice, but on a selective fantasy of Catholicism. However, this resort to melodrama deprived Ultra-Protestantism of the support of many of those who regarded themselves as taking a rational stand on religious questions. There was also an important side effect: the enjoyment gained from blackening the reputation of Roman and Anglo-Catholics brought the whole enterprise within the sphere of sensation, entertainment, and commodification, since getting the dirt on William Bennett, Robert Liddell, and their associates helped to sell tracts, newspapers, and books. It was not only Protestant ministers who stood to gain but also some of the commercially active members of their congregations.

Texts and Profits

With the waning of aristocratic power came the enfranchisement of people of middling wealth, and it was their values, including their work ethics, that increasingly formed the basis of social respectability.[28] The middle-class values of stability and responsibility were meant to ensure the safety of the newly emerging social order.[29] Such people are mostly seen today as the product and expression of economic relations, but in the period up to 1850 they were much more than that: they were 'a moral, cultural and political force whose identity was registered in and through the workings of the liberal public sphere'.[30] The evolving discourse of respectability functioned to disempower those who indulged in aristocratic self-indulgence or working class imp(r)udence.[31] Roman Catholicism was accused of being an elite conspiracy to dupe the ignorant masses. Literature that focussed on the transgressions of Catholics formed a crucial element in a booming market for fiction that combined the titillating opportunity for the voyeuristic enjoyment of the sins of others with varying degrees of reassuring moralism. The power of this market-driven encounter was immense. Patrick O'Malley has highlighted the way in which 'the nineteenth century constructed English Catholicism itself as an essentially literary phenomenon, a Gothic narrative played out in historical time'.[32] In other words 'experience could be read like a Gothic novel'.[33]

It is important to clearly distinguish the Gothic of the Gothic Revival from the Gothic of Gothic literature. The former is associated with a morally affirmative engagement with medieval art and architecture; the latter, with ambivalent fantasies that hinge on the fear and desire for some aspect of the primitive. Gothic literary transgression gained its power from the admixture of delight and disgust. It provided a 'language of forbidden desire'.[34] It was popularly believed, for much of the twentieth century, that sexual repression was a keystone of bourgeois Victorian hypocrisy. Notions of repression have since been replaced by a focus on discourse, which suggests that sexuality was not so much denied as discovered, defined, categorised, and regulated as an area of public knowledge through scientific, technological, medical, psychological, and legal understandings. These were mechanisms of community and 'anyone who wants to criticise rampant individualism should remember how a real community works, the censorship it deploys, the exclusions and downgradings and ostracisms'.[35] Sexual relations could, in other words, easily fall into the category of social danger; how, then, to explore such possibilities in safety?

I examine literary Gothic as more than style—as a mode of imagining that aimed to deliver thrills without spills.[36] One of the most intense experiences that the genre offered was the quasi-orgasmic moment of sensational revelation: when the demon, the Jesuit, the vampire, bursts in on the maiden. In Gothic literature, as with pornography, there is the desire to experience that point over and again, which is why it is perhaps ultimately devalued. Recognition of that fact may lead to the 'admixture of disgust and ecstasy [which] is typical of our uncanny response' to this false sublime with its short-term fix of excitement.[37] J. M. Neale and Benjamin Webb's neo-Gothic church that I referred to in my introduction could therefore be read by their opponents as representing an encounter not with the sublime but with debasing architectural erotica. The difference in opinion derives from the two forms of the Gothic gaze.

The delicious and sickly horror of encountering the false sublime, and the boost in our self-esteem that the reader gains by appreciating it as such, underlies the literary genre of the Gothic. According to the cultural theorist, Fred Botting, the 'Enlightenment, which produced the maxims and models of modern culture, also invented the Gothic'.[38] Good versus evil was supplemented, if not replaced, by reason versus unreason. And as in the earlier binary, emphasis on the one element created the importance of its opposite. Botting links the French Revolution with the development of the powerfully ambivalent fear that nothing was secure and yet also with the delight that anything was possible. This produced an intense love–hate relationship with boundary transgression. Gothic castles ceased to arouse horror in such a world, and there was a process of internalisation, a production of 'homely Gothic', in which Gothic came in from the moors and into the Victorian household. It 'became part of an internalised world of guilt, anxiety, despair, a world of individual transgression interrogating the uncertain bounds of imaginative freedom and human knowledge'.[39] Lurking behind all of this was the uneasy juxtaposition of moral goodness and divine power in a world in which God had apparently allowed revolution, at least temporarily, to succeed. Julia Kristeva has talked of a link between horror and the divine as being involved in a process of reverting 'to a primordial indistinction...[which] negates any ethical notion of the divine as unequivocally good'.[40] When Christian tenets conflicted with reason, the only explanation for spiritual efficacy was the presence of uncanny power. Such mysteries delighted the Gothic imagination. Ritualists might have followed the neo-Gothic visual tradition that stressed the uniting of visual pleasure and moral truth in architecture, but their opponents could employ the Gothic literary tradition to understand such constructions as stage sets for the fearfully amusing dances of unreason.

The opponents of ritualism were inspired by and participated in the Gothic literary tradition and thus became complicit, as I argue below, in the commodification of a saleable interpretation of Catholicism as entertainment. The romantic attractions of the Middle Ages became combined with the delights of demonising it, with the result that the reception of the past became incorporated into the commercial practices of modernity through the sale of tracts, scandal sheets, newspapers, and novels. Iconoclasm did not happen—it was not necessary. Victorian England incorporated Catholic spectacle through sublimating it into text. In this way, Catholicism and its material and bodily culture were constructed as the kind of dirt that could be recycled into profit.

To summarise, early Victorian society was caught between the presence of conflicting desires: to wallow in moral (especially sexual) dirt and to avoid it like the plague. Keeping a very strong boundary between private actions and public knowledge was one means of coping with this situation. Another was the consumption of the transgressions of others, a process that could be accompanied with more or less heavy doses of moral protestation as the need for self-distancing was perceived to be more or less acute. This privileged texts over images. For instance, in the case of the ritual of the washing of the feet of the poor, Victorian England would stomach a textual description with an accompanying denunciation, but they would not accept a painting of the subject, since the latter carried with it the suspicion of the viewer's public acceptance and collusion.

Life in the modern metropolis was unprecedentedly complicated, and the English were learning how to scrutinise it in safety. In the process, rationality was invoked to privilege the evolving disciplines of 'science' as cultural spaces in which techniques and discourses of safe engagement could take place. But this had momentous implications for enjoyment. For example, the weight of antiquarian classification rendered the interpenetration of sexuality and religion into a dry landscape for scholars. The search for pleasure was thus best pursued via the imagination and its literary products. It is important to realise that the resulting textual tradition overlapped with those of Protestant institutional structures such as tract societies. The denunciation of Catholic abuses fed into an avalanche of published sermons, the effect of which was primarily to reinforce self-esteem and loyalty in chapel rather than feeding into authorial profits. Nevertheless, theological debate bled into a world of scandalous novels and newspaper headlines, the aim of which was the entertainment of the reader and the generation of financial profit. As Norman Vance has commented, '[T]hen, as now, other people's purple sins coloured the grey spaces of the days'.[41] To illustrate this, I use the example of the spiritual equivalent of foot washing: the cleansing of souls in the confessional.

Confession, as practiced by Anglo-Catholics, was a vital medium for obtaining appropriate penances from a priest and returning to the path of righteousness. Those who defended such 'auricular confession' took it very seriously, as did many of their opponents. That it was a highly problematic practice was evidenced even by Alfred Poole, a curate attached to St. Barnabas', who admitted, when in trouble over the practice with Archibald Campbell Tait, the bishop of London, that the abuse of confession could lead to a 'morbid' state of mind.[42] Of course, those who defended private confession—Pusey, Bennett, Wagner of

Brighton, and Alexander Heriot MacKonochie of Holborn being some of the most (in)famous—assured the sceptical public that they conducted confession with an eye to scrupulous moral purity.

One way in which to understand this ritualist focus on private confession was that it was a borrowing from Roman Catholicism. This was certainly the way in which many people saw it at the time. However, we may think about this in the context of the rise of rival technologies of discussion and control of the body and self: judicial, medical, and psychological. In these discourses, as famously identified by Michel Foucault, 'under the authority of a language that had been carefully expurgated so that it was no longer directly named, sex was taken charge of, tracked down as it were, by a discourse that aimed to allow it no obscurity, no respite'.[43] His unfinished volume of the *History of Sexuality* was the *Confessions of the Flesh*, the key topic of which was to be the ways in which sex was harnessed by discourse. In this respect, the worries about the Anglo-Catholics were not that they were talking about sex but that, under the cover of 'privacy', they were not employing suitably 'expurgated' language. Moreover, priests were not, in many people's opinions, professional experts able to deal with such issues without danger to themselves and their patients.[44] This is not, of course, how things were expressed at the time. One was more likely to find bystanders turning to Biblical justifications such as Ephesians 5: 12, 'it is a shame even to speak of those things which are done of them in secret'.[45]

The vital text in use for Roman Catholic confession was the *Garden of the Soul* (1755) by the vicar apostolic Richard Challoner (1691–1781), which was the most important Catholic Prayer Book in England of the period. Its importance can be seen from the fact that it had far more editions than the official Roman *Raccolta*, which appeared in Latin in 1807, but not in English until 1857.[46] The method of confession was for the penitent to kneel down at the side of the priest, to make the sign of the cross, to ask his blessing, and then to list any sins. The priest then gave absolution and penance. The sort of questions that gave Protestants thrills and nightmares were, for example, have you been 'guilty of self-pollution? Or of immodest touches of yourself? How often?'; 'have you looked at immodest objects with pleasure?'; 'kept indecent pictures?'; 'have you abused the marriage bed by any actions contrary to the order of nature? Or by any pollutions? Or been guilty of any irregularity, in order to hinder your having children?' and (ironically?) 'have you taught anyone evil which he knew not before?'[47] In a correspondence between a Catholic and a Protestant, the argument made by the antiquarian Riland Bedford, Rector of Sutton Coldfield, was that the *Garden of the Soul* ranged across the whole realm of sexual experience, asking, in summary, whether you have 'ever been guilty of fornication, of adultery of incest, or any other sin against nature, either with a person of the same sex, or with any other creature'. This, said Bedford, would be placed into the hands of a 'Protestant Female of eighteen. . . . I now leave it to the reader whether or not I was wrong in styling them "disgustingly beastly interrogatories"'. Because past Popes have 'indulged in every kind of sensual abomination', how should he suppose that modern priests will be better?[48] This material was intended by Roman Catholic priests for someone to meditate upon so that they might know what to bring up at confession, but opponents thought of it as simply polluting innocent minds with evil thoughts and suggestions. This material was thus read as immoral and pornographic.

In 1858, 'that fearful engine of vice and depravity, the confessional' claimed another victim in Pimlico: a priest.[49] That man was Alfred Poole, who has been mentioned as a curate at St. Barnabas'. He believed that confession was essential, together with penance, in purifying sinners. But at the time, it was alleged that the true victims were those who had come to make their confessions to him. The supposed scenes were the subject of lurid tracts that attempted, for the benefit of their horrified, intrigued, or amused readers, to bring to light the 'scenes enacted in the darkened chambers of St. Barnabas College'. The accusation was that the ritualist clergy were 'such adepts in the mysteries of sensual enjoyments as to fit them for examiners of the secrets of vice, as apt searchers out of the hidden thoughts and fleeting fancies of unfortunate penitents.' Such a man as Poole was a whitened sepulchre, apparently pure without but ashen within: 'It might prove injurious to his character were the curtain withdrawn, and his conduct in the confessional openly contrasted with that pureness of demeanour, that outward sanctity of deportment which so remarkably adorn his character in his public walk'. Jesus asked people to repent to God, but the 'polluted minds of the modern Pharisee' sought to usurp that role.[50]

The victims were seen as being the women of the parish. Surely it was impossible that Poole, who had received confessions, had been able to do so without impropriety:

> Surely these pretenders to purity are surely tried? Fancy the lovely
> beauties, the courtly ladies of Belgravia, the blood still boiling, the
> bosom still heaving, from the exciting amusements of the previous
> night, the brain still reeling under the influence of the voluptuous
> dance; fancy such a one at the feet of the Satanic confessor ... Cast
> out the reptile; let him no longer darken your doors, pollute your
> sanctuary, or sully by his presence the sunshine of your peace-
> ful abode; avoid the confessional and the dark minister of impure
> thoughts as you would the foetid atmosphere of the pest-house.[51]

The confessional was here reinvented into a place of sensual delirium, disease, and Gothic mystery. In place of the sorrowing lover seeking to reclaim his morally and sexually fallen consort, as depicted in Dante Gabriel Rossetti's *Found* (c. 1869–81, unfinished), confessors were depicted as fallen males polluting respectable young women (figure 5.4). Wives, it was urged, must confide in their husbands rather than in such priests from meretricious churches, and they must reject councils to do otherwise:

'You must not tell your husband what has passed'. Bah! The unclean, unholy thing offends the laws of God, destroys the oneness of the

FIGURE 5.4. Dante Gabriel Rossetti, *Found* (c. 1869–81, unfinished). By permission of Delaware Art Museum, Samuel and Mary R. Bancroft Memorial, 1935.

married state, infects the very air he [i.e., the priest] breathes, pollutes the very ground on which he treads. Well may he seek the shroud of darkness, the secrecy of the secret chamber.[52]

Charles Westerton had raised with Tait the allegation that Poole had been hearing private 'auricular confessions'.[53] The formal accusation and case derived from Rev. Frederick Baring (who was in cahoots with Westerton), who called a public meeting at St. James' Hall on Friday June 11, 1858, at which he read out the letters he had sent to the bishop of London. By this point, Poole had been investigated by Tait, his licence having been suspended on May 18, and Baring was attempting to create negative publicity in the context of the appeal. That same month, a pamphlet appeared, written by one 'Fairplay', that gives us a hostile account of the proceedings. The anonymous author commented that the investigations were a mucky business: 'Through what vile waters must you have dragged your net, what slimy productions must you have brought to light, before you succeeded in landing the object you sought, in the shape of the evidence of Susan B——! [Buckingham]'. He thus argued that such interrogations were almost as debasing as those of the confessional themselves.[54]

This lady's motives in testifying against Poole were financial gain, as were those of the other witness 'Elizabeth S—— [Shiers]'. Buckingham alleged that the confession had taken place in a 'dark room'. Neither we, nor many people at the time could know what he had asked her since the printed account says that 'he then asked me [* * * * * * * *]. He told me not to be ashamed to tell my holy father these things'.[55] Poole then stood behind her and gave her absolution with his hands on her head. The same thing happened to Shiers. There was the further suggestion that Miss Joy, a district visitor, had given alms after having undergone the experience of confession. 'Fairplay' said that he was also worried about auricular confession but 'the place for discussing so important a subject is not at all events a music hall, hired by unknown persons, and filled with an audience collected together by placards and advertisements, stimulating enough in their terms, and appealing to the morbid sympathies if not to the lowest passions of the crowd'. Moreover, a sober subject required sober language. By contrast, Baring told the audience that, concerning Miss Joy and the other ladies who had catered for Mr. Poole, 'it is probable that these ladies themselves "had gone through a most searching examination"'. According to 'Fairplay', 'this statement is reported as having been received by your audience with "cheers and laughter". The audience thoroughly appreciated all the delicacy of your *double entendre*'.[56] Imagining the confessor's investigation of the women was most entertaining. The transformation into public pleasure was well underway.

The Times, although no friend of 'Puseyites', as discussed in chapter 3, criticised Tait's condemnation of Poole without giving him a chance to explain himself. As an Englishman, 'were Mr. Poole ten times a Jesuit he has a right to be heard', even though the views of the mass of Englishmen were (allegedly) so clear that the newspaper saw that the result must be a formality.[57] Liddell stood by his curate. Poole had not used a Gothic 'darkened chamber', but simply a room in the vestry. Poole had denied that he had put these 'indecent and disgusting questions'.[58] One 'F. D.' argued in his defence that although auricular confession was un-English, it was better a wife confide in a priest than in a male friend who will end as a paramour. Moreover, the recent Divorce and Matrimonial Bill, which had led to 'abundantly granted' divorces, demonstrated that 'our social condition, *without confession*, is not too pure'.[59] A further anonymous tract promptly responded to 'F. D.' This writer did think that Poole had been made a scapegoat, but because the practice was widespread amongst the ritualists, this was unlikely to stop the practice. Confession, he also admitted, was allowed by the Prayer Book, but he claimed that the people did not like it, and therefore, the Book must be altered or the Church would be overthrown by the people, the problem being not that of jealousy in connection with wives, but that the 'Prayer Book breathes the spirit of Roman Catholicism'.[60]

Poole was one of a number of clerics who got into trouble due to administering private confession. The scenes in St. James' Hall and the following refutations were repeated across Britain. For example, one may directly compare the account given by 'Fairplay' to that provided by 'A Churchman', in his *Reply to the Lecture of the Rev. Canon Stowell, on Confession, Delivered in the Free Trade Hall, Manchester, on Tuesday Evening, September 28, 1858*, which ran to at least four editions. The writer alleged that it was a slur on British womanhood to suggest that they were in any real danger: 'Ladies, do you not see the stigma on your own sex! If a man were base enough, when you were pouring out your sins into his ears, to make an attempt upon your chastity, have you not moral courage to resist him!'[61] Yet the anti-Catholic Anglican Hugh Stowell (1799–1865), like Baring, had apparently conjured up ghoulish phantoms when, against the supposed importation of Roman practices, he cried out that 'there is a ghostly inmate in every faithful popish family. The shadow of the priest haunts every place; it is behind the bed curtains, behind the chairs and tables, in the secret closet'.[62] Even if he has not got 'the body' of the woman, he has her soul. In effect, if you marry her, she is married already: therefore, 'you marry a corpse!' At this point in Stowell's vividly imaginative Gothic discourse, we are informed that a 'titter' ran round the room.[63] The implication is that those who found the situation most entertaining, or at least most consciously pleasurable, were the least threatened by it or, at least, defused their fear through laughter. The distrust of the private investigator, be he the confessor or he who would investigate the confessions, was thereby replaced by an acceptable mood of public consumption through the pleasures of amusement at the expense of both species of cleric.

We do not know exactly what Baring and Stowell said, but we can quote for other descriptions and denunciations of auricular confession, such as a splendid example by T. H. Lowe (1797–1861), Dean of Exeter: *Auricular Confession: A Sermon Preached in the Cathedral Church of Exeter, Sunday November 7th, 1852.* Yet again, the proximity of Guy Fawkes Night set off a rant against Rome and its 'apish imitators'. And, as appropriate with apes, argued Lowe, confessors revelled in bestial scenes. Would you want to find out what was said, he asks:

> Would you bear to have the screen of the confessional thrown open,
> that you might listen to the disgusting details of the minute question-
> ings to which the priestly confessor subjects his unhappy penitents;
> thus suggesting to their minds thoughts of evil, which otherwise
> would never have been harboured there, and making them familiar
> with images of pollution, which continue to haunt their imagina-
> tions, and to corrupt their hearts, and too often lead them on to the
> commission of open acts of impurity and sin?[64]

No! You would not want to hear more, he exclaims, about those for whom priestly celibacy is simply leading to inflamed desires. Yet we must be brave and imagine the scene as, in the words of another anticonfession campaigner, we see 'the tender maid, pure as the morning dew that sparkles in the glassy glade, her simple mind like the drifted snow, untainted with defiling stains, in blissful ignorance of sin'. Then we turn in revulsion to her confessor: 'If there be on earth a loathsome object of contemplation, that can sicken the heart of man, it is that of a sensual, bloated Priest, whose mind has been debauched by the pages of Rome's obscenest casuistry, sitting in sly and watchful contact beside a delicate maiden'.[65] Since it was never known for sure exactly what was being said in the confessional, the interested public turned to its imagination, assisted by journalists, novelists, and evangelical and Dissenting ministers. A use had been found for Catholicism as the vehicle of public pleasure.

It can therefore be demonstrated that the wider cultural role of anti-Catholicism represented much more than a clash of theological systems. It became a fantasy of wish fulfilment providing the vicarious acting out of atrocities of sex and violence. It went far beyond biased reporting. It gave fulsome new life, for example, to the fantasy of the vampire. That predatory monster and his innocent victims are clichés of melodramatic fiction. In 1855, Henry Bunn, curate of Calne, Wiltshire, dedicated a tract to the Earl of Shaftesbury, champion of Protestant causes, who, as a subscriber, got six copies. It was called *The Vampire of Christendom*, chapter 3 of which was on the 'sanguinary character of the Papacy'. Bunn talked of the bloody wars caused by the Popes, the tortures, the women seized in the night: 'Oh! How that distracted husband is convulsed with agony as he contemplates her the innocent victim of a long and living death' in the ecclesiastical prison. He then passed swiftly on to Irish mobs attacking Protestants in Ireland. The Papal aggression must be resisted, the wolf and the whore defied; we should 'form no association with the tyrant that drank their [the martyrs of the Reformation's] blood, and who is now thirsting for the blood of their children'.[66] Through such invective, the nightmare world of the vampiric Inquisition was directly associated with modern Popery and thus with its dupes the Tractarians and ritualists.

The secret spies and advance guard of contemporary Rome were understood to be the Jesuits. Like vampires, they originated from filthy, sinful foreign places such as Spain, 'the odious and unclean lurking place of all the worst enormities of Popery'.[67] It was believed of Jesuits that 'they like to have the weaker sex to deal with', since it is easier to 'bleed' money out of them, and likewise they prey on the rich. 'Is our moral atmosphere to be thus polluted? Are these demon-spirits to enter our dwellings—to find a place by our fireside—to tamper with the fidelity of our wives'? Are they to continue 'contaminating the minds of the youth of both sexes'?[68] In a further twist of perverse fantasy, male Jesuits, like vampires, could also be associated with gender indeterminacy, or at least effeminacy. For example, Luke, the Catholic cousin of Lancelot in Charles Kingsley's novel *Yeast*, talks of the Jesuits as those who would teach a 'fast young man'. He writes of Jesuits to Lancelot: 'Ay, start and sneer, at that delicate woman-like tenderness, that subtle instinctual sympathy'![69]

Such fears found their expression in some extraordinary novels that posed as true stories. In John Russell's (not the Prime Minister) *The Jesuit in England* of 1858, the Jesuit Garcino, come to minister to the Catholic Letty, is found snooping around in her sister's bedchamber and is driven out at poker point by the hero, Charles. The narrative abounds with references to gold crucifixes, that is, until we find one of grim iron on the wall of the cell in which the sisters are imprisoned, having unwisely ventured to Italy. The hero, in due course locked up elsewhere by bandits, finds he has an English companion, with whom he exchanges the following dialogue (this is *not* a well-written novel): '"May I venture to inquire if you have embraced the Tractarian-Puseyite opinions, and consequently been led away to the Vatican?" "Not I, sir; I am fully aware of the dangerous, evil tendency of those opinions"'.[70] In the context of the Papal Aggression, the *Liverpool Mercury* said of the Puseyites that 'if they are not Jesuits, they are worse than Jesuits because they are disguised Romanists in the pay of the Church of England'.[71]

According to another writer, there were more Jesuits in England than in Italy, and in order to convert the people, they concealed themselves even as 'Protestant priests'. Since there was a limit to the numbers who would be fooled by this,

> the Jesuits of England tried another plan. This was to demonstrate from history and ecclesiastical antiquity the legitimacy of the usages of the English Church, whence, through the exertions of the Jesuits concealed among its clergy, might arise a studious attention to Christian antiquity. This was designed to occupy the clergy in long, laborious and abstruse investigations and to alienate them from their Bibles.[72]

Thus, the Jesuits could be regarded as also being at the root of Tractarianism and Ecclesiology.

The perils of falling into the clutches of the Jesuits derived from the fact that they were thought to have been brainwashed, so that they lost their human sympathy. During their training (and we may note that both vampires and Jesuits were changed from normal people), they 'convert him into the creature, the victim, the tool of a society framed for universal domination, and founding that domination on the ruin on humanity, the bondage of the soul of man'.[73] Pseudoscience stepped in here, for 'experts' suggested that Jesuits had specific physiognomy such as tightly compressed lips as appropriate to those sworn to secrecy; following our vampire analogy, the tightly compressed lips also of those with toothy points to conceal.[74]

Jesuits, according to one study, 'glide' through Victorian fiction. They are awful figures. The only thing worse was the 'Jesuitess'. One such, supposedly true example, was the star turn of Jemima [née Thompson] Luke's *The Female Jesuit: Or the Spy in the Family* (1851) and *A Sequel to the Female Jesuit; Containing Her Previous History and Recent Discovery* (1852).[75] We read in the 1851 volume that a woman, having being brought up in various convents, was taken into Luke's household and there plotted against it. She was discovered and, at the time of writing, was on the loose in London. It was suggested that she 'was only an agent, and her plot some part of a greater system'. The peril was that 'feminine tact, combined with Jesuit cunning, could scarcely miss the attainment of any desired object'.[76]

The follow-up book of 1852 outlines various possibilities for who the woman really was. It finally appears that she was not a Jesuit, and that this must be admitted since 'truth can never be sustained upon false pretences, and they [the Lukes] would be the last to wish to be guilty of unfairness, *even* to the *Jesuits'* [emphasis original]. The question was asked, not only who she was, but also 'what' she was.[77] Of course, even though it was now made clear that the woman was simply an impostor, the book's sales continued to be promoted by the use of 'female Jesuit' in the title.

Hobart Seymour, who never had much doubt about anything, let alone about this, declared that 'I look on the order of the Jesuits as a grand conspiracy, conducted by the greatest talent, managed with the profoundest secrecy, and carried out with ablest agency—a grand conspiracy to bring the nations under the ecclesiastical empire of Rome'.[78] This theme, especially in relation to the national danger posed by Anglo-Catholicism glooms out from both novels and tracts of this period. For example, in another novel undercover Jesuits are aided by a ritualist priest, 'a zealous but mistaken young clergyman, who imagines he is a true and earnest Churchman, because he imitates the Church of Rome as much as he dares in her rites, ceremonies and rituals; he is one of those semi-Papists who will lead her at least half-way to Rome'.[79] Very occasionally someone Protestant says something charitable. William Carus Wilson (1792–1859), rector of Whittington, Lancashire, albeit in a tract against Mariolatry (!), confided that he had a Jesuit friend, H. Ramière, who was learned and amiable and whom he met at that 'admirably arranged institution', the Jesuit house at Le Puy.[80] Fear and excitement, however, was the usual pattern, late into the nineteenth century. In a publication of 1883, the Anglican priest Mourant Brock is still to be found arguing that, until the second coming, 'whether Dr. Pusey, and the other leaders of the movement, actually belonged to the Society of Loyola or not, will never be disclosed'.[81] And we hear that paranoid conspiracies featuring Edward Pusey, John Keble, and John Henry Newman as secret members of the order were played out, for example, amongst the Methodist 'rank and file'.[82]

Fantasies of bloody ecclesiastical conspiracies are, today, very big business. Dan Brown has been able to make a reported $250,000,000 from his novels, primarily due to the phenomenal sales of his bishop- and monk-infested *The Da Vinci Code* (2003).[83] Whilst the authors I have been mentioning were, needless to say, not nearly so successful, it is important to stress that sensation drama and the money-spinning author were phenomena born in the first half of the nineteenth century. It was 'during the era that began with Scott and ended with George Elliot, [that] publishing became a major, multi-million-pound industry'.[84] Intellectual property law was notably strengthened in 1842 when, by Act of Parliament, copyright was extended to the author's life plus seven, or forty-two years, whichever was the longer, albeit that there was not suitable international protection until the late nineteenth century. Sir Walter Besant (1836–1901) was able to claim, in 1899, a then reading public in English of 120 million, which he compared with 50,000 in the 1830s. This cannot be accurate, but it does give a perception of the revolution in progress.[85] It was during the 1850s that the reality of a mass reading public began to be felt; Wilkie Collins wrote in 1858 of the discovery of an '"unknown public" as dramatically as if he had come upon the sources of the Nile'.[86] In 1852, thousands and upon thousands of copies of *Uncle Tom's Cabin* were flying from the presses. The publication of periodicals boomed, too, at this time. Meanwhile, hundreds of thousands of sermons were also being sold as well as given away. The estimated totals for best-selling authors such as Charles Haddon Spurgeon (1834–92), the famous Baptist preacher, are in the millions.[87]

It is important to emphasise that all sides of Christian opinion criticised covetousness. The Protestant author of *Mammo-Mania: The Apostacy of the Age Unveiled* (1841) raises familiar complaints against worldliness in all its forms as he denounces 'a world given to antichrist, to idolatry, to mammonism . . . a world of principalities, of powers, and rulers of spiritual deceits in high places'.[88] Meanwhile, in 1850 we find Pusey emphasising that 'covetousness is idolatry'.[89] From the point of view of ritualists, those who spent much of their energy denouncing altar clothes and rood screens as the focus of idolatry had become diverted from addressing the problematic issues raised by individual wealth. It is interesting in this regard to consider R. Lawrence Moore's summary of the success of Protestant, and especially evangelical, piety in the modern United States. He concludes that such religion in that country has not acted as a break on commercial development; rather, it rode with change and helped to influence it, but was not, in the end, economically countercultural.[90]

The date of the advent of metropolitan consumer culture has been pushed back steadily in the academic literature. It is now understood that there was a substantial mass market in consumer goods and consumption for pleasure rather than need in the eighteenth century.[91] The degree to which life, including religious life, was influenced by the market is an important issue, as is the way in which that influence was perceived. For instance, it has been commented of Paris in the 1860s that it was 'a modern city born of the commodity'.[92] The period of the present study was also the age during which Marx was producing his theories of commodity fetishism in which he attempted to reveal what he regarded as the hidden truths of modern capitalism. It is worth bearing in mind his questioning of the value of commodities when we think about the burgeoning world of Victorian publishing. Books are not the same as texts. For instance, it has been noted that 'there hovered over a first edition in three stately tomes an aura of dignity and worth' that supported its high price.[93] Andrew Miller has charted the way in which the commoditisation of society and of the novel was of increasing importance to writers, such that narratives sometimes actively engaged with the dynamics of their own purchase.[94] Moreover, novels provided a 'carefully delimited space for the entertainment of fantasies of the commodity's power'.[95] Commercial books, therefore, could become uncannily animate to the extent that they were able to comment on their own fetishistic commodification.

Harriet Martineau (1802–76), musing on her experiences in Egypt and the Holy Land in 1846, wondered whether 'our current idolatry' will be succeeded by 'bibiolatry', in the sense of the worship of the early records of religion, rather than of their spirit.[96] Perhaps it was already happening? The fearful danger of the fetishising of texts by Protestants, especially the Bible, could be displaced by a focus on the supposed ritualistic and Catholic fetishisation of objects. Anglo- and Roman Catholicism were, in this process, popularly reinvented through Gothic themes in literature from novels to poems and newspaper stories.[97] The consumption of such texts should be seen as a respectable counterpart to the use of Catholic scenes in eighteenth-century erotica. A way had been found to safely reintegrate the primitive (including primitivising religious movements, e.g., ritualism) into the mainstream categorisations of capitalist society by giving them a place in the entertainment industry and thereby providing them with commodity value.

What I am suggesting is that the belief system that was becoming predominant was not any form of Christianity, but of capitalism. Ultimate power was no longer in the pulpits of the Church of England, be they Low or High. This was the position taken by George Cotton (1813–66), then master of Marlborough and future bishop of Calcutta, when preaching at the consecration of Tait as bishop of London in 1856. He claimed, as I mentioned in the introduction, that in the Church of England 'less interest and excitement is shown in the struggle against positive wickedness, than in some dispute about a cross, a vestment or a candlestick'. While we are disputing these 'minute points . . . the newspaper writer, the satirist, the popular novelist are labouring to correct those evils which the Church was designed to cure'. 'The press', he declared, 'is the chief spiritual power in England'.[98]

The form of discourse that ultimately predominated in popular culture, therefore, was not that of social science, nor of theology, but of entertainment. If commerce was the underlying structuring principle in nineteenth-century society, then the most serious impurity was what offended not God but the market. Those who believed in sacred material culture saw it as being exceptional in its potency: once the Eucharist was being performed, the communion wafer, to give an extreme example, could no longer be valued by reference to the cost of the flour of which it was made. But the logocentric commercial imperatives of Protestant England were able to reinterpret and dematerialise this magical material world into profitable Gothic texts. The primitive idols were, ultimately, disempowered, that is, cleansed of their power as abominations, not by Protestant faith, but by the belief in money. Therefore, over time, they lost their power to disturb and, with that semiotic decay, faded into commercial irrelevance as the objects of popular entertainment. Anglo-Catholicism was eventually accepted and forgotten by mainstream society precisely because it had become immaterial to its happiness.

Conclusion: The Convenient Despot

There is a horrid little story told of an old she-cannibal who had converted into a pious and exemplary Christian...as the poor creature lay on her death-bed early associations resumed their sway, and to the tender inquiries of the missionary after her spiritual welfare, she replied, 'I think if you could broil the fingers of that little child, I could just manage to pick them'. There you have the very image of the doting, plaintive, sentimental, half beseeching, half despairing tone in which a small knot of Protectionist peers every now and then ask to pick once more the savoury integuments of a corn law. The natural food of free trade becomes very insipid to those whose tastes are formed in a stronger school. Corn fetish was abolished five years ago, and there has been plenty of time for all people to practise a diet more consistent with humanity, but scarce a day passes without some inveterate *gourmand* of the old *régime* confessing once more to a longing after food wrung from the grasp of the poor...It scarcely amounts to a serious and deliberate wish once more to revel in the orgies of a legislative dearth, but it is rather a dreamy and delirious recollection of former scenes, expressed of course, in the language of desire.[1]

The writer of this piece, which appeared in *The Times* on March 21, 1851, knew very well that people loved to read 'horrid little stories about primitives and their terrible appetites. In a remarkable analogy, the death-bed hunger pangs of an 'old she-cannibal' are conjured up to explain the Parliamentary moves of peers attempting to reverse the repeal of the Corn Laws in 1846. Nature is assimilated to free-trade modernity, leaving the primitive as the realm of unnatural, sensual, and perverse horror. These British aristocrats are imagined as dreaming of *ancien régime* despotism and, thereby, displaying a level of primitivism so extreme as to suggest the supposedly fetishistic beliefs of savages and cannibals. This was not just a one-off association. In *The Times* of December 18, 1856, we find a discussion of economic beliefs running from prohibition of economic exchange between nations, to protectionism, and finally to free trade:

> The first and rudest of these states of mind resembles nothing so nearly as the fetishism of the African tribes. Just as these rude nations believe every object in nature to be instinct with a mischievous activity, and endowed with an existence opposed and hostile to their own, so they live in constant terror of the unreal dangers that their superstition conjures up.[2]

In modernity, by contrast, the material realm is not seen as dangerously alive. It is passive and subservient, a resource of commodities that God intended us to trade. The peers are accused of expressing themselves in the 'language of desire', but *The Times*, by its very invocation of a lurid primitive realm, was in fact summoning up the very 'dreamy and delirious recollection of former scenes' that it was affecting to condemn.

The spirit of *The Times* editorial stance in this article was close to that evoked by Robert Dick (1810–78), a Scottish doctor practising in London, who expressed himself thus in *The Spiritual Dunciad; Or Oxford 'Tracts' to Popery*, published by Charles Westerton in 1859:

> Poor stagnant spirits, anchor'd in the Past,
> Rooted upon the bank; while sweeping fast,
> Broad, bright and glorious, under Truth's glad beam,
> Rolls ever onwards PROGRESS' mighty stream![3]

The problem with Peers, Tractarians, and their Tory fellow travellers was, in this view, their opposition to progress. They evoked stagnant matter that gave off poisonous vapours or wasted resources that should be gleaming and pouring through the sluices of profitable investment.

I do not want to imply that ritualism should not be studied in terms of law, theology, or institutional church history. This has been done by others with great force and rigour, notably in relation to the slabs of Parliamentary time that Disraeli would devote to the passing of the Public Worship Regulation Act (1874).[4] But I do think that the wave of uproar generated over ritualistic innovation in the Church of England from 1840 to 1860 can be connected to much wider concerns in society, notably, those relating to class and the value of material goods and money. The case study of Pimlico revealed that the centre of opposition in that parish emerged not just from evangelicalism and Dissent, but also from Chartism. The Members of the London Association, of which Charles Westerton was secretary in the 1840s, published the *National Association Gazette*, the stance of which was squarely against the revenues of the 'corrupt papistical Anglican church'.[5]

When low churchmen projected moral pollution onto their ritualistic colleagues, they built up a relationship with a tainted Other that legitimated their own moral stance. In so doing, they were attempting to deflect danger from themselves and fasten it elsewhere. I have used the testimony of M. Hobart Seymour on a number of occasions, partly because he has a splendid turn of phrase, and partly because he practiced such projection of corruption in a particularly unself-conscious manner. For example, he tells us in his *Mornings among the Jesuits at Rome* (a title that in our day might equate to something like *Meetings with Al-Qaida*) that he was shown down into the Roman catacombs by a monk who 'looked like a moving plague—a personification of the malaria—a walking pestilence. There he was, an attenuated thing, a living skeleton'. The nightmare Other, in this account, is that horrific thing, a 'stagnant spirit' animated to life and power. Like the 'old she-cannibal', it is an abomination with a terrible appetite. What drove these monsters of corruption was greed. The sale of relics, 'a traffic of the most disgraceful and degraded nature' led to frenzied figures in cowls and wimples pillaging the underground caverns, ripping bones out of graves and pounding them into splinters. And when these seams of perverse gold were worked out and the supply of 'lawful relics of ecclesiastical merchandise' ran low, 'the monks who were the merchants in this matter' manufactured fake relics, and thus 'the demand of the market called forth an adequate supply'.[6]

It should be clear that, although the anti-Catholic clichés go back to the Reformation, this is a displacement of contemporary nightmares about mining and industrial production in the modern capitalist economy. And just as 'primitive' religion could be rethought as a horrific counterpart of Victorian production, so it could appear in relation to consumption. At the height of the Irish Potato famine, whilst hundreds of thousands were losing their lives, *Punch* entertained its readers with a discussion of claims that the 'Lepus Vastator' (the ravaging rabbit or, to be precise, Lepus Europaeus, the harrowing hare) was responsible.[7] Four years later, the amusement returned with a 'lecture addressed to the National Entomological Society' presenting the real culprit as 'Episcopus Vastator' (bellying bishop, or in the case of one very plump grub, consuming cardinal) (figure 6.1).[8] Science, even if in mock form, was being invoked in order to label pestilential consumption of resources that had, supposedly, caused physical death and destruction on a vast scale.

This piece, or others like it, appears to have provided inspiration for the introduction to *Monachologia*, a satire published anonymously in 1852 in Edinburgh, which played on the developing practices of biological classification. The original text was ascribed to Ignaz von Born (1742–91), who supposedly wrote it in 1782 in Augsburg having left the Jesuit order to pursue geological science. Nevertheless, the introduction is clearly new material, and the whole was cheerfully dedicated to Mr. Punch of Fleet Street. Robert Chambers, the author of *Vestiges of the Natural History of Creation* (1844), is advised that we have now solved the mystery of what lies between man and 'ourang-outang': 'a new genus, which connects *man*, the most perfect of mortal beings, with the *monkey*, the most silly of all animals.... I mean the *monk*, a genus of mammalia, whose outward appearance is almost identical to that of man, though in every other respect there is an immeasurable distance which separates *man* from *the monk*'. We are told that modern governments are moving to get rid of them as 'very noxious animals to mankind' and that this book will be a service to future scientists who 'seeing painted or sculpted representations of various kinds of monks, would be quite at a loss, not only how to define and to class, but even how to name the various species of these extinct animals'. However, in advance of such sanitary eradication these animals are now, by contrast, flourishing and infest Ireland, doing more damage than the potato blight.[9]

In 1851, Parliament bestirred itself and passed the Ecclesiastical Titles Act, which was intended to make the reestablishment of the Roman Catholic episcopacy illegal if based on specific locations (i.e., Bishop of Thistown). In the event, the law was never enforced, but *Punch*, meanwhile, looked forward to the demise of Nicholas Wiseman's pretentions (figure 6.2). In 'Selling off!!' the disconsolate cardinal is depicted as a shopkeeper who, in a situation of 'alarming failure!!!', is forced to sell off all his stock at knockdown prices. The shop had sold a wide range of ecclesiastical garments, candles, and 'winking pictures' and had advertised itself as offering 'real popery'. Clearly, business had gone very badly. People had not been deceived into buying relics, since they realised that they were just 'a quantity of old bones and rags'. Who would buy? 'Young ladies and children' were invited to purchase 'pretty little gimcracks'. Beyond that, another potential market was provided by theatrical managers and purveyors of fake Popery: 'Puseyites now is your time'. In the event, even these customers were not forthcoming, and Wiseman was forced to sell his own clothes

FIGURE 6.1. 'The Episcopus Vastator', *Punch* 20 (1851), p. 112. Photograph by the author, with permission, from the edition held at the library of Birkbeck College, London.

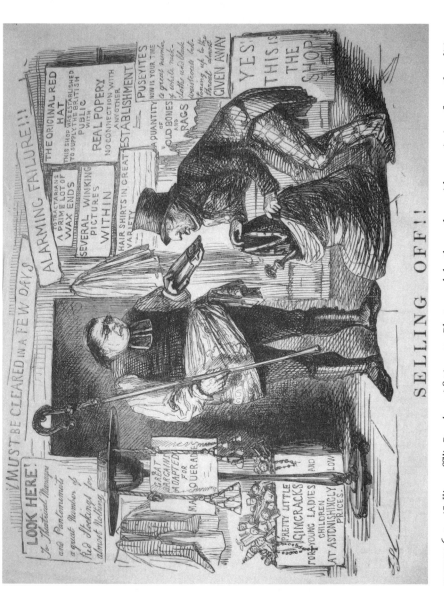

FIGURE 6.2. 'Selling off!!', *Punch* 20 (1851), p. 77. Photograph by the author, with permission, from the edition held at the library of Birkbeck College, London.

to that favourite racist stereotype, the hook-nosed, Jewish, old-clothes man (a favourite mode of depicting Disraeli, who mocked but also voted for the Act).[10]

In Nathaniel Hawthorne's *The Marble Faun* (1859), there is a vivid description of fakery at a carnival in Rome at which onlookers were fleeced by local children. Not only were bonbons made of chalk being hawked, but flowers were sold, thrown down, picked up, and sold again: 'muddy, too, having been fished up from the pavement, where a hundred feet have trampled on them...these venal and polluted flowers, therefore, and these deceptive bonbons, are types of the small reality that subsists in the observance of the Carnival'.[12] The ultimate hideous and yet alluring commerce was that of those 'venal and polluted flowers', the prostitutes, that haunted the streets of the metropolis, just as did the churches not only of the Whore of Rome, but also of her meretricious dupes. Why such mockery? Why such fear? Anglo-Catholicism was, as I have argued, a particularly dangerous conceptual pollution because it represented deviation within the English Protestant body itself. It is therefore no surprise to find that if Roman Catholicism was conceptualised as a fraudulent business enterprise, then Anglo-Catholicism was a worse one. The virtuous manly energy of successful commercial enterprise was quite missing in what *Lloyd's Weekly Newspaper* referred to as 'at best a wretched, mincing, harlotry imitation of the Church of Rome'.[11]

The consumer needed to be educated in order that he might avoid purchasing goods that, with the misleading packaging removed, were not worth the price. Morality had been associated with 'taste' since the eighteenth-century advent of that term in England. In the wake of the Great Exhibition of 1851, the aim of which was to improve the standard of British manufactures, a 'Chamber of Horrors', providing choice examples of bad taste in design, was opened at the Museum of Ornamental Art, Marlborough House, Pall Mall, from 1852 to 1853. A similar exercise was carried out by government fiat a century later by the Council of Industrial Design at the 'Britain Can Make It' Exhibition in 1946.[13] Associated with this later drive for improvement in consumer taste was the publication of *The Things We See: Indoors and Out* by Alan Jarvis, the future director of the National Gallery of Canada (from 1955 to 1959). To illustrate 'vulgarity', he contrasted a blond, heavily made-up woman with a pair of ceramic jugs, all of which exhibited a 'crude shape poorly decorated' (figure 6.3). David Matless has summed up Jarvis's views as referring to 'misguided beauty on a wronged anatomy...here was a lack of visual education, a wrong design for a wrong life'.[14] This was precisely the moralising aesthetic criticism made of the ritualistic designs on the body of the Church: they were meretricious marketing designed to bamboozle the uninformed punter, thence came the English disgust.

I want to restate the quote from Peter Stallybrass and Allon White that I mentioned in chapter 5: '[D]isgust always bears the imprint of desire'.[15] From meretricious draperies to phallic candles, this study has highlighted the intensely sexualised nature of readings of Anglo- and Roman Catholic material culture. But, for some observers, a sense of terrible and fascinating carnality hung over the world of art and commerce in general. For instance, the (in)famous attack on aesthetes and sensualists made by the Scottish poet Robert Buchanan (1841–1901) in his article 'The Fleshly School of Poetry' (1871, revised 1872), reflects panic at the thought of the irrepressibly carnal nature of the commercial world, and an intense desire to find someone to blame. Walking in London, Buchanan sees erotica everywhere:

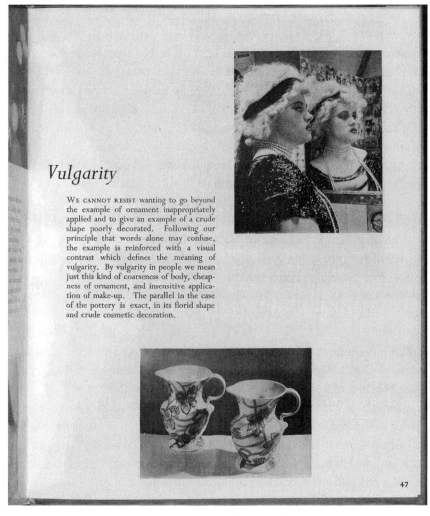

FIGURE 6.3. Alan Jarvis, *The Things We See: Indoors and Out* (Harmondsworth: Penguin Books, 1947), p. 47. Copyright British Library Board, all rights reserved, WP.2117.1. Reproduction by permission of Penguin Books Ltd.

> photographs of nude, indecent, and hideous harlots, in every attitude
> that vice can devise, flaunt[ing] from shop windows…it has [even]
> penetrated into the very sweet shops; and there, among the com-
> moner sorts of confectionary, may be seen this year's model of the
> female Leg, the whole definite and elegant article as far as the thigh,
> with a fringe of paper in imitation of the female drawers.

He asserts that there is nothing wrong with legs in themselves, but they can become a 'spectre, a portent, a mania…we see a demon resembling the Manx coat-of-arms' (i.e., a symbol made of three legs linked together at the hip).[16] Just as Seymour plunged into lurid fantasies of industrial bodily commerce in the catacombs, so Buchanan conjured up a demon of female flesh to whirl before him.

Blame, in these accounts, is thrust away from the viewer and fastened upon the polluted, whirling commodity and its vendors. This was much more difficult to do when all parties were manly. For example, Buchanan tells us that he was asked (and it is a very good question) why he liked Walt Whitman, despite people in America seeing him as bestial. Buchanan's answer was that Whitman was intensely 'spiritual' apart from fifty lines that were silly, 'silly as Shakespere's [sic] dirt is silly'; in those fifty lines he was 'talking nonsense, as is the way of all wise men at some unfortunate moment or other'.[17] This pathetic excuse for an answer should be replaced by the obvious explanation: manliness was pure, and because Whitman was undoubtedly manly, his im-purity must be an unrepresentative aberration. To be spiritually manly was to be in control of one's body as of one's prose, and it is precisely that control that Buchanan felt he would lose in the presence of those alluring, sickly, all too comestible legs.

It should be clear by now that much of this cultural critique was carried out through the construction of the Other as a female or feminised abomina-tion that could then be easily attacked. *Punch* was only exceptionally blatant in this regard when it 'published' a highly affected letter, supposedly from 'Fleur de Belgravie', defending the Catholic position on aesthetic principles under the headline 'The Genteel View of the Papal Aggression'. Decadent aristocrats in general, as we saw from *The Times* piece on free trade, and their wives in partic-ular, were thought most prone to 'dreamy and delirious' effeminacy. Mr. Punch then commented below the letter in an editorial footnote:

> I flatter myself to know what 'aesthetic' principle is, pretty well. A cer-
> tain calf of gold was made once, I believe, on that 'principle'. So were
> various hawk-headed, and other sculptures from Egypt in the British
> Museum. Diana of the Ephesians too, I rather think was adored on

the 'aesthetic principle'. And on precisely the same principle, I take it, does the negro grovel before his *fétiche*.[18]

Such aesthetic qualities, which were powerfully expressed in Anglo-Catholic worship, were thus objectified, feminised, exoticised, and eroticised.

We have seen how theories of comparative religion, which today appear culturally marginal, had, at this time, achieved a wide currency in popular culture. The reason for this may be that they colluded in the notion that fetishism was a feature of primitive rather than of modern society (the view that Marx wrote to correct) and that modern material commodity culture was, by contrast, founded on a rational and, therefore, an unquestionable base. The desire to identify the primitive through classification was lauded as a mechanism of progress—witness the comment of *The Times* correspondent in Madrid in 1875 when the progressive Spanish politician Antonio Romero Ortiz (1822–84) placed a piece of the clothing of St. Teresa of Avila in a museum rather than a Church:

> The very fact that a 'reprobate' like...Orta [*sic*] is allowed, in spite
> of all the croaking and scolding of the *Espana Catolica*, to place so
> valuable a fetish as the *troza de camisa* [relic] of Spain's greatest saint
> among the Indian idols, pagan amulets, and other profane knick
> knacks of an old-world repository, is a fact by which we may gauge
> the progress of modern inquiry even in this once so sadly-benighted
> and priest-asphyxiated Spanish community.[19]

Such viewpoints valued antiquities not so much as aesthetic treasures as evidence of the superiority of British modernity. This is how *Punch* made fun of oriental antiquities in a column discussing 'Punch's papist relics': the accompanying drawing showed a slab, supposedly found in the cellar of *Punch*'s offices. This find displayed an Assyrian bull wearing the triple crown, with Pope Pius IX's face, being goaded and mocked by the British lion on its back (figure 6.4). The style is reminiscent of the colossal human-headed bull excavated in Khorsabad, northern Iraq, and bought by Henry Rawlinson, the British Resident in Baghdad, from the French consul in 1849 and sent to the British Museum. The anti-Semitic discourse of the time found Assyrians, like Phoenicians, 'difficult to separate from the Jews'.[20] In this way, the Roman nose of Pius IX is assimilated to the hooked nose of the Semite in an image of the oriental Other, just as Wiseman was smeared by his commercial association with the Jewish peddler.[21]

The Pope was also depicted by *Punch* as an oriental despot in relation to a dispute over a contact relic (an object touched by a saint) (figure 6.5). This was the *Cathedra Petri*, the 'first Pope's' chair that had come to be enshrined in St. Peter's in Rome. Supposedly, it was given by a senator to Peter. The novelist and Irish Protestant aristocrat Lady Sydney Morgan (c. 1783–1859) wrote critically on the history of St. Peter's chair, was rebuffed by Wiseman, and wrote again in defiance (published by Westerton). 'Is it probable, my Lord,' she asks the cardinal, 'that St. Peter, the humble fisherman of Galilee, permitted himself to be seated or carried in this gorgeous chair, on the shoulders of slaves…If they [Christians] sat upon a raised seat, it was a stone concealed in the catacombs or in caverns, as their perilous position dictated'.[22] Anthony Rich (1803–91), a classicist and historian, then wrote to say that the chair was likely to be Byzantine, since its back was in the form a series of arches sup-

FOUND IN THE CELLAR OF THE PUNCH OFFICE.

FIGURE 6.4. 'Found in the cellar of the Punch Office', *Punch* 20 (1851), p. 84. Photograph by the author, with permission, from the edition held at the library of Birkbeck College, London.

FIGURE 6.5. 'The Pope in his Chair, with Mr Punch's compliments to Lady Morgan',
Punch 20 (1851), p. 37. Photograph by the author, with permission, from the edition
held at the library of Birkbeck College, London.

ported on columns and it included old panels with what appeared to him to be Zoroastrian mystical imagery.[23] This chair is now thought to have been made for the imperial coronation of the ninth-century Carolingian emperor Charles the Bold.[24] *Punch*'s take was to ignore the shape of the chair itself in order to render the Pope into a decadent Ottoman, puffing pleasurably on his water pipe.

Orientalism, following the work of Edward Said, is often thought of as referring to the western construction of the east. However, the effect of rendering the Pope as a Turk was to orientalise much of Europe. Moreover, the implication was, perhaps, that there was not, in fact, a clear boundary between west and east at all, or between Protestant and Catholic, masculine and feminine, self and Other. Such discourse in England can therefore be understood in relation to contestation of the nature and values of English patriarchy itself. After all, Anglo-Catholicism was not, in fact, a copy of Roman Catholicism, but represented a particular local fantasy of the late medieval English past.

In 1979 Alain Grosrichard outlined his understanding of orientalism as a functional fantasy in *Structure du sérail: La fiction du despotisme asiatique dans l'Occident classique*, which was translated as *The Sultan's Court: European Fantasies of the East*.[25] The key impact of Grosrichard's work on colonial and postcolonial theory has been to enable readings of western orientalist texts as bearers of information about their own society rather than about those which they claim to be documenting.[26] In a fascinating introduction to the English translation, the philosopher Mladen Dolar elaborates on some of the key issues that are raised by Grosrichard's work. Dolar emphasises that 'fantasy is not just some realm of pure ideas and representation, for it ultimately relies on enjoyment'. Moreover, the fantasy of oriental despotism relies upon the construction of a 'place of unalloyed excitement':

> What else is the entire despotic machine but a gigantic system of organisation, regimentation...?
>
> The machine is fuelled by a one-way stream of goods, produced by an infinite self-sacrifice of all subjects, which rolls toward the despotic centre for the sole enjoyment of the despot. Ultimately it is epitomised by the flux of 'sexual goods' reserved for the exclusive use of the despot.[27]

In this fantasy, the image of humans toiling on earth while their minds are on the perfect happiness that is heaven is morphed into an image of humans toiling on earth for an evil earthly sovereign. This is a nightmare of a life under an absolute monarchy. Since that monarchy is based on a monopoly of pleasures, the limitation of such rule implies their sharing. Under capitalism, we are both despot and subject depending on whether we are earning or spending. Hence, we both embrace the pleasure of despotic consumption and also despise it when, as in the fantasy, it is not accompanied by the suffering that is work. We are poised, thereby, in the uncomfortable position of being both the despised tyrant and the despised subject. This is where projection steps in. We know we are despotic, so we single out those who appear more so, and we know we are inferior, so we look for those who seem worse. I am arguing that orientalising fantasy was not simply a matter of the invention of non-Europeans by Europeans, but also a structuring element of thought within Europe itself. Comparative religion in both its antiquarian and theological manifestations provided the means by which the textual and material culture of Catholicism was constructed as an orientalist fantasy. Indeed, it would be fascinating to investigate further the ways in which anti-Catholicism was a *basis*, as well as a variant, of orientalist fantasies involving the projection of sin and excitement.

I have identified several examples of such 'projection', such as that of sin onto Catholics or that of the fetishistic fear of an animated material world onto African tribes people. Drawing on ideas formulated by Sigmund Freud at the end of the nineteenth century, Peter Gay explains his use of the notion of projection in his analysis of aggression in nineteenth-century bourgeois life:

> [Freud] argued that so far as they are not justified by real exploitation or real persecution, people making an enemy will adopt the psychological manoeuvre of projection. They defend themselves against their unacceptable thoughts or wishes by expelling them from their own mind into the outside world, onto the convenient Other. This mechanism provides a highly supportive way of living with one's failings; it permits the denial that one is subject to those failings in the first place and then opportunely discovers them in strangers or adversaries, real or imagined.[28]

I mentioned in my introduction that John Wolffe has argued that anti-Catholicism was a 'rational, if extreme, response to contemporary circumstances'.[29] But were 'respectable' people really in danger from the exotic cultural relatives of the fearful working-class 'home heathen' such as ritualists, Jesuits, Jews, and vampires?

Anti-Catholicism was a tool in a struggle for moral authority. The ability to deflect criticism by fastening the blame on others was an enormously powerful strategy in Victorian Britain, and it remains so to this day. A recent review of

Margo Jefferson's *On Michael Jackson* (2006) commented, in the light of the singer's epic trial on child abuse charges, that

> Our [British] tabloid media have a paedophile element to their subconscious, a child-abusing energy at the heart of their own anger... You can't read the British papers without feeling polluted, not only by the stories, but by the degree to which the writers and editors of these stories appear to want them to be true, even before the evidence has proved it. Beyond this, a carnival of sensationalism vies with a deadly prurience, matched by a creepy populist appeal to the 'common decency' of the mob. You feel that the hacks are getting off on the horrors they ascribe, getting high on the pseudo-democratic vengeance their stories might excite.[30]

Opposition to Catholic material culture in the Church of England, in sum, involved the construction of an orientalist fantasy in which the objects themselves were cast as adjuncts of the Papal despot. This meant that they were read as playing a role in his sensual immorality. In this way, apparently unerotic objects, such as crosses and crucifixes, were giving a directly sexual interpretation. That this was a culturally constructed process of sexual fetishisation can be seen from the fact that, conversely, an artwork that was, on the face of it, straightforwardly erotic (in this case, a female nude) could be constructed as asexual in relation to a narrative that associated it with opposition to Turkish (oriental) despotism: *The Greek Slave* by the American sculptor Hiram Powers, which was, arguably, one of the most commercially successful artworks of the century.

The first version of this sculpture was produced in 1844 and, complete with a moralising explanatory booklet, toured America before going to the Crystal Palace, and was viewed by millions of people in the process.[31] There were to be six full-size versions in total, as well as an abundant mass production of small replicas. The object is all the more remarkable because it is a female nude and, as such, might be expected to have been the subject of considerable moral opprobrium. However, quite the contrary, she assumed the role of 'an ikon of the domestic ideal'. Even the substance of which she was made, an especially fine form of marble, was celebrated as 'organically pure, free from foreign elements and permanent'.[32] This was despite the image being dependent on a sexual narrative: she was a slave in a Turkish market about to be purchased and consigned to the effeminate pleasures of the harem (silk divans, eunuchs, and general depravity).

Modern accounts focus on what today appears as the obvious eroticism of the chains draped round the crotch, and it has even been commented that

the column supporting the figure is an obvious phallus: 'The Greek cap sur-
mounting it forms the glans, and the slave's clothing draped beneath forms the
skin of the shaft'.[33] Moreover, it has been commented that 'while insisting that
the sculpture did not evoke "vulgar" passions, [contemporary] descriptions of
the sculpture and its reception throb with desire'.[34] Vivien Green, for instance,
quotes an undated cutting from the *New York Express* that was pasted into Powers' own scrapbook: 'To us she looks like one who had by rough and ruthless
hands been torn from her home, and dragged to the private slave market...She
knows she is of a trampled race, that the iron grasp of the master is upon
her...that his heart is hot with lust'.[35]

It is instructive to compare the image of *The Greek Slave* as drawn in the
Illustrated London News with the skit, the *Virginian Slave*, published in *Punch*
(figures 6.6 and 6.7).[36] The latter is an artefact of the sustained critical barrage
that satirised American attachment to slavery. In discussing the latter drawing, Green argues that it 'shows a partially clothed Negro whose expression
of imploring despair animates the *Greek Slave*'s calm resignation'.[37] However,
attractive young women in *Punch* are typically coquettes. Much was popularly
made of the demure downcast gaze of the *Greek Slave*, whereas her Virginian counterpart bats her eyelids upward. The latter's breasts are emphasised
by being squeezed together by her arms, and the erotic thrust of her hips is
also exaggerated. Even the supporting pillar seems to have swollen up, inviting
thoughts of what will be revealed if the flag covering it and the slave's skimpy
shift are pulled away. By contrast, *The Greek Slave* was wearing nothing but a
pair of manacles, a detail that was understood to express that she had nothing
to hide. I have also previously mentioned Saarti Baartman (1789–1815), the so-
called 'Hottentot Venus' who was paraded for European fascination as a result
of her unusually large buttocks and breasts.[38] *Punch*, with its Baartman-like
cartoon, evokes exactly that sense of sexual voyeurism that the many proponents of *The Greek Slave* as a model of propriety were so keen to deny. Crucially,
the lust of viewers of the statue could be displaced onto the imaginary Turkish
tyrant. Readers of *Punch* could therefore, at a further remove, revel in the amusing suggestion that the real despot was the United States.

The Greek Slave was therefore not primarily what it was pretending to be, a
noble comment on the plight of women during of the Greek War of Independence (1821–31). It was, by contrast, a highly successful and duplicitous commercial proposition. Part of the reason that it was so successful was that it
provided erotic excitement in a way that was morally defensible. The despotic
power of men over women, and the viewer over the object, was projected onto
the oriental Other, which played the necessary role of scapegoat, so allowing
voyeuristic prurience. In this way, an object that was sexually arousing found

THE VIRGINIAN SLAVE.

INTENDED AS A COMPANION TO POWER'S "GREEK SLAVE"

FIGURE 6.6. 'The Virginian slave', *Punch* 20 (1851), p. 236. Photograph by the author, with permission, from the edition held at the library of Birkbeck College, London.

For beauty of design and delicacy of execution, this exquisite statue is inferior to nothing in the Great Exhibition. It represents an historical fact in all but the chains, for it *was* the custom to expose female slaves in the bazaar of Constantinople. Observe the shame and scorn, the sad melancholy rebuke, upon the face of the beautiful girl exposed to such ignominy: see with what modesty the pure, high-minded Greek stands before her voluptuous purchasers:—verily, the purpose of the sculptor was aimed high when he conceived this noble idea. He has failed not in his task of reading a lesson of shame and scorn to the traffickers in the dreadful trade. Appealing to the sensibilities of our better nature, rather than to those feelings which yield delight, he has successfully overcome the difficulties of his subject, and won our admiration by the touching beauty and unexaggerated ideality of his subject. It was no easy task to place a young, beautiful, and high-minded female in such a position without a chance of offending; but the great charm of Mr. Powers' statue is, that it repels all thoughts but those of sympathy and compassion for the victim, and execration of those who could make merchandise of the beauty and innocence of the fairest of GOD's creatures:

"As if their value could be justly told
By pearls and gems, and heaps of shining gold."

The Greek Slave was first exhibited in 1845, in the rooms of Messrs. Graves, of Pall-mall, and excited universal approbation by the excellence of its execution and the beauty of its conception.

While admitting the truth that genius exclusively belongs not to age nor race, and that its elements are as likely to dwell in the minds of the untutored savage as in the more favoured inhabitant of a civilised state, the first sight of this statue—coming from the hand of a sculptor whose country has hitherto made comparatively little progress in this, the highest department of Art—afforded us no little surprise, but it also gave us infinite pleasure. We had not often heard of the name of Hiram Powers, and were consequently astonished to find so fine a work from one whose fame had not already reached the shores of England. But we subsequently learned that he had been studying for a considerable time in Florence. In his studio here, Captain Grant

THE GREEK SLAVE.

saw a small model of the Greek Slave in plaster, and was so struck with the beauty of the subject, that he immediately gave a commission to the sculptor to execute it in marble. The result was triumphant.

FIGURE 6.7. Hiram Powers's *The Greek Slave* in *The Illustrated Exhibitor* 2, June 14th (1851), p. 37. Copyright British Library Board, all rights reserved, 606*48*DSC, October 3, 2008.

widespread popular support and moral approval. The attempt at such projection in the case of Anglo-Catholic material culture was more difficult because its ambiguity generated cultural pollution by blurring the boundaries of male and female, east and west, self and other. It was, therefore, often approached via the literary Gothic interpretive mode. But what *The Greek Slave* shared with such objects as the controversial cross and notorious crucifix was that it gained much of its power by reference to fantasies of despotism that remained at the level of generalised horror and scandal. Too much accurate knowledge would undermine such fantasies of, as Dolar, put it 'unalloyed excitement'.[39] It was essential, therefore, that the fantasised Other with its load of sin should be denounced rather than understood; it should be pilloried for its effects rather than being the centre of systematic analysis. Profit was to be made by the sale of inaccurate sensationalising narratives.

It is important to stress that that commercial success was based upon the social violence of acts of scapegoating. In 1854, William Holman Hunt (1827–1910) took himself to the Holy Land. There, he spent much of his time attempting to paint a goat dying of thirst against a scrupulously detailed study of the landscape around the Dead Sea (figure 6.8). The goat is meant to look pathetic and the landscape, the supposed site of Sodom and Gomorrah, to be steeped in evil desolation. Hunt's aim was to use Old Testament texts referring to the expulsion of the scapegoat bearing the sins of the people as a symbolic type of Christ's crucifixion. The frame of the painting is inscribed with Isaiah 53:4, 'Surely he

FIGURE 6.8. William Holman Hunt, *The Scapegoat* (1854–86). Copyright National Museums Liverpool, Lady Lever Art Gallery.

hath borne our Griefs, and carried our Sorrows/Yet we did esteem him stricken, smitten of GOD, and afflicted', and Leviticus 16:22, 'And the Goat shall bear upon him all their iniquities unto a Land not inhabited'. In one version (now in Manchester City Art Galleries), Hunt attempted to express the contrast between heroic abjection and transcendence by contrasting a black goat with a rainbow; in the other, the beautiful colours of a sunrise on the bleak landscape, contrasting with the white of the beast's coat, attempt to do the same work.

The painting did not get a positive reception.[40] For the critic of *The Times*, 'the scene is not impressive, and were it not for the title annexed it would be rather difficult to divine the nature of the subject'.[41] John Ruskin, in his review of the Royal Academy Exhibition of 1856, showed that he understood what Hunt was trying to do, commenting that 'the appointed sending forth of the scapegoat into the Wilderness...represented the carrying away of their sin into a place uninhabited and forgotten'. He notes, in a significant compliment, that it 'lights the room, far away, just as Turner's used to do', but he thought it lacking in qualities of composition.[42] Modern commentary agrees with him. As George Landow puts it, many did not appreciate the symbolism, but even if one does 'one comes upon a mere goat'.[43] By making the sacrificial creature into something that seemed so unimpressive, Hunt threatened to reveal the moral abjectness of the whole exercise of scapegoating by which the 'disabled [the culturally marginal] becomes the deformed [the fantastic horror]'.[44] For when the scapegoat is viewed clearly, it will be revealed as nothing more than the mirror of the moral wretchedness of those who have deployed it.

These acts of persecution were, however, also of benefit to the ritualists. Scapegoating involves attributing power [albeit for harm] to the powerless. This process thereby enhanced the perceived importance of ritualism. Furthermore, insofar as ritualists regarded the obloquy of the worldly as placing them in imitation of Christ, so it also enhanced their sense of glorious martyrdom. In the longer term, the increasing familiarity of the English with ritualists' practices led to the latter's gradual assimilation into the general life of the country, a process that drew many of them back to their Tory roots. Thus, Anglo-Catholicism faded, even as it was born, from a national scandal to a sectarian eccentricity. The entertainment industry looked elsewhere for business as new threats to the nation and bourgeois self were duly discovered.

But there was nothing insignificant, at the time, about the Victorian fears and hopes that I have been describing. Taking leave of the church of St. Barnabas that he had founded, William Bennett preached the last of his published *Farewell Sermons* on the evening of March 23, 1851. His text was John 9:4, 'I must work the works of Him that sent Me while it is day, the night cometh, when no man can work'. It was clearly a very emotional occasion. Bennett told his congregation that 'we have *all* had a bright, shining day—a short one indeed. But while it pleased GOD to let it last, a bright one'. There was so much good work and prayer left to be done, yet for now that work had stopped. That was a kind of death. But we should remember that the night's coming was also a blessing from God. There would be another dawn tomorrow, for the parish, and for us each at the end of that day which was our life on this earth. 'There *is* a place', he assured them. 'May we all meet together, and have our portion *there*, when GOD may please to call us in the eternal night of His Judgment'. Out of that undifferentiated darkness, light and sight will again be reborn, 'for there, verily we shall see Him in the dwellings of His thousand saints, amid the myriads of His heavenly hosts—there we shall see Him face to face—hear Him—yea, even touch him'.[45] Bennett, and many of his congregation, believed quite sincerely, that we would no longer have to make do with oil and greasepaint of however radiant a hue. The perversity of longings for ambiguous worldly bodies and the related cries of idolatry would be banished at last, for, at that moment, the struggle for purity would end forever in the immaculate, tangible, presence of God.

Notes

CHAPTER ONE

1. Neale and Webb (1843), pp. cxxviii–ix.
2. Neale and Webb (1843), p. cxxxii.
3. Conybeare (1999) [original publication 1853].
4. Yates (1999), p. 49.
5. Chadwick (1971), vol. 1, p. 213, White (1962) and Webster and Elliot (2000).
6. Wheeler (2006), p. 250.
7. E.g., in Pugin (1843b).
8. J. Reed (1996).
9. Wauzzinksi (1993) and Wolffe (1994), p. 24.
10. Hilton (1988), p. 28.
11. Voll (1963), p. 30.
12. On the 'Protestant evangelical awakening' across Europe in the eighteenth century, see W. Ward (1992).
13. Hilton (2006), p. 182.
14. Toon (1979), p. 203.
15. Wolffe (1991), pp. 114–16.
16. Portal (1854), p. 18.
17. Marotti (2005); see also Shell (1999).
18. Chadwick (1971), vol. 1, p. 365.
19. F. Knight (1995) explores this as a key theme.
20. Seymour (1843), pp. 382–83.
21. Wolffe (1991), p. 121.
22. Anon., *Invocation of Saints* (1846).
23. For example, Anon., *Image-Worship* (1849).

24. Wolffe (1991), p. 107 and, for anticatholicism in general, Drury (2000).

25. Wolffe (1991), pp. 198 and 290.

26. Cumming (1850), pp. 3 and 5; see also Ellison and Engelhardt (2003), and Wheeler (2006), p. 24.

27. *The Times*, July 19, 1854, p. 12.

28. Hoppen (1998), p. 257.

29. Cotton (1856), p. 12.

30. Chadwick (1971), vol. 1, pp. 496–97.

31. E.g., Bentley (1978), J. Reed (1996), Yates (1999), and Whisenant (2003).

32. Strachey (1918), pp. 36–37.

33. Benson (1985), p. 29 [original publication 1932].

34. J. Reed (1996), p. 28.

35. Ryle (1851), p. 66.

36. De Gruchy (2001), p. 50.

37. Yates (1999), p. 380.

38. Poole (1840), pp. 17 and 35.

39. White (2006), p. 102.

40. Buchli (2002).

41. Tilley (2002), p. 52.

42. Byrne (1998), p. 47.

43. Boudewijnse (1998), pp. 277–79 and 282.

44. Burke (2001), p. 16.

45. Appadurai (1986), Briggs (1988), De Grazia and Furlough (1996), and Pasztory (2005).

46. E. Moore (1857), p. 81.

47. O'Malley (2006), p. 41.

48. Hawkes (2001), pp. 53 and 71.

49. Milligan (1912), pp. 219–63.

50. De Brosses (1760).

51. Logan (2003), p. 559.

52. Ruether (2005), p. 251.

53. James (1986), p. 207 [original publication 1875].

54. Pietz (1985, 1987, 1988).

55. McLellan (1995), p. xvii discussing Marx (1995), pp. 42–50 [first volume original publication 1867].

56. Taussig (1980).

57. Stallybrass (1998), p. 184.

58. Finn (2001).

59. Pinch (1998), p. 139.

60. Masuzawa (2000), p. 261.

61. Daly (1994).

62. Graeber (2005), p. 415.

63. Freud (1961), p. 157 [original publication 1927].

64. Kristeva (1982)

65. Steele (1996), p. 14 and Krips (1999).

66. Cocks (2006) discusses the overlap between sex and spirituality in the nineteenth century.

67. Hawkes (2001), p. 52.

68. Marx (1995), p. 49 [first volume original publication 1867].

69. Hawkes (2001), p. 75.

70. Billig (1999).

71. Hilton (2006), p. 183.

72. Porter (2001), pp. 201 and 222, with quote at p. 273.

73. Ironside (1850).

74. McClintock (1995), p. 47.

75. M. Douglas (1984).

76. W. Miller (1997), p. 106.

77. Hacking (2006).

78. Nead (1992), p. 6.

79. M. Douglas (1984), pp. 36 and 165.

80. Gallagher (2006), p. 110.

81. Otter (2004).

82. Robinson (2004), p. 53.

83. Wallis (2005), p. 2.

84. Grassby (2005).

85. Canning (1999), p. 499.

86. Kantorowicz (1957).

87. Porter (2003), p. 247.

88. Dekker (1607).

89. Bernstein (1994), p. 227.

90. A. Anderson (1993), p. 60.

91. Gilman (1995), p. 66.

92. Newman (1848), pp. 176–77.

CHAPTER TWO

1. Brooks (1999), is a good overview of the Gothic Revival; see also Lewis (2002), Chapman (1992), Chandler (1971) and R. Smith (2002).

2. Balleine (1951), pp. 6–7 [original publication 1908].

3. Hall (2002), p. 21; see also Arnstein (1982).

4. Ellis (2000), pp. 22–27.

5. Aldrich (1994), pp. 69 and 141. Compare O'Donnell (1983), p. 12, for a similar testament to his influence on Catholic Liturgical practice.

6. Hill (2002), p. 161; (2007), pp. 169–76 and Chadwick (1971), vol. 1, p. 283. Note the view that Ultramontanism never became dominant in the nineteenth-century English Roman Catholicism in general; see Heimann (1995), p. 165.

7. Hill (2002), p. 180; Fraser (1986), p. 64; and Aldrich (1995), p. 39.

8. Meara (1995), pp. 55–57 and 60.

9. Pugin (1841a), p. 9 [original publication 1836].

10. Pugin (1843a), pp. 23–24.

11. Pugin (1841a), p. 17 [original publication 1836].

12. Pugin (1841b), p. 34.

13. Pugin (1843a), pp. 49–50.

14. Pugin, Letter to Lord Shrewsbury, c. April 20, 1843, in Pugin (2003), p. 43.

15. O'Donnell (1983), p. 16.

16. Pugin (1843b).

17. Lewis (2002), p. 85. Compare with Skinner (2004) on Tractarian responses to social change and the industrial revolution.

18. Pugin (1841a), p. 57 [original publication 1836].

19. Brooks (1999), pp. 233–34.

20. Watkin (1977).

21. Watkin (1977), p. 18.

22. Coldstream (1998), p. 24.

23. England (1845), p. 8.

24. Wiseman (1856b), p. 37.

25. Wiseman (1853), p. 39.

26. Wiseman (1856b), p. 18.

27. Wiseman (1856a), p. 4.

28. See chapter 1 and Brooks (1999), pp. 246–47.

29. Neale (1841), p. 12.

30. Neale (1842), p. 4; see also Neale (1843). For an introduction to the society and reprint of these important texts, see Webster (2003). On Neal in general, see Rowell (1983), pp. 98–115, especially p. 101; and M. Chandler (1995).

31. Neale (1842), p. 12.

32. Neale and Webb (1843), p. xxi.

33. Pugin (1843b), p. 51. This was highlighted and condemned in Close (1844), p. 13, with plate opposite p. 32. This writer is discussed below.

34. O'Donnell (2000), p. 106.

35. Neale and Webb (1843), p. xxvii.

36. O'Donnell (2000), p. 99.

37. Close (1844), p. 23.

38. Montalembert (1844), p. 3.

39. Close (1844), pp. 4 and 17; see also Toon (1979), p. 67; and Whisenant (2003), p. 20.

40. Barr (1846) [original publication 1842].

41. Christmas (1845), pp. 120–21.

42. Brandwood (2000), p. 69.

43. J. Reed (1996), pp. 16, 20, and 23.

44. Fraser (1986), p. 63.

45. Pattison (1991), p. 28.

46. Newman in Wells (1840), p. v.

47. W. Bennett (1845), pp. 316 and 333.

48. Anon., *Puseyism in London* (1843), p. 35.

49. W. Bennett (1845), p. 351.

50. W. Bennett (1843), pp. 119 and 232–33.

51. Herring (1984), p. 92.

52. J. Reed (1996), p. 99.

53. Seymour (1848), p. 560.

54. Morgan (1851), p. 18.

55. Paley (1848), p. 12.

56. Guthrie (1858), pp. 14 and 17. This does not refer to the Catholic notion of saints, but to the Protestant notion of the elect.

57. Wood (1846), pp. 342 and 344.

58. Morgan (1999), p. 268.

59. Clark (1969), p. 284. Note also the ritualist Richard Littledale's insouciant, and misleading, dismissal of those who were against colour in church decoration as being no more than a few Manicheans in Littledale (1857), pp. 1–2.

60. Anon., 'A Churchman of the Reformation' (1850), p. 13.

61. Schimmelpenninck (1859), pp. 123 and 126; and see the discussion of Cowling (1989).

62. Ruskin (1849), pp. 17–18.

63. Ruskin (1853), vol. 2, p. 386.

64. Wheeler (2006), pp. 205–9.

65. Buc (2001), p. 4.

66. Bocock (1974).

67. F. Lee (1860a), p. ix.

68. Newman (1848), p. 26.

69. *The Times*, Dec. 12, 1850. See chapter 3 for detailed discussion.

70. Palmer (1839) [original publication 1832]; and J. Reed (1996), p. 26.

71. Beal (1850).

72. Quoted and discussed in Blackley (1850), pp. 26–30, as he builds his case for the danger.

73. Davenport (1855), pp. 2–3, which may be compared with Jebb (1856).

74. Klaus (1987), p. 138; and Conybeare (1999) [original publication 1853].

75. E.g., Anon., 'A Churchman' (1866), and I. Brock (1866).

76. J. Reed (1996), pp. xxi, 137, 183, 205, and 215.

77. Liddell (1852), p. 9.

78. Hook (1849), p. 44.

79. Jebb (1856), pp. 14 and 25.

80. White (1854), p. 45.

81. W. Bennett (1851a), p. 3.

82. W. Bennett (1845), p. 5.

83. W. Bennett (1851a), p. 23, referring to C. Blomfield (1842).

84. W. Bennett (1846), p. 2.

85. Lambeth Palace, ms. 1922.

86. Lambeth Palace, ms. 1923, f. 70 v.

87. Westerton (1854), pp. 10–11.

88. W. Bennett (1845), p. 5.

89. W. Bennett (1843), p. 246.

90. W. Bennett (1842), p. 9.

91. Skinner (1856a), pp. iv and 46.

92. Skinner (1856b), pp. 3, 5, 12, 14–15, and 18. Note that this emphasis on symbolism could be associated with Jesuitical casuistry, see Parsons (1988b), p. 196.

93. Skinner (1857), pp. 9, 12–13, and 15.

94. Skinner (1857), pp. 9, 12–13, and 15. For a detailed examination of these issues, see Janes (2007b).

95. W. Bennett (1851a), pp. 145–46, 150, 152, 156–57, and 186.

96. Greeley (2000), pp. 6 and 10.

97. Purchas (1858), pp. vii, xii, xxiv, and 62–63.

98. Greeley (2000), p. 145.

99. Anon., *A Christian Woman* (1871), p. 13.

100. Littledale (1865) and (1866b), p. 35.

101. Littledale (1866b), p. 39.

102. Parsons (1988a), p. 34.

103. Godfrey (1847), p. 7.

104. Harington (1852), pp. 8 and 21.

105. Godfrey (1847), pp. 10 and 17.

106. Harington (1852), pp. 28 and 32.

107. E.g., Newland (1851).

108. Maccall (1851), p. 34.

109. Anon., 'A Protestant' (1858), p. 32.

110. Garbett (1847), p. v.

111. Beeman (1868), p. 162.

112. J. Bennett (1838), p. 34.

113. J. Reed (1996), pp. 226 and 232.

114. Peace (1857), p. 31.

115. Bailey (1868), p. 45.

116. Bradford (1860), p. 4.

117. Rawlings (1863), p. 119.

118. Cumming (1851), p. 37.

119. Kingsley (1851), pp. 63–64.

120. Paull (1867), p. 472. Note that not everyone liked Saxons; for Muir (1860), pp. 40–41, they were 'sorry adventurers', and modern reference to them was so much 'Saxon Cant'. For him it was 'our Norman blood that has given us Genius, and Enterprise'.

121. Winslow (1840), p. 170.

122. Peacock (1866), p. 23.

123. Anon., *The Prince of the Power* (1868), p. 39.

124. Bailey (1868), pp. 18–19, 38, and 44.

125. Lea (1867), p. 21.

126. Anon., 'A Protestant' (1848), pp. 26 and 30.

127. Shout (1851).

128. Garbett (1847), p. 35. For a discussion of gold and the god of the Christians, see Janes (1998).

129. Bailey (1868), p. 41.

130. Anon., 'A Protestant' (1848), pp. 5–6.

131. Garbett (1847), p. 35.

132. Garbett (1844), p. 8.

133. Anon., 'A Clergyman' (1868), p. 24.

134. Anon., 'A Protestant' (1848), pp. 4 and 52.

135. Drummond (1857), p. 24.

136. This happened in the 1860s, so slightly later than the main events discussed in this chapter. I have therefore not explored the issue of queer readings of Anglo- and Roman Catholicism. For discussion on this, see Hilliard (1982), O'Malley (2006), and Janes (forthcoming).

137. Wiseman (1850b), pp. 9–10 and 19.

138. Pugin (1843b), p. 9; see also p. 41.

139. Heimann (1995), p. 25; she discusses *190th Thousand: The Explanatory Catechism of Christian Doctrine Chiefly Intended for the Use of Children in Catholic Schools* (London, 1880) at p. 28, and *Large Type Edition: Catechism of Christian Doctrine, Approved for the Use of the Faithful in all the Dioceses of England and Wales* (London, 1876), which is the same text as the edition of 1859, at p. 32.

140. Heimann (1995), p. 23

141. Bellett (1853), pp. 64–65.

CHAPTER THREE

1. Parsons (1988a), pp. 223–27.

2. Parsons (1988b), p. 10.

3. Englander (1988), pp. 19 and 24.

4. Curl (1990), p. 18.

5. Englander (1988), p. 20.

6. Yates (1999), p. 222 and Wolffe (2005).

7. Hilton (1988).

8. See the character portrait of Blomfield in Chadwick (1971), vol. 1, pp. 133–34. On Blomfield's reputation and the William Bennett case, see Pinnington (1967).

9. C. Blomfield (1842), pp. 22, 30, and 54; see also Yates (1999), pp. 178–79; and Chadwick (1971), vol. 1, pp. 214–15.

10. Welch (1954), p. 335. Nockles (1994), p. 217, points out that 'the essential difference between the old High Church and later ritualist rubrical campaigns' lay not simply in the nature of the ceremony advocated, but also in the willingness of the latter to undermine Episcopal authority where they held it hostile to catholicity. It was this change that made Blomfield's position increasingly difficult.

11. Anon., *A Few Reasons* (1843), p. 6 n; see also P. Laurie (1843).

12. Anon., *Puseyism in London* (1843), pp. 5, 7, 10, 21, 23, and 33.

13. F. Bennett (1909), pp. 13, 19–23, and 29.

14. Kennedy (1851), p. 28.

15. Griest (1965), pp. 110–11.

16. Anon., *Puseyism in London* (1843), p. 35.

17. Carter (1900), p. xiii.

18. W. Bennett (1843), pp. 311–21

19. Yates (1999), p. 91.

20. W. Bennett (1846), pp. vi–vii.

21. Anon., 'Caustic' (1847), p. 13, on W. Bennett (1847).

22. Anon., 'A Protestant' (1848), p. 62.

23. Herring (1984), p. 54.

24. W. Bennett (1850c), p. xiii.

25. E. Moore (1857), p. 14.

26. British Library, add. ms. 39863, with St. Barnabas' discussed at ff. 48–49.

27. Macneile (1849), p. 19.

28. Anon., *More Disclosures* (n.d.), pp. 8–10.

29. Burgess (1848), pp. 7–9.

30. Anon., 'A Barrister' (1851), pp. 9 and 20–21.

31. Janes (2007b).

32. Rowell (1983), p. 123.

33. W. Bennett (1851a), p. 98, Sellon (1852), Williams (1950), Anson (1955; 1973) and Mumm (1999).

34. Letter printed in W. Bennett (1851a), pp. 100–2.

35. Anson (1955), p. 271 n.1. For an analysis of the precarious countercultural position of orders of religious women, Fessenden (2000).

36. Anon., *History of S. Barnabas* (1933), p. 17.

37. F. Bennett (1909), p. 58.

38. W. Bennett (1850c), p. xxxii.

39. Ellsworth (1982), p. 16.

40. W. Bennett (1850c), p. liii.

41. Saint (1977), p. 1476.

42. F. Bennett (1909), p. 59; and Anon., *History of S. Barnabas* (1933), p. 16.

43. Powell (1985), p. 1502.

44. NADFAS (1999), Record of Church Furnishings, St. Barnabas, Pimlico, cat. nos. 100–1, 189, 211, and 508.

45. Bennett, Letter to Gladstone, May 25, 1850, British Library, add. ms. 44369, f. 223.

46. Richards (1850); and Kennaway (1850), pp. 166–67.

47. *Illustrated London News*, June 15, (1850), p. 428.

48. *Illustrated London News*, Sept. 20 (1851), p. 363.

49. *The Ecclesiologist* 11 (1850), pp. 112–14.

50. The text of his 1850 charge was reprinted rapidly by Charles Westerton, and there were several further editions by other publishers.

51. C. Blomfield (1850), pp. 26 and 32–33.

52. Wolffe (1991), p. 243.

53. F. Bennett (1909), pp. 99–100; quote from Klaus (1987), p. 178.

54. Lord John Russell (1850).

55. Paz (1982), p. 63.

56. Yates (1999), p. 204.

57. Klaus (1987), p. 144.

58. Wallis (1993), p. 81.

59. Anon., *The Parish Priest* (1851), p. 8.

60. Scherer (1999), p. 190.

61. Prest (1972), pp. 319–23; Norman (1968), p. 59; and Machin (1977), pp. 196–210.

62. Klaus (1987) is a monograph study of the 'Aggression'. See Norman (1984), p. 104; and *The Times*, Oct. 14 (1850).

63. Brown (1985), p. 27.

64. 'Principal Clergy of London', Bodleian Library, add. ms. C290, ff. 4 r. and 6 r.

65. *The Times*, Nov. 4 (1850), p. 4.

66. Anon., *The Parish Priest* (1851), p. 29.

67. *The Times*, Nov. 18, 1850, p. 2; and F. Bennett (1909), p. 110.

68. F. Bennett (1909), p. 107; and McNees (2004), pp. 21–27.

69. *Punch* 19 (1850), p. 215.

70. Chadwick (1971), vol. 1, p. 445.

71. F. Bennett (1909), p. 108.

72. Browne (1861), p. 201.

73. Girard (1986), p. 16.

74. On relations with Bennett, see Pinnington (1967), p. 292; and A. Blomfield (1863), vol. 2, pp. 136–60.

75. For an introduction to these issues, see Norman (1984), pp. 16–22.

76. Parsons (1988a), p. 150.

77. Ralls (1974), p. 256.

78. *The Tablet*, Nov. 30 (1850), p. 760.

79. Wiseman (1850a).

80. Wiseman (1850c).

81. Paz (1992), p. 148.

82. Spencer (1850).

83. Turnley (1850), p. iv.

84. *The Tablet*, Dec. 7 (1850), p. 777.

85. *The English Churchman*, Dec. 19 (1850), p. 770.

86. *John Bull*, Dec. 14 (1850), pp. 792–93.

87. W. Bennett (1850a), pp. 4, 7, 8, and 61.

88. *The Times*, Dec. 30, 1850, p. 4.

89. Blomfield 55, f. 222 v.

90. Blomfield 50, f. 285 v.

91. Phillpotts (1851), p. 61.

92. Anon., 'A Simple Protestant' (1851), pp. 5 and 17.

93. Anon., *The Bells* (1851), p. 13.

94. Thomas Bastard, Chairman of the Poor Man's Committee, in Gibson, Humphrey, and Bastard (1851), p. 6.

95. W. Bennett (1852).

96. Bennett, Letter to Gladstone, Apr. 15, 1852, British Library, add. 44371, f. 304.

97. W. Bennett (1852), pp. 6–8.

98. McIlhiney (1988), p. 24; Rowell (1983), p. 120; and Yates (1999), p. 71.

99. *Illustrated Times*, Dec. 27 (1856), p. 438.

100. Skinner (1881), pp. 4–6; and Ellsworth (1982), p. 15.

101. Liddell (1853), p. 4.

102. Liddell (1852), p. 10.

103. Liddell (1858b), pp. 16 and 19.

104. *Grounds of Objection to Prostration at the Holy Communion*, in Lambeth Palace Library, Tait 154, ff. 31–32.

105. Klaus (1987), p. 183

106. Drummond (1855), p. 182.

107. Mason (1994), p. 124.

108. Ellsworth (1982), p. 16.

109. Christodoulou (1992), p. 609.

110. Skinner (1881), p. 16.

111. Westerton (1849), inside cover of part 1, with quote at p. 121.

112. Westerton (1854), p. 37.

113. Davidson and Benham (1891), vol. 1, p. 216.

114. Lentin (1988), p. 104.

115. Westerton (1854), pp. i–iv.

116. F. Knight (1995), pp. 182–83.

117. Anon., *Case of the Churchwarden* (1854), p. 4.

118. Westerton (1853), p. 3.

119. Liddell (1881), pp. 4–5.

120. Westerton (1854), p. 48.

121. Anon., *Case of the Churchwarden* (1854), p. 13.

122. Westerton (1854), pp. 6 and 11.

123. J. Reed (1996), p. 41.

124. *Liddell and Horne v. Westerton*, 1855: the Hon. Robert Liddell, vicar of St. Barnabas', Pimlico, Middlesex, and Jason Thomas Horne, churchwarden v. Charles Westerton, churchwarden, faculty to remove altar furnishings (London); and *Liddell, etc. v. Beal*, 1855: the Hon. Robert Liddell, vicar of St Barnabas', Pimlico, Middlesex, and William Parke and George Evans, churchwardens v. Jason Beal, legality of altar furnishings (London).

125. Yates (1999), pp. 214–15.

126. Transcript and commentary of the cases appears in E. Moore (proctor for the appellants and official reporter) (1857). For modern legal discussion of these cases, see Waddams (1992), pp. 288–97.

127. E. Moore (1857), pp. 4 and 6.

128. Hulbert (1842), p. 46.

129. E. Moore (1857), pp. 8–9.

130. Goode (1851).

131. Toon (1979), pp. 117 and 175.

132. Goode (1851), p. 9.

133. E. Moore (1857), p. 20..

134. E. Moore (1857), pp. 16–21, referring to J. Robertson (1845).

135. E. Moore (1857), pp. 26, 32, 41, 45, 48, 50, 52, 54, 55, 73, 76–77, and 81.

136. Phillpotts (1856), p. 35.

137. Anon., *Dr Lushington's Judgment* (1855), pp. 5 n. 1, 10–12, 15, and 17–18.

138. *The Times*, May 3, 1854, p. 11.

139. Anon., *Case of the Churchwarden* (1854), p. 3.

140. *The Times*, July 17, 1854, p. 9.

141. Anon., *More Disclosures* (n.d.), pp. 5 and 11.

142. Liddell (1858b), pp. 24–25.

143. Anon., *More Disclosures* (n.d.), p. 9.

144. Guild of Saint Alban (1856), rule 11.

145. Letter to Westerton, undated, c. November 1857, Lambeth Palace Library, Tait ms. 154, f. 79.

146. Littledale (1866a), p. 19.

147. Anon., *More Disclosures* (n.d.), p. 7.

148. E. Moore (1857), p. 103.

149. Liddell (1856).

150. Baring, letter to Tait, Jan. 5, 1857, Tait 154, f. 6 r.

151. Liddell, letter to Tait, Apr. 4, 1857, Tait 154, f. 8 r.

152. *The Times*, Mar. 23, 1857, p. 10.

153. E. Moore (1857), pp. 139, 149, 161, 163, 172, and 187–88.

154. Perry (1857), p. 1; compare with Purchas (1858).

155. Liddell (1857), p. 15.

156. Peace (1857).

157. Anon., 'A Protestant' (1858), pp. 10 and 13. For subsequent legal developments, notably the Public Worship Regulation Act, 1874, see Bentley (1978) and Graber (1993).

158. B. King (1877) and P. Smith (1986).

159. 'Principal Clergy of London', Bodleian Library, add. ms. C290, f. 7 r.

160. B. King (1860), p. 8.

161. Anon., 'A Layman', *The Riots* (1860), p. 5.

162. Crouch (1904), p. 66.

163. B. King (1860), p. 14.

164. Anon., 'Alpha' (1860), p. 4.

165. B. King (1860).

166. F. Lee (1860b), pp. 4, 8, and 12. Note that Westerton was also supposed to have had the backing of victuallers.

167. George W. E. Russell, in Crouch (1904), p. viii..

168. Tait, quoted in B. King (1860), p. 12.

169. Crouch (1904), pp. 88, 112, and 136.

170. Anon., 'Alpha' (1860), p. 1.

171. Kingsley (1851), p. 371.

172. Yates (1999), p. 93.

173. Anon., *History of S. Barnabas* (1933), p. 51.

174. Yates (2000a), p. 127.

175. Anon., *Dr Lushington's Judgment* (1855), pp. 15–16.

176. *Lloyd's Weekly Newspaper*, Nov. 16 (1856), reprinted in Westerton (1857), p. 24.

177. Freud (1961), p. 153 [original publication 1927].

178. E. Moore (1857), p. 54.

179. Anon., *Important Protestant Demonstration* (1856), p. 6.

180. Lovett (1876), p. 259.

181. Westerton (1859), pp. 104–40, with quote at p. 128. For general background on anticlericalism, Evans (1983).

182. This is from 'Sir Bulwer Lytton and his principles of art in fiction', in Westerton (1859), pp. 159–210 at p. 193.

183. Westerton (1859), pp. 135 and 139–40.

CHAPTER FOUR

1. Seymour (1869), p. 11. For the Church of Ireland and the evangelical campaigns there, see Bowen (1978).

2. Seymour (1869), p. 6.

3. Seymour (1868), p. 33.

4. Seymour (1870), pp. 65–73. For the Victorian reception of medieval penitentials, see Janes (2007a).

5. Seymour (1835), p. 4.

6. Seymour (1836).

7. Anon., *Truth versus Popery* (1838).

8. Kollar (2001).

9. Seymour (1874), p. 5.

10. *English Review* 12 (1849), pp. 30–50; *Church of England Quarterly Review* 24 (1848), pp. 353–61.

11. Seymour (1849b), pp. 5 and 19.

12. Seymour (1850), pp. 6 and 259ff.

13. Seymour (1849a), pp. 6–9.

14. Anon., 'A. M.' (1849), pp. 17, 25–26, and 35.

15. Seymour (1849a), p. 24.

16. Seymour (1854), pp. 239–44.

17. Seymour (1849a), p. 21.

18. Anon., 'A. M.' (1849), p. 21.

19. *Church of England Quarterly Review* 24 (1848), p. 360.

20. Seymour (1866), pp. 17–18.

21. Seymour (1870), p. 152.

22. Seymour (1867), p. 4.

23. Seymour (1838), pp. 97–98.

24. Foxe (1838); Wolffe (1991), p. 112.

25. Bonwell (1846), pp. 27 and 57.

26. J. Carlile (1854), p. 13.

27. Hobson (1840), p. 7.

28. Pollock (1858), p. 36; and Ainslie (1837), p. 220.

29. Ryle (1851), p. 59.

30. Pollock (1858), p. 5; and Peter (1907), p. 67.

31. Pollock (1858), p. 16.

32. Ryle (1851), p. 64.

33. Anon., 'A Quiet Looker-On' (1851), p. 4.

34. J. Taylor (1857), p. 41.

35. Maguire (1840), p. 5.

36. England (1845), pp. 13 and 27.

37. Rivenall (1848), p. 4.

38. H. Ward (1871), p. 24; and Rivenall (1848), p. 6.

39. England (1845), p. 42.

40. R. Taylor (1847), pp. 127 and 296–304.

41. Blackley (1850), p. 24.

42. R. Taylor (1847), p. 178.

43. Berard (1849).

44. Kidd (1851), pp. 8–9.

45. Ruskin (1853), vol. 2, pp. 386–88.

46. Pollock (1858), pp. 18 and 33.

47. H. Ward (1871), p. 11.

48. Cumming (1851), p. 32.

49. Wordsworth (1851), p. 41.

50. Anon., 'E. I. O.' (1852), p. xv.

51. Wordsworth (1851), p. 33.

52. Desprez (1856).

53. E.g., Kay (1857).

54. Moule (1868), p. 6.

55. Knox (1857), p. 19.

56. Jones (1801), p. 221.

57. Weaver (1840), p. 137.

58. Tomkins (1850), pp. 250–51.

59. Guthrie (1858), p. 17.

60. Said (1978), p. 4; see also the discussion of Alain Grosrichard in chapter 6.

61. Van der Veer (2001), p. 26; see also R. King (1999a), p. 183, (1999b), p. 98: '[T]he notion of 'Hinduism' is itself a Western-inspired abstraction'.

62. For further reading, see Copley (1997).

63. Quote is the subtitle of Gould (1987).

64. Rodriguez (1841–45), pp. iii and 204.

65. Nash (1999), p. 65.

66. Cannadine (2001), p. xix.

67. Bearce (1961), pp. 61 and 80.

68. Callaway (1993), p. 40.

69. Macintyre (1858), p. 5.

70. Leoshko (2003), pp. 112–13.

71. Metcalf (1994), p. 14.

72. Legrew (1845), pp. 88.

73. Legrew (1845), pp. 94 and 96.

74. J. Taylor (1857), p. 33. We should, of course, be quite clear than any notion of classical polytheism as a 'national faith' is completely anachronistic, but Taylor's use of this term is very revealing. Good belief systems were, in his worldview, meant to be 'faiths' and shared on a national basis.

75. J. Taylor (1857), pp. 29–30.

76. Logan (2003), p. 559.

77. E. Robertson (1849).

78. W. Laurie (1850), p. xvi.

79. Poynder (1837), p. 6.

80. Gurney (1848), p. 19; black faces and red mouths were clearly not a social advantage!

81. Dhall (1997), pp. 237 and 250; and Kulakkatt (2002), p. 25.

82. E.g., Anon., 'Petition of the undersigned' (1852).

83. Piggin (1984), p. 117; and Rodriguez (1841–45), p. iii.

84. Baggaly (1845), p. 18.

85. The connections between drink, moral degradation and physical destruction were vital themes in Victorian cultural politics and literature, T. Reed (2006).

86. Anon., *Heathen Books* (c. 1850), p. 4.

87. Morgan (1851), p. 18.

88. Pattison (1991), p. 44.

89. Droit (2003).

90. Kieschnick (2003), pp. 6 and 13.

91. Newstead (1838), p. 5.

92. Tennent (1850), p. 95.

93. Rev. J. Davies, who was a Baptist missionary in Ceylon, quoted in Tennent (1850), p. 116.

94. Kerns (1851), pp. 18–19.

95. Poynder (1835), pp. 34 and 83.

96. Wiseman (1836), pp. 1 and 10.

97. W. Bennett (1843), p. 206.

98. Anon., *The Gospel* (1864), pp. 14 and 49.

99. Hawley (1839), pp. 56–62, with quotes at p. 60.

100. Earlier versions of this section have appeared as Janes (2008a, 2008b).

101. J. Reed (1996), p. 151. For background on 'south-coast' ritualism, see Yates (1983) and Cowl (1996).

102. Anon., *Pictorial Crucifixes* (1852), pp. 9–10.

103. Tomlinson, *Queen Elizabeth's Crucifix* (n.d.), p. 13.

104. Aston (2002), p. 272.

105. Anon., *Offer of a Seat* (1856).

106. Trower (1857), p. 44.

107. Liddell, letter to Tait, June 29, 1857, Lambeth Palace Library, Tait 154, f. 46.

108. Montpincon (1895), pp. 9, 11, 30, and 36.

109. Charles (1848), pp. 7, 11, 15, and 18.

110. Anon., 'A London Curate' (1850), p. 35.

111. Nugée (1856), pp. 81–82.

112. Anon., 'A London Curate' (1850), p. 4.

113. Anon., 'A Puseyite' (1858), p. 8.

114. Peace (1857), p. 21.

115. Seymour (1848), pp. 375–76.

116. Quoted in Landow (1979), p. 118.

117. Maas (1984), pp. 33–34.

118. Anon., 'Didymus' (1905), pp. 114–15 and 123–24. Compare with Kee (1982).

119. M. Brock (1879), pp. 3–5, 16–17, 36–38, 57, 66, 86, and 115.

120. Rock (1851), pp. vii, 352, 355, and 360–63. Compare Tennent (1851), p. 486.

121. Anon., 'Investigator Abhorrens' (1858) and Nye (1994), p. 97.

122. Anon., 'Investigator Abhorrens' (1858), pp.iii–iv.

123. Anon., 'Investigator Abhorrens' (1858), pp. 1, 11, 13, 15, 24, 28, 35, 37, 39–40, 42–43.

124. Anon., 'Investigator Abhorrens' (1858), pp. 46–48, using Seymour (1854).

125. Anon., 'Investigator Abhorrens' (1858), p. 17.

126. M. Brock (1879), p. 40.

127. McCalman (1988), pp. 209–11, discusses the links between radicals and libertines.

128. Gaimster (2000), p. 13.

129. O'Connor (1989), p. 39.

130. Benedict (2002), p. 269.

131. Leonard (2006), p. 198.

132. Kendrick (1996), p. 2; and Sigel (2002).

133. Carabelli (1996a), p. 112.

134. Stone (1927), vol. 1, p. 95.

135. Carabelli (1994) and (1996b).

136. R. Knight (1865) [original publication 1786]. See the discussion of Knight's understanding of phallic symbolism in architecture in Ponte (1992).

137. Stumpf-Condry and Skedd (2004).

138. Mitter (1977), p. 85; Haskell (1984), p. 190; and Hancarville (1785).

139. Rousseau (1987), p. 102.

140. Barnett (2003), p. 11.

141. Larkin (2005), p. 146.

142. Daily (1999), pp. 33 and 56.

143. Paine discussed in Larsen (2004), p. 46; and Davidson and Scheick (1994).

144. Clifford (1993).

145. Dupuis (1794): vol. 1, pp. 308 and 382; vol. 4, pp. 491–516; vol. 5, p. 260.

146. Mitter (1977), p. 86.

147. Estlin (1797), pp. 48–49.

148. J. Smith (1841), p. 152.

149. R. Carlile (1826), p. 43 [original publication 1826].

150. Wright in R. Knight (1865), p. 248.

151. Astle (1800).

152. Mason (1994), p. 183.

153. Inman (1869), pp. xii, xiv–v, 9, and 10.

154. Pike (1873), p. 24.

155. Perceval (1851), p. 5. This issue is developed further in chapter 5.

156. H. Ward (1871), p. 75.

157. Denby (2004).

158. Rock (1851), pp. 118 and 168.

159. See the refutation of such views by the Irish Roman Catholic priest Maguire (1840), p. 6.

160. Beeman (1868), pp. 164–66.

161. Anon., 'A Churchman of the Reformation' (1850), p. 22.

162. Macghee (1853), p. 57.

163. Härdelin (1965), p. 156.

164. Parsons (1988a), p. 36.

165. W. Bennett (1842), p. xi.

166. W. Bennett (1846), pp. vi–vii and 99.

167. W. Bennett (1857).

168. Parsons (1988a), pp. 37–38.

169. Keble (1857), p. 21.

170. Anon., 'A Layman', *The Doctrine* (1838), p. 27.

171. Bird (1839), p. 16.

172. W. Bennett (1851a), pp. 352 and 415.

173. Wreford (1846), pp. 4, 31, 33, and 271–72.

174. King, quoted in Crouch (1904), p. 166.

175. Hewison (1914), p. 97.

176. The erotic, and particularly homoerotic, potentials of this are explored in Janes (forthcoming).

177. Valeri (1999), pp. 43, 70, and 102.

178. Kristeva (1982), pp. 3–4.

179. Young (2000).

180. Flint (2000), p. 63.

CHAPTER FIVE

1. Inman was the author of several medical works, e.g., *Foundation for a New Theory and Practice of Medicine* (1861) and *On the Restoration of Health* (1872).

2. Inman (1872), pp. vi and xi.

3. Inman (1868), p. 68.

4. Inman (1875), p. xv.

5. Inman (1868), p. vi.

6. Cox (2004), p. 246.

7. Hobson (2005); and Ryan (1997), p. 145.

8. Stallybrass and White (1986), p. 191.

9. Bellasis (1851), discussed in Wheeler (2006), pp. 29–30.

10. Seymour (1843), pp. 376 and 382.

11. Dr. Lee (1843), p. 526.

12. Anon., 'Adam Bede' (1860), p. 5.

13. Anon., 'Will o' the Wisp' (1843), pp. 8–9. A questman collected parish rates and assisted the churchwardens.

14. W. Anderson (1995), pp. 640 and 668–69.

15. Brown (1981), p. 82.

16. Perceval (1851), p. 5.

17. Curtis (1992), p. 629 and Landow (1972).

18. Seymour (1849b), p. 23.

19. Ford Madox Brown, exhibition catalogue entry, 191, Piccadilly, 1865, in Bendiner (1998), p. 135.

20. Freedman (1990), p. 210.

21. Danahay (2005), p. 108.

22. Haskins (1993), pp. 346–47; and Reay (2002), pp. 86–87.

23. *Punch* 7 (1844), p. 182.

24. Herbert (2002), p. 201.

25. NADFAS (1999), cat. no. 512.

26. Neale and Littledale (1887), vol. 3, pp. 49–50 [original publication 1860).

27. Reay (2002), p. 65.

28. Douglas and Isherwood (1996), p. 13.

29. Thompson (1988).

30. Gunn (1999), p. 16.

31. A. Ward (1980).

32. O'Malley (2006), p. 94.

33. Tropp (1990), p. 75.

34. O'Malley (2006), p. 95.

35. Douglas and Isherwood (1996), pp. xxi–ii.

36. Botting (1996), p. 14.

37. Kearney (2002), p. 89.

38. Botting (2000), p. 3.

39. Botting (1996), p. 113, with quote at p. 10.

40. Kearney (2002), p. 88.

41. Vance (1997), p. 260.

42. Poole, letter to Tait, Aug. 11, 1858, Lambeth Palace Library, ms. Tait 154 f. 167 v.

43. Foucault (1979), p. 20.

44. Carrette (2000), pp. 26 and 32.

45. Anon., *The Roman Catholic Confessional* (1837), p. 27.

46. Heimann (1995), pp. 72–73 and 80–81. The nineteenth-century editions of Challoner's *Garden of the Soul* preserved the core of the original text of 1755 while making various rearrangements and additions.

47. Challoner (1801), pp. 202–3 and 215–16 [original publication 1755].

48. Bedford (1836), pp. 32 and 49.

49. Godfrey (1847), p. 23.

50. Anon., 'A Protestant' (1858), pp. 14–16.

51. Peschier (2005), pp. 10–42, argues that anti-Catholic discourses were strongly structured around patriarchal anxieties over the control of women who, if taught too intensively, questioned, confined, or otherwise maltreated, were liable to lapse into 'hysterical' mental states. As such, it was highly dangerous to subject them to the confessional.

52. Anon., 'A Protestant' (1858), pp. 17–18.

53. Westerton, letter to Tait, Nov. 19, 1857, in Lambeth Palace Library, ms. Tait 154, ff. 73–77.

54. Anon., 'Fairplay' (1858), p. 4.

55. Poole quoted in Liddell (1858a), p. 39.

56. Anon., 'Fairplay' (1858), pp. 6–7.

57. *The Times*, Jan. 31, 1859. For modern legal discussion of the case, see Waddams (1992), pp. 297–302.

58. Liddell (1858a), pp. 33 n. and 41.

59. Anon., 'F. D.' (1858), pp. 4, 8, and 13.

60. Anon., *A Plea* (1858), p. 5. There was a lively, if divided, movement for the reform of the Prayer Book.

61. Anon., 'A Churchman' (1858), p. 10.

62. Stowell, quoted in anon., 'A Churchman' (1858), p. 11.

63. Anon., 'A Churchman' (1858), p. 13.

64. Lowe (1852), pp. 3 and 11–12.

65. Fox (1854), p. 25.

66. Bunn (1855), pp. 22–37 and 179–80.

67. R. Taylor (1847), p. 276.

68. Anon., 'A Barrister' (1851), pp. 33, 41, and 43.

69. Kingsley (1851), p. 87.

70. Russell (1858), pp. 183 and 378.

71. *Liverpool Mercury*, Dec. 10, 1850, p. 796.

72. Desanctis (1852), p. 134.

73. Tweedie (1851), p. 16.

74. Klaus (1987), p. 290.

75. Luke (1851, 1852) discussed in Maison (1961), p. 174.

76. Luke (1851), pp. iv and 432.

77. Luke (1852), pp. 187 and 204.

78. Seymour (1848), p. 272.

79. Paull (1867), p. 464.

80. Wilson (1856), p. iv.

81. M. Brock (1883), p. 268.

82. Selén (1992), p. 57.

83. Figures from *The Times*, cited on Wikipedia: http://en.wikipedia.org/wiki/ Dan_Brown, accessed January 10 2007 (I am happy to use this source since I am simply indicating widespread rumours of vast wealth).

84. Diamond (2003), pp. 84–87; and Mays (2002), p. 12.

85. Mays (2002), pp. 19 and 22; see also the extended discussion in Bossche (1994).

86. Altick (1954), p. 5.

87. Ellison (1998), p. 61.

88. Anon., 'Anti-Mammon' (1842), p. 8 [original publication 1841].

89. Pusey (1850), p. 20.

90. R. Moore (1994), p. 275.

91. White (2006), p. 93; Brewer, McKendrick, and Plumb (1982); and Brewer (1997).

92. Eisenman (1994), p. 241.

93. Griest (1965), p. 117.

94. A. Miller (1995), p. 8.

95. Daly (1994), p. 46.

96. Martineau (2004), vol. 3, pp. 97–98.

97. Mighall (1998), p. 26.

98. Cotton (1856), pp. 12 and 18.

CHAPTER SIX

1. *The Times*, Mar. 21, 1851, p. 5.

2. *The Times*, Dec. 18, 1856, p. 6.

3. Dick (1859), p. 7.

4. Bentley (1978).

5. *National Association Gazette*, Jan. 22, 1842, p. 28.

6. Seymour (1850), pp. 300 and 330.

7. *Punch* 12 (1847), p. 258.

8. *Punch* 20 (1851), p. 112.

9. Anon., 'A Naturalist' (1852), pp. 3, 8, and 13.

10. Nicolay (2003), pp. 122–23, with quote at p. 129.

11. *Lloyd's Weekly Newspaper*, Nov. 16 (1856), reprinted in Westerton (1857), p. 24.

12. Hawthorne (2002), p. 342 [original publication 1859].

13. Yasuko (2004), pp. 47 and 56.

14. Matless (1998), p. 264.

15. Stallybrass and White (1986), p. 191.

16. Buchanan (1872), pp. 3–4. On the sale of pornography in London at this time, Nead (2000), pp. 164–65 and 178–89.

17. Buchanan (1872), pp. 96–97.18. *Punch* 20 (1851), p. 37.

19. *The Times*, May 24, 1875, p. 6.

20. Champion (2001), p. 462.

21. One might also compare the *Punch* drawing of the same year showing the Pope cross-legged and smoking a water pipe (figure 6.5).

22. Morgan (1851), pp. 13–14.

23. Rich (1851), p. 20.

24. Nees (1991).

25. Grosrichard (1979) and (1998).

26. Ahiska (2003), p. 370 n. 5.

27. Dolar (1998), pp. xi and xvi.

28. Gay (1995), p. 70.

29. Wolffe (1991), p. 107.

30. O'Hagan (2006), p. 18.

31. Yagou (2003), p. 86.

32. Reynolds (1977), p. 403.

33. Herbert (1991), pp. 124–25; see also Kasson (1998).

34. Kasson (1998), p. 80.

35. Green (1982), p. 36.

36. Cunliffe (1951), p. 121.

37. Green (1982), p. 37.

38. Hobson (2005); and Ryan (1997), p. 145.

39. Dolar (1998), p. xi.

40. Landow (1979), p. 108.

41. *The Times*, May 3, 1856, p. 9.

42. Ruskin (1856), pp. 29 and 31 n.

43. Landow (1979), p. 111; see also Sussman (1968), p. 88; and Roskill and Sussman (1969), pp. 466 and 470.

44. Girard (1986), p. 22; see also T. Douglas (1995).

45. W. Bennett (1851b), pp. 84 and 89–90.

Bibliography

MANUSCRIPTS AND ARCHIVED RECORDS

Bodleian Library, Oxford

Ms. add. C290, 'Principal Clergy of London'

British Library, London

Ms. add. 44369, 44371, 44652, W. J. E. Bennett to Gladstone, Gladstone
   papers
Ms. add. 39863, 'History of Pimlico', W. H. Husk papers

Lambeth Palace Library, London

Ms. 1922, W. J. E. Bennett, 'Directory for the Celebration of the Holy
   Communion'
Ms. 1923, W. J. E. Bennett, Mass Book
Blomfield 50, Fulham Palace archives, Charles James Blomfield, bishop
   of London 1828–1856, papers
Tait 154, Fulham Palace archives, correspondence on St. Paul's and
   St. Barnabas', Archibald Campbell Tait, bishop of London 1856–68,
   papers

City of Westminster Archives, London

NADFAS (National Association of Decorative and Fine Arts Societies),
   Record of Church Furnishings, St. Barnabas, Pimlico (London:
   NADFAS, 1999)

PRIMARY SOURCES: PRINTED

Periodicals

Church of England Quarterly Review
Dublin Review
The Ecclesiologist
Edinburgh Review
The English Churchman
English Review
Fraser's Magazine
John Bull
Illustrated London News
Illustrated Times
Liverpool Mercury
National Association Gazette
National Review
Punch
The Rambler
The Tablet
The Times

Books and Articles

Ainslie, Robert, 'British idolatry in India. A sermon', in Anon., ed., *The Pastoral Echo. Nineteen Sermons by Eminent Dissenting Ministers, and Others* (London: W. Harding, 1837), pp. 215–36.

Anon., *The Bells of S. Barnabas. Suggested by Reading in the Papers of the Remonstrance Addressed to the Bishop of London, Complaining that the Bells of the above Church 'Annoyed Thousands of the Inhabitants of the Parish'* (London: W. J. Cleaver, 1851).

Anon., *The Case of the Churchwarden and Incumbent of St. Paul's, Knightsbridge; And a Review of the Letters of the Bishop of London and the Archdeacon of Middlesex*, 2nd ed. (London: Seeleys, 1854).

Anon., *A Christian Woman* (London: Elliot Stock, 1871).

Anon., *Dr Lushington's Judgment in the Case of Westerton v. Liddell upon 'Ornaments of the Church' Considered by a Parish Priest Who Has Not in Use the Articles Complained of* (London: John Masters, 1855).

Anon., *A Few Reasons for Deprecating the Attempt of the Bishop of London to Alter the Service of the Church* (London: C. and E. Layton, 1843).

Anon., *The Gospel According to the Heathen. Bacchus Elucidated. By the Author of 'Evidences of a Belief in the Doctrine of the Holy Trinity'* (London: A. Hall and Co., 1864).

Anon., *Heathen Books and Christian Tracts* (London: Religious Tract Society, c. 1850).

Anon., *The History of S. Barnabas, Pimlico* (London: Catholic Literature Association, 1933).

Anon., *Image-Worship*, What Is Romanism? vols. 17–26 (London: Society for Promoting Christian Knowledge, 1849).

Anon., *Important Protestant Demonstration* (London, 1856).

Anon., *More Disclosures about Saint Barnabas' and the Tractarians*, 6th ed. (London: W. M. Clark, n.d.).

Anon., *Offer of a Seat in Parliament, etc* [poster with reprinted correspondence and extracts from newspapers relating to the re-election of Mr. Westerton as Churchwarden at St. Paul's, Knightsbridge] (London, 1856).

Anon., *On the Invocation of Saints and Angels*, What Is Romanism? vols. 3–7 (London: Society for Promoting Christian Knowledge, 1846).

Anon., *The Parish Priest and the Prime Minister. Being an Article Rejected by a Leading Review, Founded on Lord John Russell's Letter to the Bishop of Durham, and Rev. N. J. E [sic] Bennett's Letter to Lord John Russell.* (London: John Murray, 1851).

Anon., 'Petition of the undersigned ministers of the gospel resident in Calcutta', *The Chrisitian Intelligencer, Including a Quarterly Missionary Intelligencer* (1852), pp. 183–86.

Anon., *Pictorial Crucifixes, A Letter to the Lord Bishop of Chichester, by a Priest of the Parish*, 2nd ed. (London: Joseph Masters, 1852).

Anon., *'The Prince of the Power of the Air:' Being Thoughts Concerning the Past, Present and Future* (London: William Macintosh, 1868).

Anon., *Puseyism in London* (London: Edwards and Hughes, 1843).

Anon., *The Roman Catholic Confessional Exposed: In Three Letters to a Late Cabinet Minister* (Dublin: Philip Dixon Hardy, 1837).

Anon., *Truth versus Popery. A Report of the Discussion Which Took Place at a Special Meeting of the Protestant Association, Held at the Town Hall, Guildford…between the Rev, Messrs. Seymour and Page, Clergymen of the Church, and the Rev. Joseph Sidden, a Priest of the Romish Sect* (London: Seeleys, 1838).

Anon., 'Adam Bede', *The Natural History of Puseyism: With a Short Account of the Sunday Opera at St. Paul's, Brighton* (Brighton: G. Smart, 1860).

Anon., 'Alpha', *The 'Outrages' at St. George's in the East: A Letter to Sir George Cornewall Lewis* (London: Joseph Masters, 1860).

Anon., 'A. M.', *A Brief Review of the Rev. Hobart Seymour's 'Pilgrimage to Rome'* (London: Longman and Co., 1849).

Anon., 'Anti-Mammon', *Mammo-Mania: The Apostacy of the Age Unveiled, Dedicated to Sir Robert Peel, Bart.*, 2nd ed. (London: John Templeman, 1842).

Anon., 'A Barrister', *A Letter to the Lord Bishop of London on the Promulgation of the Recent Papal Bull* (London: J. Ridgway, 1851).

Anon., 'Caustic', *Strictures on a Sermon Entitled 'Apostacy': A Sermon in Reference to a Late Event at S.Paul's Knightsbridge, Preached on the Twenty-second Sunday after Trinity, 1847, by the Rev. William J. E. Bennett, M.A., Perpetual Curate* (London: Trelawney W. Saunders, 1847).

Anon., 'A Churchman', *A Reply to the Lecture of the Rev. Canon Stowell, on Confession, Delivered in the Free Trade Hall, Manchester, on Tuesday Evening, September 28, 1858*, 4th ed. (Manchester: Abel Heywood, 1858).

————, *An Example of Extreme Ritualism in the Church of England. A Short Account of What Took Place in One of the London Churches on Ascension Day, May 10, 1866* (London, William Macintosh: London, 1866).

Anon., 'A Churchman of the Reformation', *Tractarian Practices in Protestant Churches: Three Letters, Reprinted from the 'Christian Guardian', and Now Addressed to the Right Hon. and Right Rev. the Lord Bishop of London, and the Protestant Churchmen of the Diocese* (London: J. H. Jackson, 1850).

Anon., 'A Clergyman', *Ritualism, What It Is, and What It Teaches, with Other Matter, and Suggestions for a Remedy* (London: William Macintosh, 1868).

Anon., 'Didymus', *The True Christian, Or, The Cross Instead of the Crucifix* (London: James Speirs, 1905).

Anon., 'E. I. O.', *The Scarlet Book; Showing the Connection of the Roman Catholic Ceremonies with the Pagan Rites. With an Account of the Bishops, Patriarchs, and Popes of Rome, from A.D. 60. Also an Explanation of the Revelation of St. John the Divine, as It Applies to Modern Events… By E. I. O., Author of 'The Reply to Cardinal Wiseman's Manifesto'* (London: Piper Brothers and Co., 1852).

Anon., 'F. D.', *A Plea for Saint Barnabas. The Confessional versus the Social Evil* (London: Alfred William Bennett, 1858).

Anon., 'Fairplay', *Letter to the Honorable and Reverend F. Baring, with Reference to the Statements* [on the use of the confessional by the Rev. Alfred Poole] *Reported to Have Been Made by Him, at St. James Hall, on Friday, the 11th of June, 1858* (London, 1858).

Anon., 'Investigator Abhorrens', *Idolomania; Or, The Legalised Cross Not the Instrument of Crucifixion, Being an Inquiry into the Difference between the Cross Proper and the Symbol of Heathen Processions* (London: Effingham Wilson, 1858).

Anon., 'A Layman', *The Doctrine of Transubstantiation Refuted* (London: T. C. Savill, 1838).

————, *The Riots at St. George's East: A Letter to the Lord Bishop of London* (London: Basil Montagu, 1860).

Anon., 'A London Curate', *Pestilence, in Relation to Christian Duties and Natural Laws: Conveyed in a Series of Consecutive Sermons* (London: Francis and John Rivington, 1850).

Anon., 'A Naturalist', *Monachologia: Or, Handbook of the Natural History of Monks Arranged According to the Linnaean System* (Edinburgh: Johnstone and Hunter, 1852).

Anon., 'A Protestant', *Protestantism and Puseyism. Strictures on the Rev. W. J. E. Bennett's 'Principles of the Book of Common Prayer'; With an Examination of His Sermon Lately Preached at St. Paul's, Knightsbridge* (London: Charles Ollier, 1848).

————, *The Belles, Belgravia, and the Bellman. Observations upon a Pamphlet Entitled 'More Disclosures about St. Barnabas and the Tractarians'* (London: Partridge and Co., 1858).

Anon., 'A Puseyite', *Plain Words to Protestants* (London: G. J. Palmer, 1858).

Anon., 'A Quiet Looker-On', *The Worship of Saints, Images, and Relics*, Letters to a Romanist 5 (Scarborough: A. Russell, 1851).

Anon., 'A Simple Protestant', *Reflections Arising out of the Popish Aggression, for the Consideration of the Church, Laity, and Parliament, with Comments on the Dispute* between the Rev. W. J. E. Bennett, of Saint Barnabas, Pimlico, and the Bishop of London (London: J. H. Kendall, 1851).

Anon., 'Will o' the Wisp', A Paper Lantern for Puseyites (London: Smith Elder and Co., 1843).

Astle, Thomas, 'Observations on stone pillars, crosses and crucifixes', Archaeologia 13 (1800), pp. 208–22.

Baggaly, William, The Juggernaut of Popery. The Narrative of a Visit to Lough Dearg, in the County of Donegall, Ireland, in the Month of August, 1845 (London: J. Bakewell, 1845).

Bailey, E., Priestism: The Question of the Day (London, Whittaker and Co., 1868).

Balleine, George Reginald, A History of the Evangelical Party in the Church of England, new ed. (London: Church Book Room Press, 1951).

Barr, James, Anglican Church Architecture with Some Remarks upon Ecclesiastical Furniture, 3rd ed. (Oxford: John Henry Parker, 1846).

Beal, William, An Analysis of Palmer's 'Origines Liturgicae; Or the Antiquities of the English Ritual'; And of His 'Dissertation on Primitive Liturgies'. For the Use of Students at the Universities, and Candidates for Holy Orders, Who Have Read the Original Work (Cambridge: John Deighton, 1850).

Bedford, W. M. Riland, ed., The Indelicacy of Auricular Confesssion, as Practised by the Roman Catholic Church Treated in a Correspondence between the Hon. and Rev. George Spencer, and the Rev. W. M. Riland Bedford (Birmingham: William Hodgetts, 1836).

Beeman, Thomas Oyler, Ritualism: Doctrine not Dress. Notes of Lectures on Ritualism, the Development of Tractarianism, with Additions, Including Remarks on the Charge of the Bishop of Salisbury (Cranbrook: Geo. Waters and Son, 1868).

Bellasis, Edward, [Anon.], The Anglican Bishops versus the Catholic Hierarchy: A Demurrer to Further Proceedings (London: James Toovey, 1851).

Bellett, George, The City of Rome, Considered Chiefly in Reference to the Remains of Heathen Antiquity; The Memorials of the Early Church; The Present Character of the Roman Church. A Lecture (Bridgenorth: Rowley Bros., 1853).

Bennett, Frederick, The Story of W. J. E. Bennett, Founder of S. Barnabas', Pimlico and Vicar of Froome-Selwood and of His Part in the Oxford Church Movement of the Nineteenth Century (London: Longmans, Green, and Co, 1909).

Bennett, John B., The Evil of Theatrical Amusements, Stated and Illustrated in a Sermon Preached in the Wesleyan Methodist Chapel, Lower Abbey Street, on Sunday, November 4th, 1838; With an Appendix (Dublin: John Fannin and Co., 1838).

Bennett, William J. E., The Duty of Associating against the Profanation of the Sabbath Day (Bath: Printed by Benjamin Higman, 1842).

——, Letters to my Children on Church Subjects, vol. 1 (London: W. J. Cleaver, 1843).

——, The Principles of the Book of Common Prayer Considered. A Series of Lecture Sermons (London: W. J. Cleaver, 1845).

——, The Eucharist, Its History, Doctrine and Practice, 2nd. ed. (London: Cleaver, 1846).

——, Apostacy. A Sermon in Reference to a Late Event at S. Paul's Knightsbridge, Preached on the Twenty-second Sunday after Trinity, 1847, 2nd ed. (London: W. J. Cleaver, 1847).

———, *A First Letter to the Right Honorable Lord John Russell, M.P. on the Present Persecution of a Certain Portion of the English Church, with a Sermon, Preached at S. Paul's Knightsbridge, on Sunday Morning and Evening, November 17, 1850*, 7th ed. (London: W. J. Cleaver, 1850a).

———, ed. *Sermons Preached at S. Barnabas, Pimlico, in the Octave of the Consecration, M.DCCC.L* (London: W. J. Clefaver, 1850b).

———, *A Farewell Letter to His Parishioners* (London: W. J. Cleaver, 1851a).

———, *Three Farewell Sermons Preached at S. Barnabas', Pimlico*, 2nd ed. (London: W. J. Cleaver, 1851b).

———, *A Second Letter to the Right Honorable Lord John Russell, M.P. on the Present Persecution of a Certain Portion of the English Church, in Which Some Debates in the Last Parliament are Considered*, 7th ed. (London: W. J. Cleaver, 1852).

———, *An Examination of Archdeacon Denison's Propositions of Faith on the Doctrine of the Holy Eucharist. With a Prefatory Letter to the Lord Bishop of Bath and Wells* (London: Whittaker and Co., and J. Cleaver, 1857).

Berard, S., *The Union of Church and State: A Heathen Principle* (London: Partridge and Oakey, 1849).

Bird, Charles S., *Transubstantiation Tried by Scripture and Reason Addressed to the Protestant Inhabitants of Reading* (London: Hatchards, 1839).

Blackley, William, *Pastoral Letter to a Rural Congregation; With Peculiar Reference to the Special Danger of the Times* (London: J. Hatchard, 1850).

Blomfield, Alfred, *Memoir of Charles James Blomfield, D.D., Bishop of London, with Selections from His Correspondence*, 2 vols. (London: John Murray, 1863).

Blomfield, Charles James, *A Charge Delivered to the Clergy of the Diocese of London at the Visitation in October, MDCCCXLII*, 2nd ed. (London: B. Fellowes, 1842).

———, *The Charge of the Bishop of London to the Clergy of His Diocese, Assembled in the Cathedral of St. Paul's, on the Occasion of His Sixth Visitation* (London: Charles Westerton, 1850).

Bonwell, James, *The Corruptions and Idolatry of the Church of Rome and of the Popish Sect in this Land, Contrasted with the Pure Faith of the Catholic and Apostolic Church of England; Being Two Sermons* (London: George Bell, 1846).

Bradford, W., *Another Candle for Puseyites. By Which They May See How Their System Is Based on Idolatry and Materialism in Religion, and Treason in the State* (London: W. Mattocks, 1860).

Brock, Isaac, *Extreme Ritualism. The Language of Dogmas Condemned by the Church of England. A Sermon* (London: Sutter, Alexander and Co., 1866).

Brock, Mourant, *The Cross: Heathen and Christian. A Fragmentary Notice of Its Early Pagan Existence, and Subsequent Christian Adoption* (London: Seeley, Jackson and Halliday, 1879).

———, *Rome: Pagan and Papal* (London: Hodder and Stoughton, 1883).

Brown, Ford Madox, *The Diary of Ford Madox Brown*, ed. Virginia Surtees (New Haven: Yale University Press, 1981).

Browne, E. G. K., *Annals of the Tractarian Movement from 1842 to 1860*, 3rd ed. (London: E. G. K. Browne,, 1861).

Buchanan, Robert, *The Fleshly School of Poetry and other Phenomena of the Day* (London: Strahan and Co., 1872).

Bunn, Henry, *The Vampire of Christendom: A Book for the Times* (London: Hamilton, Adams and Co., 1855).

Burgess, Richard, *The Sixth Biennial Letter to the Parishioners of Upper Chelsea* (London: Jacques and Robinson, 1848).

Carlile, James, *The Station and Occupation of the Saints in Their Final Glory* (London: James Nisbet and Co., 1854).

Carlile, Richard, *Every Woman's Book, or What Is Love*, 4th ed. (London: R. Carlile, 1826).

Carter, T. T., 'Introduction', in A. F. A. Hanbury-Tracy, ed., *Faith and Progress. The Witness of the English Church during the last Fifty Years. Being Sermons Preached at the Jubilee of the Consecration of S. Barnabas', Pimlico. A.D. 1900. With an introduction by the Rev. T. T. Carter and a Preface by the Rev. the Hon. A. F. A. Hanbury-Tracy* (London: Longmans, Green, and Co., 1900), pp. xi–xvi.

Challoner, Richard, *The Garden of the Soul; A Manual of Spiritual Exercises and Instructions for Christians, Who, Living in the World Aspire to Devotion* (Wolverhampton: J. Smart, 1801).

Charles, Elizabeth, *Rest in Christ, Or, The Crucifix and the Cross* (London: J. J. Guillaume, 1848).

Christmas, Henry, 'Of the furniture and ornaments of churches', in James Cottle, ed., *Some Account of the Church of St. Mary Magdalene, Taunton, and the Restoration Thereof: Together with Several Notices on Ecclesiastical Matters* (London: Vizetelly Brothers and Co., 1845), pp. 119–28.

Close, Francis, *Restoration of Churches Is the Restoration of Popery, Proved and Illustrated from the Authenticated Documents of the 'Cambridge Camden Society'. A Sermon Preached in the Parish Church, Cheltenham, on Tuesday, November 5th, 1844*, 2nd ed. (London: Hatchard and Son, 1844).

Conybeare, W. J., *Church Parties*, 3rd ed., edited by Arthur Burns, in Stephen Taylor, ed., *From Cranmer to Davidson: A Miscellany*, Church of England Record Society 7 (Woodbridge: Boydell, 1999), pp. 215–385.

Cotton, George Edward Lynch, *The True Strength and Mission of the Church. A Sermon, Preached in the Chapel Royal, Whitehall, at the Consecration of the Right Reverend Archibald Campbell Tait, D.C.L., Bishop of London, and the Right Rev. Henry Cotterill, D.D. Bishop of Grahamstown, on Sunday, November 23, 1856* (London: Rivingtons, 1856).

Crouch, William, *Bryan King and the Riots at St. George's-in-the-East* (London: Methuen and Co., 1904).

Cumming, John, *Dr Cumming's Lecture on the Papal Aggression. Delivered at the Hanover Square Rooms on Thursday, November 7th* (London: Charles Westerton, 1850).

——, *Rome, the Babylon of the Apocalypse. A Lecture Delivered on Thursday, May 29th, 1851, in Exeter Hall (Authorized Edition, Revised and Corrected, with the References Verified, by the Author)* (London: British Society for Promoting the Religious Principles of the Reformation, 1851).

Davenport, J. S., *Ritualism. A Letter to a Clergyman* (1855).

Davidson, Randall Thomas, and William Benham, *Life of Archbishop Campbell Tait*, 2 vols. (London: Macmillan and Co., 1891).

De Brosses, Charles, *Du culte des dieux fétiches, ou parallèle de l'ancienne religion de l'Égypte avec la religion actuelle de Nigritie* (Paris, 1760).

Dekker, Thomas, *The Whore of Babylon, as It Was Acted by the Princes Seruants* (London: Nathaniel Butter, 1607).

Desanctis, L., *Popery and Jesuitism at Rome in the Nineteenth Century. With Remarks on the Influence in England* (London: Wertheim and Macintosh, 1852).

Desprez, P. S., *Babylon the Great, Neither Rome Pagan, nor Papal, but Jerusalem* (London: Joseph Masters, 1856).

Dick, Robert, *The Spiritual Dunciad; Or Oxford 'Tracks' to Popery. A Satire; With Notes and Appendix* (London: Charles Westerton, 1859).

Drummond, Henry, *Reply to the Rev. R. I. Wilberforce's 'Principles of Church Authority'* (London: Thomas Bosworth, 1855).

———, *The Rationale of Liturgies and of Public Worship* (London: Bosworth and Harrison, 1857).

England, John, *Explanation of the Construction, Furniture and Ornaments of a Church, of the Vestments of the Clergy and of the Nature of the Mass* (Rome: Monaldini, 1845).

Estlin, J. P., *The Nature and the Causes of Atheism* (Bristol, 1797).

Fox, George Townshend, *Priestly Celibacy Exposed. A Lecture Delivered in the Borough Hall, Stockton-upon-Tees, on Wednesday Evening, 11th October 1854* (London: John Farquhar Shaw, 1854).

Foxe, John, *The Acts and Monuments of the Church; Containing the History and Sufferings of the Martyrs*, ed. M. Hobart Seymour, 2 vols. (London: Scott, Webster and Geary, 1838).

Garbett, James, *The Sense, the Mind and the Spirit. A Sermon Preached at the Cathedral of Chichester for National Schools, May 31st, 1844* (London: J. Hatchard and Son, 1844).

———, *Popery and Infidelity in the Last Times. A Sermon Preached before the University of Oxford, November 5th, 1847* (London: J. Hatchard and Son, 1847).

Gibson, J. H., W. G. Humphrey, and Thomas Bastard, *Correspondence between the Hon. Secretary to the General Committee [J. H. Gibson] and the Right Honorable and Right Reverend the Lord Bishop of London, on the Subject of a Proposed Deputation from the Committee of the Poor of the Parish to Present to His Lordship an Address from the Poor; With the Address Which It Was Intended to Present on the Occasion* (London: J. T. Hayes, 1851).

Godfrey, N. S., *The British Church Not Originally a Popish Church. A Sermon Preached in Trinity Church, Swansea, on Thursday Evening, November 4th, 1847* (London: Wertheim, 1847).

Goode, William, *Aids for Determining some Disputed Points in the Ceremonial of the Church of England*, 2nd ed. (London: Thomas Hatchard, 1851).

Guild of Saint Alban, *Rules of the Westminster and Pimlico Church Burial Society, Conducted by the Guild of S. Alban* (London: J. T. Hayes, 1856).

Gurney, William Brodie, *A Lecture to Children and Youth on the History and Character of Heathen Idolatry; With Some References to the Effects of Christian Missions* (London: London, 1848).

Guthrie, Thomas, *Christ and the Inheritance of the Saints: Illustrated in a Series of Discourses from the Colossians* (Edinburgh: Adam and Charles Black, 1858).

Hancarville, P. d', *Recherches sur l'origine, l'esprit at les progress des arts de la Grèce*, 2 vols. (London, 1785).

Harington, Edward Charles, *The Purity of the Church of England and the Corruptions of the Church of Rome. A Sermon* [on Acts 24: 14] (London: F. and J. Rivington, 1852).

Hart, Ernest, *London, Old and New: A Sanitary Contrast* (London: Allman and Son, 1884).

Hawley, Richard Maddock, *Genuine Christianity Contrasted with Its Corruptions, with Idolatry, and with the Religion of Mahomet* (Edinburgh: John Lindsay and Co., 1839).

Hawthorne, Nathaniel, *The Marble Faun* (Oxford: Oxford University Press, 2002).

Hewison, James King, *The Runic Roods of Ruthwell and Bewcastle with a Short History of the Cross and Crucifix in Scotland* (Glasgow: John Smith and Son, 1914).

Hobson, S., *The Sin and Danger of Forsaking God and Following Idols* (Norwich: Isaiah Fletcher, 1840).

Hook, Walter Farquhar, *The Nonentity of Romish Saints and the Inanity of Romish Ordinances* (London: John Murray, 1849).

Hulbert, Charles Augustus, *Theotokos: Or the Mother of Our Lord. A Sermon on the Song of the Blessed Virgin* (London: Henry Washbourne, 1842).

Inman, Thomas, *Foundation for a New Theory and Practice of Medicine*, 2nd ed. (London: John Churchill, 1861).

——, *Ancient Faiths Embodied in Ancient Names: Or an Attempt to Trace the Religious Belief, Sacred Rites, and Holy Emblems of Certain Nations by an Interpretation of the Names Given to Children by Priestly Authority, or Assumed by Prophets, Kings and Hierarchs* (London: Trübner, 1868).

——, *Ancient Pagan and Modern Christian Symbolism Exposed and Explained* (London: Thomas Inman, 1869).

——, *On the Restoration of Health; Being Essays on the Principles upon Which the Treatment of Many Diseases Is to Be Conducted*, 2nd ed. (Liverpool: H. K. Lewis, 1872).

——, *Ancient Pagan and Modern Christian Symbolism*, 2nd ed. (London: Trübner, 1875).

Ironside, Nestor, *Old England's Letter on Our State Church Provocation, or the Papal Aggression, Addressed to Young England at Oxford* (London: Effingham Wilson, 1850).

James, Henry, *Roderick Hudson* (Harmondsworth: Penguin, 1986).

Jarvis, Alan, *The Things We See: Indoors and Out* (Harmondsworth: Penguin Books, 1947).

Jebb, John, *The Principle of Ritualism Defended. A Sermon* [on Rev. 5: 11–12] (London: Rivingtons, 1856).

Jones, William, 'On the gods of Greece, Italy, and India', *Asiatick Researches* 1 (1801), pp. 221–75.

Kay, John, *Our Home Heathen! What Is to Be Done for Them? Who Is to Do It? How Is It to Be Done?* (London: Judd and Glass, 1857).

Keble, John, *On Eucharistical Adoration* (Oxford: John Henry and James Parker, 1857).

Kennaway, Charles E., 'The socialism of the early church', in W. Bennett (1850b), pp. 143–74.

Kennedy, Jane, *Sketches of Character. Julian; Or Reminiscences of Affection* (London: Charles Westerton, 1851).

Kerns, Thomas, *Analogia; Or, Brief Notes of Pagan Idolatry and the Church of Rome*, 2nd ed. (Sheffield: Ridge and Jackson, 1851).

Kidd, George Barrow, *The Idolatry of the Church of Rome Proved from Cardinal Wiseman's Third Lecture on the Catholic Hierarchy* (London: John Snow, 1851).

King, Bryan, *Sacrilege and Its Encouragement, Being an Account of the S. George's Riots and of Their Successes, in a Remonstrance to the Lord Bishop of London* (London: Joseph Masters, 1860).

———, *The S. George's Mission with the S. George's Riots and Their Results* (London: Rivingtons, 1877).

Kingsley, Charles, *Yeast: A Problem* ['reprinted, with corrections and additions, from *Fraser's Magazine*'] (London: W. J. Parker, 1851).

Knight, Richard Payne, *A Discourse on the Worship of Priapus, and Its Connection with the Mystic Theology of the Ancients…A New Edition. To Which Is Added an Essay* [by Thomas Wright and others] *on the Worship of the Generative Powers during the Middle Ages of Western Europe* (London: Chiswick Press, 1865).

Knox, John, *The Masses Without! A Pamphlet for the Times, on the Sanitary, Social, Moral, and Heathen Condition of the Masses Who Inhabit the Alleys, Courts, Wynds, Garrets, Cellars, Lodging-Houses, Dens and Hovels of Great Britain, with an Appeal for Open-Air Preaching, and Other Extraordinary Efforts to Reach the Perishing Masses of Society* (London: Judd and Glass, 1857).

Laurie, Peter, *Puseyism: Or, An Address to the Wesleyan Methodists* (London: G. Mansell, 1843).

Laurie, William Ferguson Beatson, *Orissa, the Garden of Superstition and Idolatry: Including an Account of British Connexion with the Temple of Jagannath: To Which are Added, Lighter Literary Recreations of a Critic Abroad* (London: Johnstone and Hunter, 1850).

Lea, Henry Charles, *An Historical Sketch of Sacerdotal Celibacy in the Christian Church* (Philadelphia: Lippincott, 1867).

Lee, Dr., 'Tractarianism: On Dr Pusey's late sermon', *The Pulpit* 44, Dec. 21 (1843), pp. 525–26.

Lee, Frederick George, *The Beauty of Holiness. Ten Lectures on External Religious Observances* (London: G. J. Palmer, 1860a).

———, *The S. George's Riots, a Plea for Justice and Toleration: A Letter to the Right Hon. W. E. Gladstone* (London: Joseph Masters. 1860b).

Legrew James, *A Few Remarks on the Sculpture of the Nations Referred to in the Old Testament, Deduced from an Examination of Some of Their Idols* (London: Whittaker and Co, 1845).

Liddell, Robert, *Matins, Litany, and Holy Communion-Three Distinct Offices, the Division of them Lawful and Expedient. A Sermon* [on Isaiah 51:3] (London: J. T. Hayes, 1852).

———, *A Pastoral Letter to the Parishioners of S. Paul's, Knightsbridge, and S. Barnabas', Pimlico* (London: J. T. Hayes, 1853).

———, *Christian Moderation. A Sermon Preached in the Fourth Sunday in Advent, 1855, in St. Paul's Church, Knightsbridge* (London: J. T. Hayes, 1856).

———, *The Commemorative Sacrifice of the Eucharist; A Profession of Our Faith to Be Held Fast without Waverings: A Sermon* [on Hebrews 10:23–24] (London: J. T. Hayes, 1857).

———, *A Letter to the Lord Bishop of London, on Confession and Absolution, with Special Reference to the Case of the Rev. Alfred Poole, with an Appendix Containing Mr. Poole's Appeal to His Grace the Archbishop of Canterbury* (London: J. T. Hayes, 1858a).

———, *A Pastoral Letter to the Parishioners of St. Paul's, Knightsbridge and St. Barnabas', Pimlico* (London: J. T. Hayes, 1858b).

———, *A Pastoral Letter to the Parishioners of St. Paul's Knightsbridge* (London: J. T. Hayes, 1881).

Littledale, Richard Frederick, *On the Application of Colour to the Decoration of Churches: A Paper Read before S. Patrick's Ecclesiological Society, April 8, 1856* (London: Joseph Masters, 1857).

———, *Catholic Ritual in the Church of England, Scriptural, Reasonable, Lawful*, 2nd ed. (London: G. Palmer, 1865).

———, *Early Christian Ritual, a Lecture, Read before the Guild of S. Alban the Martyr*, 2nd ed. (London: Charles Cull, 1866a).

———, 'The missionary aspect of ritualism', in Orby Shipley, ed., *The Church and the World: Essays on Questions of the Day by Various Writers* (London: Longmans Green, 1866b), pp. 25–50.

Lovett, William, *The Life and Struggles of William Lovett in His Pursuit of Bread, Knowledge and Freedom* (London: Trübner, 1876).

Lowe, T. H., *Auricular Confession: A Sermon Preached in the Cathedral Church of Exeter, Sunday November 7th, 1852*, 2nd ed. (Exeter: A. Holden, 1852).

Luke, Jemima, *The Female Jesuit: Or the Spy in the Family* (London: Partridge and Oakey, 1851).

———, *A Sequel to The Female Jesuit; Containing Her Previous History and Recent Discovery* (London: Partridge and Oakey, 1852).

Maccall, William, *The Idolatry of the Church of Rome* (London: T. K. Gorbell, 1851).

Macghee, Robert James, *The Church of Rome Proved Unable to Justify the Sacrifice of the Mass, or the Idolatry of the Wafer. A Lecture Delivered at Exeter Hall on Wednesday, April 20th 1853* (London: Arthur Hall, Virtue and Co., 1853).

Macintyre, J. J., *A Plan for the Military Seizure and Occupation of the Temple and City of Mecca, as Defensive and Offensive Measure for the War in Asia. With an Appendix of Remarks* (London: Charles Westerton, 1858).

Macneile, Hugh, *National Sin—What is It? A Letter to the Right Honorable Sir George Grey, Bart., M.P., Her Majesty's Secretary of State for the Home Department*, 3rd ed. (London: J. Hatchard and Son, 1849).

Maguire, Thomas, *Important Lecture in Answer to a Protestant, on Images and Relics, Delivered by the Rev. T. Maguire, on Good Friday Evening Last, in Adam and Eve Chapel* (Dublin: M'Mullen, 1840).

Martineau, Harriett, *Eastern Life, Past and Present (1848)*, in Deborah Logan, ed., *Harriet Martineau's Writing on the British Empire*, vols. 2 and 3 (London: Pickering and Chatto, 2004).

Marx, Karl, *Capital*, ed. David McLellan (Oxford: Oxford University Press, 1995).

Montalembert, Charles Forbes René de, *Letter to the Rev. Mr. Neale (a Member of the Cambridge Camden Society) on the Architectural, Artisitical and Archaeological Movements of the Puseyites* (London: J. Ringrose, 1844).

Montpincon, Allard, *My Crucifix, Or, Thoughts at a Prie-Dieu* (London: W. Knott, 1895).

Moore, Edmund F., *The Cases of Westerton against Liddell (Clerk), and Horne and others, St. Paul's, Knightsbridge and Beal against Liddell (Clerk), and Parke and Evans, St Barnabas, Pimlico': As Heard and Examined by the Consistory Court of London, the Arches Court of Canterbury and the Judicial Committee of Her Majesty's Most Honorable Privy Council* (London: Brown, Green, Longmans and Roberts, 1857).

Morgan, Lady Sydney, *Letter to Cardinal Wiseman in Answer to His 'Remarks on Lady Morgan's Statements Regarding St. Peter's Chair'*, 3rd ed. (London: Charles Westerton, 1851).

Moule, Henry, *Our Home Heathen: How Can the Church of England Get at Them?* (London: William Hunt and Co., 1868).

Muir, W. J. Cockburn, *Pagan or Christian? Or, Notes for the General Public on Our National Architecture* (London: Richard Bentley, 1860).

[Neale, J. M.], Cambridge Camden Society, *A Few Words to Church Builders* (Cambridge: Cambridge University Press, 1841).

[————], Cambridge Camden Society, *A Few Words to Churchwardens on Churches and Church Ornaments, II. Suited to Town and Manufacturing Parishes*, 5th ed. (Cambridge: Stevenson, 1842).

[————], Cambridge Camden Society, *A Few Words to Churchwardens on Churches and Church Ornaments, I. Suited to Country Parishes*, 13th ed. (Cambridge: Stevenson, 1843).

Neale, J. M., and R. F. Littledale, *A Commentary on the Psalms*, 3rd ed., 4 vols. (London: Joseph Masters, 1887).

Neale, J. M., and Benjamin Webb, 'Introductory essay', in William Durandus, *The Symbolism of Churches and Church Ornaments: A Translation of the First Book of the 'Rationale Divinorum Officiorum'*, trans. J. M. Neale and Benjamin Webb (Leeds: T. Green, 1843), pp. xvii–cxxvi.

Newland, Henry, *Increase in Romanism in England* (London: Joseph Masters, 1851).

Newman, John Henry, *Loss and Gain* (London: James Burns, 1848).

Newstead, Robert, *Notices Relative to the Idolatry and Devil-Worship of Ceylon, Designed to Impress upon the Minds of Youth a Concern for the Salvation of the Heathen* (London: J. Mason, 1838).

Nugée, George, *The Words from the Cross as Applied to Our Own Death-Beds: Being a Series of Lent Lectures Delivered at S. Paul's Knightsbridge, MDCCCLIII* (London: John Masters, 1856).

Paley, Thomas, *On the Church, the Great Power of God, Seen in the Faith and Patience of the Saints; Not in Successions, Forms, and Ceremonies. A Sermon* (Stamford: W. Langley, 1848).

Palmer, William, *'Origines Liturgicae' or Antiquities of English Ritual, and a Dissertation on Primitive Liturgies*, 3rd ed., 2 vols. (Oxford: Oxford University Press, 1839).

Paull, Mrs. Henry H. B., *The Means and the End; Or, The Chaplain's Secret. A Tale in Which Ritualism and Its Errors Are Traced to Their Source* (London: Houlston and Wright, 1867).

Peace, William, *The Confessional: A Fragment* (London: William Edward Painter, 1853).

Peacock, Edward, ed., *English Church Furniture, Ornaments and Decorations, at the Period of the Reformation* (London: John Camden Hotten, 1866).

Perceval, Arthur Philip, *On the Use of the Crucifix* (London: Privately printed, 1851).

Perry, Thomas Walter, *Lawful Church Ornaments: Being an Historical Examination of the Judgment of the Rt. Hon. S. Lushington, D.L.C., in the Case of Westerton v. Liddell, etc. and of 'Aids for Determining Some Disputed Points in the Ceremonial of the Church of England' by the Rev. W. Goode. With an Appendix on the Judgment of the Rt. Hon. Sir J. Dodson, D.C.L. in the Appeal Liddell v. Westerton* (London: Joseph Masters, 1857).

Peter, A., *A Brief Account of the Magdalen Chapel, Lower Leeson Street, Dublin* (Dublin: Hodges, Figgis and Co., 1907).

Phillpotts, Henry, *A Pastoral Letter to the Clergy of the Diocese of Exeter, on the Present State of the Church* (London: John Murray, 1851).

———, *Letter to the Right Hon. Dr. Lushington on His Judgment in the Case of Westerton v. Liddell (Clerk)* (London: John Murray, 1856).

Pike, Albert, *The Holy Triad AIN ... KL ... IH Jah: Baal-Peor, the Syrian Priapus: The City of Idolatry and Iniquity. A Reply to [Bland] the Grand Chaplain and [Chapman] Grand High Priest of the Grand Royal Arch Chapter of Massachusetts* [from *Mackeys National Freemason*] (Washington, DC: Office of Mackeys National Freemason, 1873).

Pollock, Alexander Matthew, *Idolatry, Ancient and Modern. A Lecture* (Dublin: George Herbert, 1858).

Poole, George Ayliffe, *The Anglo-Catholic Use of Two Lights upon the Altar, for the Signification that Christ Is the Very True Light of the World, Stated and Defended* (London: Burns, 1840).

Portal, G. R., *On Some of the Prevalent Objections to Ritual Observances. A Sermon Preached in S. Barnabas' Church, Pimlico, on the Second Sunday after Easter* (London: J. T. Hayes, 1854).

Poynder, John, *Popery in Alliance with Heathenism: Letters Proving That Where the Bible Is Wholly Unknown as in the Heathen World, or Only Partially Known as in the Romish Church, Idolatry and Superstition Are Inevitable*, 2nd ed. (London: J. Hatchard and Son, 1835).

———, *Speech at a General Court of Proprietors of the East India Company, on the 21st December, 1836, upon the Motion for Carrying into Effect the Letter of the Court of Directors of the 20th February, 1833, Which Ordered the Withdrawal of British Patronage and Support from the Worship and Service of Idolatry, and the Extinction of all Taxation Arising from the Superstitions of Heathenism* (London: Hatchard and Son, 1837).

Pugin, A. W. N., *Contrasts; Or, A Parallel between the Noble Edifices of the Fourteenth and Fifteenth Centuries, and Similar Buildings of the Present Day; Shewing the Present Decay of Taste: Accompanied by Appropriate Texts*, 2nd ed. (London: Charles Dolman, 1841a).

——, *The True Principles of Pointed or Christian Architecture: Set Forth in Two Lectures Delivered at St. Marie's, Oscott* (London: John Weale, 1841b).

——, *An Apology for the Revival of Christian Architecture in England* (London: John Weale, 1843a).

——, *The Present State of Ecclesiastical Architecture in England* (London: Charles Dolman, 1843b).

——, *Collected Letters*, vol. 2, *1843–1845*, ed. Margaret Belcher (Oxford: Oxford University Press, 2003).

Purchas, John, *'Directorium Anglicanum'; Being a Manual of Directions for the Right Celebration of the Holy Communion, for the Saying of Matins and Evensong, and for the Performance of Other Rights and Ceremonies of the Church, According to the Ancient Uses of the Church of England* (London: Joseph Masters, 1858).

Pusey, E. B., *The Danger of Riches: Seek God First and Ye Shall Have All: Two Sermons, Preached in the Parish Church of St. James, Bristol* (Oxford: Parker, 1850).

Rawlings, John, *A History of the Origin of the Mysteries and Doctrines of Baptism and the Eucharist, as Introduced into the Church of Rome and the Church of England; And Their Jewish and Heathen Origin Delineated in Profane and Ecclesiastical History* (London: Alfred W. Bennett, 1863).

Rich, Anthony, *The Legend of St Peter's Chair* (London: Charles Westerton, 1851).

Richards, W. Upton, 'The danger of riches' [sermon], in W. Bennett (1850bc), pp. 323–44.

Rivenall, William, *Crumbling Babylon, a Poem: in which Popery is Compared to Babylon, and Its Decline Described as Indicated in the Signs of the Times* (Stamford: 1848).

Robertson, Edward, *Idolatry, a Poem* (Edinburgh: Myles Macphail, 1849).

Robertson, J. E. P., *Stone Altar Case. The Judgment of the Rt. Hon. Sir Herbert Jenner Fust, KT. Dean of the Arches, in the Case of Faulkner v. Litchfield and Stearn, on the 31st January, 1845. Edited from the Judge's Notes* (London: William Bennning and Co., 1845).

Rock, Daniel, *'Hierurgia', or Transubstantiation, Invocation of Saints, Relics and Purgatory*, 2nd ed. (London: C. Dolman, 1851).

Rodriguez, E. A., *The Hindoo Pantheon* (Madras: Printed for the author at the Christian Knowledge Society's Press, 1841–45).

Ruskin, John, *The Seven Lamps of Architecture* (London: Smith, Elder and Co., 1849).

——, *Stones of Venice*, 3 vols. (London: Smith, Elder and Co., 1853).

——, *Notes on the Principal Pictures Exhibited in the Rooms of the Royal Academy, and the Society of Painters in Water Colours, II, 1856* (London: Smith, Elder and Co., 1856).

Russell, John, *The Jesuit in England; With the Horrors of the Inquisition* (London: Blayney and Fryer, 1858).

Russell, Lord John, *Lord John Russell's Letter to the Bishop of Durham on the Papal Aggression* (London: Charles Westerton, 1850).

Ryle, John Charles, 'Idolatry, a predicted sin of the visible Church, with its abolition at Christ's coming' [a lecture on Isaiah. 2: 18], in Edward Auriol, ed., *Popish Darkness and Millenial Light: Being Lectures Delivered During Lent, 1851, at St. George's Bloomsbury* (London: James Nisbet and Co., 1851), pp. 55–89.

Schimmelpenninck, Mary Anne, *The Principles of Beauty as Manifested in Nature, Art, and Human Character, with a Classification of Deformities. An Essay on the Temperaments, with Illustrations, and Thoughts on Grecian and Gothic Architecture*, ed. Christiana C. Hankin (London: Longman, Brown, Green, Longmans and Roberts, 1859).

Sellon, Commander, *Miss Sellon and the Sisters of Mercy*, 2nd ed. (London: Joseph Masters, 1852).

Seymour, Michael Hobart, *Popery in Ireland: A Letter to the Lord Bishop of London* (London: L. and J. Seeley, 1835).

———, *The Speech of the Rev. M. Hobart Seymour, at the Ninth Annual Meeting of the Society for Promoting the Religious Principles of the Reformation, at Exeter Hall, May 13, 1836* (London: C. Norman, 1836).

———, 'Novelty of the peculiar doctrines of the Church of Rome', in Anon., ed., *The Errors of Romanism: Six Lectures on the Errors of the Church of Rome, Delivered in Sir George Wheeler's Chapel, Near Spital Square, London, on the Wednesday Evenings of Lent, 1838* (London: Francis Baisler, 1838), pp. 97–114.

———, 'The English Communion contrasted with the Roman Mass, Preached by Rev. M. Hobart Seymour, St George's Church, Southwark, Sunday eve Nov 5th, 1843', *The Pulpit* 44, Nov. 9 (1843), pp. 375–83.

———, *A Pilgrimage to Rome: Containing Some Account of the High Ceremonies, the Monastic Institutions, the Religious Services, the Sacred Relics, the Miraculous Pictures and the General State of Religion in That City* (London: Seeleys, 1848).

———, *The Nature of Romanism, as Exhibited in the Missions of the Jesuits and Other Orders. A Lecture Delivered before the Young Men's Christian Association, in Exeter Hall* (London: James Nisbet and Co., 1849a).

———, *Romanism in Rome in the Nineteenth Century. A Lecture, Delivered before the Islington Protestant Institute* (London: Islington Protestant Institute, 1849b).

———, *Mornings among the Jesuits at Rome*, 3rd 'considerably enlarged' ed. (London: Seeleys, 1850).

———, *Moral Result of the Romish System* (London: Seeleys, 1854).

———, *The Jubilee at Rome: A Lecture Delivered at the Assembly Rooms, Bath, April, 16th, 1866* (Bath: R. E. Peach, 1866).

———, *No Peace with Rome. A Lecture, at St. James' Hall, Piccadilly, March 19, 1867*, Church Association Lectures 5 (London: William Macintosh, 1867).

———, *My Experience in the Church of Ireland: A Letter to the Earl of Derby* (London: Seeley, Jackson and Halliday, 1868).

———, *The Church and the Land of Ireland. A Lecture Delivered in the Assembly Rooms, Bath* (London: Simpkin, Marshall and Co., 1869).

———, *The Confessional: An Appeal to the Primitive and Catholic Forms of Absolution, in the East and in the West* (London: Seeley, Jackson and Halliday, 1870).

————, *The Bishop and the Rector. A Defence of the Charge of the Lord Bishop of Bath and Wells, in Reply to the Strictures of Rev. W. J. E. Bennett* (London: Simpkin, Marshall and Co., 1874).

Shout, J. T., *Case in Reference to a Late Event in the Parish of St. Paul, Knightsbridge; Illustrative of the Doctrine Contained in a Sermon Preached There by the Rev. W. J. E. Bennett* (London: J. T. Shout, 1851).

Skinner, James, *Three Suggestive Discourses* (London: J. T. Hayes, 1856a).

————, *Why Do We Praise Externals in the Service of God? Or, The Ministry of the Church Preparing Christ's Way by All Means* (London: J. T. Hayes, 1856b).

————, *Fleshly Sins: A Sermon* (London: Cleaver, 1857).

————, *Letter from the Rev. James Skinner, M. A., to the Rev. Henry Montagu Villiers, M. A. on His Appointment to the Vicarage of St. Paul's, Knightsbridge* (London: Masters and Co., 1881).

Smith, John, *The Missionary's Appeal to British Christians, on Behalf of Southern India; Comprising Topographical Descriptions of the Madras Presidency; Notices of the Moral Statistics of Its Provinces; Observations on the Character and Condition of Its Population; And Arguments in Favour of Augmented Effort for Its Evangelisation* (London: Hamilton, Adams and Co., 1841).

Spencer, W., *Papal Aggressions Aided and Encouraged by Tractarian Movements: A Sermon Preached in Princess-Street Chapel, Devonport, on the Lord's Day Evening, November 24th, 1850* (Devonport: J. Heydon, 1850).

Stone, L. A., *The Story of Phallicism with Other Essays on Related Subjects by Eminent Authorities*, 2 vols. (Chicago: Pascal Covici, 1927).

Strachey, Lytton, *Eminent Victorians* (London: Chatto and Windus, 1918).

Taylor, John James, *Two Lectures; Being the Introduction to a Course on the Early History of Christianity* (London: E. T. Whitfield, 1857).

Taylor, Robert, *The Diegesis; Being a Discovery of the Origin, Evidences, and Early History of Christianity, Never Yet before or Elsewhere So Fully and Faithfully Set Forth* (London: Richard Carlisle, 1829).

————, *Pagan and Popish Priestcraft Identified and Exposed and Popery Proved to Be Satan's Systemized Opposition to the Work of Redemption* (London: Hatchard and Son, 1847).

Tennent, James Emerson, *Christianity in Ceylon; Its Introduction and Progress under the Portuguese, the Dutch, the British and American Missions: With an Historical Sketch of the Brahmanical and Buddhist Superstitions* (London: John Murray, 1850).

————, 'The crucifix as used by early Christians', *Notes and Queries* 4.112, Dec. 20 (1851), pp. 485–86.

Tomkins, Samuel, *The Influence of the Hebrew and Christian Revelations on Ancient Heathen Writers. An Essay Which Obtained the Hulsean Prize for 1849* (Cambridge: J. Deighton and E. Johnson, 1850).

Tomlinson, John, *Queen Elizabeth's Crucifix: Its Secret History and Real Meaning Shown from Contemporary Documents* (London: Church Association, n.d.).

Trower, Charles Francis, *A Review of the Judgment of the Rt. Hon. Sir John Dodson, Knt., D.C.L. Delivered in the Arches Court of Canterbury on December 20th, 1856, in the Case of Liddell v. Westerton, Considered with Especial Reference to the Legality of Crosses as Church Ornaments* (London: J. T. Hayes, 1857).

Turnley, Joseph, *Popery in Power, or the Spirit of the Vatican: To Which Is Added, Priestcraft, or the Monarch of the Middle Ages; A Drama* (London: Effingham Wilson, 1850).

Tweedie, W. K., *Lectures on Popery: The Jesuits* (Edinburgh: Johnson and Hunter, 1851).

Ward, Henry Dana, *History of the Cross: The Pagan Origin, and Idolatrous Adoption and Worship of the Image* (London: James Nisbet and Co., 1871).

Weaver, Robert, *The Pagan Altar and Jehovah's Temple. An Essay to Excite Renewed Interest in Public Worship* (London: Thomas Ward and Co., 1840).

Wells, Edward, *The Rich Man's Duty to Contribute Liberally to the Building, Rebuilding, Repairing, Beautifying and Adorning of Churches*, with a preface by John Henry Newman (Oxford: John Henry Parker, 1840).

Westerton, Charles, *A Catalogue of the Books in Westerton's English and Foreign Library Near Albert Gate, Knightsbridge*, in 2 parts (London: Charles Westerton, 1849).

————, *A Letter to the Right Reverend the Lord Bishop of London, on the Popish Manner in which, Contrary to the Rubrics, Divine Service Is Performed on Sunday Mornings at the Parish Church of St. Paul's, Wilton Place, Knightsbridge. By One of the Churchwardens* (London: Charles Westerton, 1853).

————, *A Remonstrance Contained in a Letter to the Hon. and Rev, Robert Liddell on the Popish Practices Used in the Said Church: To Which Is Added Mr. Liddell's Reply* (London: Charles Westerton, 1854).

————, ed., *The Holy Flower Show in Belgravia, Or, Puseyism at a Discount. The Bishop of Oxford's Reception in Belgravia. The Perilous Crisis-Jesuits in the Church of England. Puseyism in a Fog. The Great Candle Question. Being a series of reprints of articles, etc.* (London: Charles Westerton, 1857).

————, *Emily Morton, a Tale; With Sketches from Life and Critical Essays* (London: Charles Westerton, 1859).

White, William, *Is Symbolism Suited to the Spirit of the Age?* (London: Thomas Bosworth, 1854).

Wilson, William Carus, *Correspondence with a Jesuit, on the Subject of Mariolatry* (London: Seeley, Jackson and Halliday, 1856).

Winslow, Octavius, *The Inquirer Directed to an Experimental and Practical View of the Work of the Holy Spirit,* (London: John F. Shaw, 1840).

Wiseman, Nicholas, *Letters to John Poynder, Esq., upon His Work Entitled 'Popery in Alliance with Heathenism'* (London: Joseph Booker, 1836).

————, *An Appeal to the Reason and Good Feeling of the English People on the Subject of the Catholic Hierarchy* (London: Thomas Richardson, 1850a).

————, *The Social and Intellectual State of England, Compared with Its Moral Condition: A Sermon Delivered in St. John's Catholic Church, Salford, on Sunday, July 28th, 1850* (London: Thomas Richardson and Son, 1850b).

————, *Three Lectures on the Catholic Hierarchy* (London: Richardson and Son, 1850c).

————, *The Highways of Peaceful Commerce Have Been the Highways of Art. An Address Delivered at Liverpool, on Tuesday, August 30, 1853, on Occasion of the Opening of the Catholic Institute* (Liverpool: Rockliff and Son, 1853).

———, *On the Influence of Words on Thought and on Civilisation. A Lecture Delivered at the Marylebone Institution, Wednesday, April 22nd, 1856* (London: Richardson and Son, 1856a).

———, *On the Perception of Natural Beauty by the Ancients and Moderns. Rome, Ancient and Modern. Two Lectures* (London: Burns and Lambert, 1856b).

Wood, Thomas, *The Origin, Learning, Religion, and Customs of the Ancient Britons: With an Account of the Introduction of Christianity into Britain, and the Idolatry and Conversion of the Saxons; Remarks on the Errors and Progress of Popery; Considerations on the Christian Church, Its Foundation, Superstructure, and Beauty* (London: William Brown, 1846).

Wordsworth, Christopher, *Is the Pope of Rome the Man of Sin? A Sermon Preached in Westminster Abbey* (London: Francis and John Rivington, 1851).

Wreford, Henry, *Rome, Pagan and Papal; By an English Resident in that City* (London: Hamilton, Adams, and Co., 1846).

Secondary Sources

Ahiska, Meltem, 'Occidentalism: The historical fantasy of the modern', *South Atlantic Quarterly* 102 (2003), pp. 351–79.

Aldrich, Megan, *Gothic Revival* (London: Phaidon, 1994).

———, 'Gothic sensibility: The early years of the Gothic Revival', in Atterbury (1995), pp. 13–30.

Altick, Richard A., 'English publishing and the mass audience in 1852', *Studies in Bibliography* 6 (1954), pp. 3–24.

Anderson, Amanda, *Tainted Souls and Painted Faces: The Rhetoric of Fallenness in Victorian Culture* (Ithaca: Cornell University Press, 1993).

Anderson, Warwick, 'Excremental colonialism: Public health and the poetics of pollution', *Critical Inquiry* 21 (1995), pp. 640–69.

Anson, Peter F., *The Call of the Cloister: Religious Communities and Kindred Bodies in the Anglican Communion* (London: S.P.C.K, 1955).

———, *Building up the Waste Places: The Revival of Monastic Life on Medieval Lines in the Post-Reformation Church of England* (Leighton Buzzard: Faith Press, 1973).

Appadurai, Arjun, 'Introduction: Commodities and the politics of value', in Appadurai, *The Social Life of Things: Commodities in Cultural Perspective* (Cambridge: Cambridge University Press, 1986), pp. 3–63.

Arnstein, Walter L., *Protestant versus Catholic in Mid-Victorian England: Mr. Newdegate and the Nuns* (Columbia: University of Missouri Press, 1982).

Aston, Margaret, 'Cross and Crucifix in the English Reformation', in Peter Blickle et al., eds., *Macht und Ohnmacht der Bilder. Reformatorischer Bildersturm im Kontext der europäischen Geschichte* (Munich: R. Oldenburg, 2002), pp. 253–272.

Atterbury, Paul, ed., *A. W. N. Pugin: Master of Gothic Revival* (New Haven: Yale University Press, 1995).

Barnett, S. J., *The Enlightenment and Religion: The Myths of Modernity* (Manchester: Manchester University Press, 2003).

Bearce, George D., *British Attitudes towards India, 1784–1858* (London: Oxford University Press, 1961).

Bendiner, Kenneth, *The Art of Ford Madox Brown* (University Park: Pennsylvania University Press, 1998).

Benedict, B. M. ed., *Eighteenth Century British Erotica*, vol. 2 (London: Pickering and Chatto, 2002), p. 269

Benson, E. F., *Secret Lives* (London: Hogarth Press, 1985).

Bentley, James, *Ritualism and Politics in Victorian Britain: The Attempt to Legislate for Belief* (Oxford: Oxford University Press, 1978).

Bernstein, Susan David, 'Dirty reading: Sensation fiction, women and primitivism', *Criticism* 36 (1994), pp. 213–41.

Billig, Michael, 'Commodity fetishism and repression: Reflections on Marx, Freud and the psychology of consumer capitalism', *Theory and Psychology* 9 (1999), pp. 313–29.

Bocock, Robert, *Ritual in Industrial Society: A Sociological Analysis of Ritualism in Modern England* (London: George Allen and Unwin, 1974).

Bossche, Chris Vanden, 'The value of literature: Representations of print culture in the copyright debate of 1837–1842', *Victorian Studies* 38 (1994), pp. 41–68.

Botting, F., *Gothic* (London: Routledge, 1996).

——, 'In gothic darkly: Heterotopia, history, culture', in David Punter, ed., *A Companion to the Gothic* (Oxford: Blackwell, 2000), pp. 3–14.

Boudewijnse, Barbara, 'British roots of the concept of ritual', in Molendijk and Pels (1998), pp. 277–96.

Bowen, Desmond, *The Protestant Crusade in Ireland, 1800–70: A Study of Protestant-Catholic Relations between the Act of Union and Disestablishment* (Dublin: Gill and Macmillan, 1978).

Brandwood, Geoffrey K., '"Mummeries of a Popish character": The Camdenians and early Victorian worship', in Webster and Elliot (2000), pp. 62–97.

Brewer, John, Neil McKendrick, and J. H. Plumb, *Birth of a Consumer Society* (Bloomington: Indiana University Press, 1982).

Briggs, Asa, *Victorian Things* (London: Batsford, 1988).

Brooks, Chris, *The Gothic Revival* (London: Phaidon, 1999).

Brown, Lucy, *Victorian News and Newspapers* (Oxford: Clarendon Press, 1985).

Buc, Philippe, *The Dangers of Ritual: Between Early Medieval Texts and Social Scientific Theory* (Princeton: Princeton University Press, 2001).

Buchli, Victor, ed., *The Material Culture Reader* (Oxford: Berg, 2002).

Burke, Peter, *Eyewitnessing: The Uses of Images as Historical Evidence* (London: Reaktion Books, 2001).

Byrne, Peter, 'The foundation of the study of religion in the British context', in Molendijk and Pels (1998), pp. 45–66.

Callaway, Helen, 'Purity and exotica in legitimating the empire: Cultural constructions of gender, sexuality and race', in Terence Ranger and Olufemi Vaughan, eds., *Legitimacy and the State in Twentieth-Century Africa: Essays in Honour of A. H. M. Kirk-Greene* (Basingstoke: Macmillan, 1993), pp. 31–61.

Cannadine, David, *Ornamentalism: How the British Saw Their Empire* (London: Allen Lane, 2001).

Canning, Kathleen, 'The body as method? Reflections on the place of the body in gender history', *Gender and History* 11 (1999), pp. 499–513.

Carabelli, G., *M560–4: Gli ex voto di Isernia al British Museum*, Annali dell'Università di Ferrara, Nuova Serie, Sezione III, Filosophia, Discussion Paper 35 (Ferrara: Università degli studi di Ferrara, 1994).

———, *In the Image of Priapus* (London: Duckworth, 1996a).

———, *Veneri e Priapi: Culti di fertilità e mitologie falliche tra Napoli e Londra nell'età dell 'Illuminismo*, Mnemosyne 9 (Lecce: Argo, 1996b).

Carrette, Jeremy R., *Foucault and Religion: Spiritual Corporality and Political Spirituality* (London: Routledge, 2000).

Carter, Grayson, *English Evangelicals: Protestant Successions from the 'Via Media', c.1800–1850* (Oxford: Oxford University Press, 2001).

Chadwick, Owen, *The Victorian Church*, 2 vols., 3rd ed., An Ecclesiastical History of England 7 (London: Adam and Charles Black, 1971).

Champion, Timothy, 'The appropriation of the Phoenicians in British imperial ideology', *Nations and Nationalism* 7 (2001), pp. 451–65.

Chandler, Alice, *A Dream of Order: The Medieval Ideal in Nineteenth-Century English Literature* (London: Routledge and Kegan Paul, 1971).

Chandler, Michael, *The Life and Work of John Mason Neale 1818–1866* (Leominster: Gracewing, 1995).

Chapman, Raymond, 'Last enchantments: Medievalism and the early Anglo-Catholic movement', *Studies in Medievalism* 4 (1992), pp. 170–86.

Christodoulou, Joan, 'The Glasgow Universalist Church and Scottish radicalism from the French Revolution to Chartism: A theology of liberation', *Journal of Ecclesiastical History* 43 (1992), pp.608–23.

Clark, Kenneth, *Civilisation: A Personal View* (London: BBC and John Murray, 1969).

Clifford, Brendan, *'Blasphemous Reason': The 1797 Trial of Tom Paine's 'Age of Reason'* (London: Bevin Books, 1993).

Cocks, H. G., 'Religion and spirituality', in Cocks and Houlbrook(2006), pp. 157–79.

Cocks, H. C. and Matt Houlbrook, eds., *Palgrave Advances in the Modern History of Sexuality* (Basingstoke: Palgrave Macmillan, 2006).

Coldstream, Nicola, 'The middle pointed revival: A medievalist's view', in F. Salmon, ed., *Gothic and the Gothic Revival* (Manchester: Manchester University Press, 1998).

Copley, Antony, *Religions in Conflict: Ideology, Cultural Contact and Conversion in Late Colonial India* (Delhi: Oxford University Press, 1997).

Cowl, Ruth, '"London, Brighton and South Coast Religion"?: Tractarianism and Ritualism in Brighton, Hove and Worthing', University of Keele, Ph.D. (1996).

Cowling, Mary, *The Artist as Anthropologist: The Representation of Type and Character in Victorian Art* (Cambridge: Cambridge University Press, 1989).

Cox, Jeffrey, 'Were Victorian nonconformists the worst imperialists of all?' *Victorian Studies* 46 (2004), pp. 243–55.

Cunliffe, Marcus, 'America at the Great Exhibition of 1851', *American Quarterly* 3 (1951), pp. 115–26.

Curl, James Stevens, *Victorian Architecture* (Newton Abbot: David and Charles, 1990).

Curtis, Gerard, 'Ford Madox Brown's "Work": An iconographic analysis', *Art Bulletin* 74 (1992), pp. 623–36.

Daily, D., *Enlightenment Deism: The Foremost Threat to Christianity and the Role That It Has Played in American Protestantism* (Pittsburgh: Dorrance, 1999).

Daly, Nicholas, 'That obscure object of desire: Victorian commodity culture and fictions and the mummy', *Novel: A Forum on Fiction* 28 (1994), pp. 24–51.

Danahay, Martin A., *Gender at Work in Victorian Culture: Leisure, Art and Masculinity* (Aldershot: Ashgate, 2005).

Davidson, E. H., and W. J. Scheick, *Paine, Scripture, and Authority: 'The Age of Reason' as Religious and Political Idea* (Bethlehem: Lehigh University Press, 1994).

De Grazia, Victoria, and Ellen Furlough, 'Introduction', in De Grazia and Furlough, eds., *The Sex of Things: Gender and Consumption in Historical Perspective* (Berkeley: University of California Press, 1996), pp. 1–10.

De Gruchy, John W., *Christianity, Art and Transformation: Theological Aesthetics in the Struggle for Justice* (Cambridge: Cambridge University Press, 2001).

Denby, David, 'Passion of the Christ' [review], *New Yorker*, March (2004), http://www.newyorker.com/critics/cinema/?040301crci_cinema, accessed November 21, 2005.

Dhall, Manjusri, *The British Rule: Missionary Activities in Orissa (1822–1947)* (New Delhi: Har-Anand, 1997).

Diamond, Michael, *Victorian Sensation: Or, The Spectacular, the Shocking and the Scandalous in Nineteenth-Century Britain* (London: Anthem Press, 2003).

Dolar, Mladen, 'Introduction: The subject supposed to enjoy', in Grosrichard (1998), pp. ix–xxvii.

Douglas, Mary, *Purity and Danger: An Analysis of Concepts of Pollution and Taboo*, Ark reprint ed. (London: Routledge, 1984).

Douglas, Mary, and Baron Isherwood, *The World of Goods: Towards an Anthropology of Consumption*, new ed. (London: Routledge, 1996).

Douglas, Tom, *Scapegoats: Transferring Blame* (London: Routledge, 1995).

Droit, Roger-Pol, *The Cult of Nothingness: The Philosophers and the Buddha*, trans. David Streight and Pamela Vohson (Chapel Hill, NC: UNC Press, 2003).

Drury, Marjule Anne, 'Anti-Catholicism in Germany, Britain and the United States: A review and critique of recent scholarship', *Church History: Studies in Christianity and Culture* 70 (2001), pp. 98–131.

Dupuis, Charles, *Origine de tous les cultes, ou religion universelle*, 7 vols. (Paris, 1794).

Eisenman, Stephen F. et al., *Nineteenth Century Art: A Critical History* (London: Thames and Hudson, 1994).

Ellis, Markman, *The History of Gothic Fiction* (Edinburgh: Edinburgh University Press, 2000).

Ellison, Robert H., *The Victorian Pulpit: Spoken and Written Sermons in Nineteenth-Century Britain* (Selinsgrove: Susquehanna University Press, 1998).

Ellison, Robert H., and Carole Marie Engelhardt, 'Prophecy and anti-popery in Victorian London: John Cumming reconsidered', *Victorian Literature and Culture* 31 (2003), pp. 373–89.

Ellsworth, L. E., *Charles Lowder and the Ritualist Movement* (London: Darton, Longman and Todd, 1982).

Englander, David, 'The word and the world: Evangelicalism in the Victorian city', in Parsons (1988b), pp. 14–37.

Evans, Eric J., 'The church in danger? Anticlericalism in nineteenth-century England', *European Studies Review* 13 (1983), pp. 177–200.

Fessenden, Tracy, 'The convent, the brothel and the Protestant woman's sphere', *Signs: Journal of Women in Culture and Society* 25 (2000), pp. 451–78.

Finn, Margot, 'Sex and the city: Metropolitan modernities in English history', *Victorian Studies* 44 (2001), pp. 25–34.

Flint, Valerie, *The Victorians and the Visual Imagination* (Cambridge: Cambridge University Press, 2000).

Foucault, Michel, *The History of Sexuality*, vol. 1, *An Introduction*, trans. Robert Hurley (London: Allen Lane, 1979).

Fraser, Hilary, *Beauty and Belief: Aesthetics and Religion in Victorian Literature* (Cambridge: Cambridge University Press, 1986).

Freedman, Jonathon, *Professions of Taste: Henry James, British Aestheticism and Commodity Culture* (Stanford: Stanford University Press, 1990).

Freud, Sigmund, 'Fetishism', in James Stratchey, ed., *The Standard Edition of the Complete Psychological Works of Sigmund Freud*, vol. 21 (London: Hogarth Press, 1961), pp. 149–57.

Gaimster, David, 'Sex and sensibility', *History Today* 50.9 (2000), pp. 10–18.

Gallagher, C., *The Body Economic: Life, Death, and Sensation in Political Economy and the Victorian Novel* (Princeton: Princeton University Press, 2006).

Gay, Peter, *The Cultivation of Hatred* (London: Fontana, 1995).

Gilman, Sander L., *Health and Illness: Images of Difference* (London: Reaktion Books, 1995).

Girard, René, *The Scapegoat*, trans. Yvonne Freccero (London: Athlone Press, 1986).

Gould, Harold A., *The Hindu Caste System: The Sacralization of a Social Order* (Delhi: Chanakya Publications, 1987).

Graber, Gary W., *Ritual Legislation in the Victorian Church of England: Antecedents and Passage of the Public Worship Regulation Act, 1874* (Lewiston: Mellon Research University Press, 1993).

Graeber, David, 'Fetishism as social creativity: Or, fetishes are gods in the process of construction', *Anthropological Theory* 5 (2005), pp. 407–39.

Grassby, Richard, 'Material culture and cultural history', *Journal of Interdisciplinary History* 35 (2005), pp. 591–603.

Greeley, Andrew M., *The Catholic Imagination* (Berkeley: University of California Press, 2000).

Green, Vivien M., 'Hiram Powers' *Greek Slave*: Emblem of freedom', *American Art Journal* 14 (1982), pp. 31–39.

Griest, Guinevere L., 'A Victorian leviathan: Mudie's Select Library', *Nineteenth-Century Fiction* 20 (1965), pp. 103–26.

Grosrichard, Alain, *Structure du sérail: La fiction du despotisme asiatique dans l'Occident classique* (Paris: Éditions du Seuil, 1979).

———, *The Sultan's Court: European Fantasies of the East*, trans. Liz Heron (London: Verso, 1998).

Gunn, Simon, 'The public sphere, modernity and consumption: New perspectives on the history of the English middle class', in Alan Kidd and David Nicholls, eds., *Gender, Civic Culture and Consumerism: Middle-Class Identity in Britain, 1800–1940* (Manchester: Manchester University Press, 1999), pp. 12–29.

Hacking, Ian, 'Making up people', *London Review of Books*, Aug. 17 (2006), pp. 23–26.

Hall, Michael, 'Introduction', in Hall, ed., *Gothic Architecture and Its Meanings, 1550–1830* (Reading: Spire Books, 2002), pp. 7–26.

Härdelin, A., *The Tractarian Understanding of the Eucharist* (Uppsala: Almquist and Wiksells, 1965).

Haskell, F., 'The Baron d'Hancarville: An adventurer and art historian in eighteenth-century Europe', in E. Chaney and N. Ritchie, eds., *Oxford, China and Italy: Writings in Honour of Sir Harold Action on His Eightieth Birthday* (London: Thames and Hudson, 1984), pp. 177–92.

Haskins, Susan, *Mary Magdalen* (London: Harper Collins, 1993).

Hawkes, David, *Idols of the Marketplace: Idolatry and Commodity Fetishism in English Literature, 1580–1680* (London: Palgrave, 2001).

Heimann, Mary, *Catholic Devotion in Victorian England* (Oxford: Clarendon Press, 1995).

Herbert, Christopher, *Culture and Anomie: Ethnographic Imagination in the Nineteenth Century* (Chicago: Chicago University Press, 1991).

———, 'Filthy lucre: Victorian ideas of money', *Victorian Studies* 44 (2002), pp. 185–213.

Herring, George William, 'Tractarianism to Ritualism: A Study of Some Aspects of Tractarianism Outside Oxford, From the Time of Newman's Conversion in 1845, Until the First Ritual Commission in 1867', University of Oxford, D.Phil. (1984).

Hill, Rosemary, '"The ivi'd ruins of fallen Grace Dieu": Catholics, Romantics and the late Georgian Gothic', in Michael Hall, ed., *Gothic Architecture and Its Meanings, 1550–1830* (Reading: Spire Books, 2002), pp. 159–84.

———, *God's Architect: Pugin and the Building of Romantic Britain* (London: Allen Lane, 2007).

Hilliard, David, 'Un-English and unmanly: Anglo-Catholicism and homosexuality', *Victorian Studies* 25 (1982), pp. 181–210.

Hilton, Boyd, *The Age of Atonement: The Influence of Evangelicalism on Social and Economic Thought, 1795–1865* (Oxford: Clarendon Press, 1988).

———, *A Mad, Bad and Dangerous People? England 1783–1846* (Oxford: Oxford University Press, 2006).

Hobson, Janell, *Venus in the Dark: Blackness and Beauty in Popular Culture* (London: Routledge, 2005).

Hoppen, K. Theodore, *The Mid-Victorian Generation, 1846–1886* (Oxford: Oxford University Press, 1998).

Janes, Dominic, *God and Gold in Late Antiquity* (Cambridge: Cambridge University Press, 1998).

———, 'Sex and text: The afterlife of medieval penance in Britain and Ireland', in April Harper and Caroline Proctor, eds., *Medieval Sexuality: A Casebook* (New York: Routledge, 2007a), pp. 32–44.

———, 'Spiritual cleaning, priests and prostitutes', in Rosie Cox and Ben Campkin, eds., *Dirt: New Geographies of Cleanliness and Contamination* (London: IB Tauris, 2007b), pp. 113–22.

———, 'Rites of man: The British Museum and the sexual imagination in Victorian Britain', *Journal of the History of Collections* 20 (2008a), pp. 101–112.

———. 'The shadow of the Passion: Protestants and the suffering Christ in nineteenth-century British art and text', *Ikon* 1 (2008b), pp. 237–44.

———, 'Seeing and tasting the divine: Simeon Solomon's homoerotic sacrament', in Patrizia di Bello and Gabriel Koureas, eds., *History and the Senses 1830 to the Present* (forthcoming).

Kantorowicz, Ernst H., *The King's Two Bodies: A Study in Medieval Political Theology* (Princeton: Princeton University Press, 1957).

Kasson, Joy S., 'Mind in matter in history: Viewing *The Greek Slave*', *Yale Journal of Criticism* 11 (1998), pp. 79–83.

Kearney, Richard, *Strangers, Gods and Monsters: Interpreting Otherness* (London: Routledge, 2002).

Kee, Alistair, *Constantine versus Christ: The Triumph of Ideology* (London: SCM Press, 1982).

Kendrick, W., *The Secret Museum: Pornography in Modern Culture*, edition with new afterword (Berkeley: University of California Press, 1996).

Kieschnick, John, *The Impact of Buddhism on Chinese Material Culture* (Princeton: Princeton University Press, 2003).

King, Richard, 'Orientalism and the modern myth of "Hinduism"', *Numen* 46 (1999a), pp. 146–85.

———, *Orientalism and Religion: Postcolonial Theory, India and 'the Mystic East'* (London: Routledge, 1999b).

Klaus, Robert J., *The Pope, the Protestants, and the Irish: Papal Aggression and Anti-Catholicism in Mid-Nineteenth-Century England* (New York: Garland, 1987).

Knight, Frances, *The Nineteenth-Century Church and English Society* (Cambridge: Cambridge University Press, 1995).

Kollar, R., 'Two lectures at Bath: The Rev. M. Hobart Seymour and Cardinal Nicholas Wiseman and the nunnery question', *Revue d'histoire ecclesiastique* 96 (2001), pp. 372–90.

Krips, Henry, *Fetish: An Erotics of Culture* (Ithaca: Cornell University Press, 1999).

Kristeva, Julia, *Powers of Horror: An Essay on Abjection*, trans. L. S. Roudiez (New York: Columbia University Press, 1982).

Kulakkatt, Augustine J., *Trade, Politics and Religion: The Religious Policy of the English East India Company (1757–1857) with Special Reference to Travancore* (Bangalore: Dharmaram Publications, 2002).

Landow, George P., 'William Holman Hunt's "The Shadow of Death"', *Bulletin of the John Rylands University Library of Manchester* 55 (1972), pp. 197–239.

———, *William Holman Hunt and Typological Symbolism* (New Haven: Yale University Press, 1979).

Larkin, E., *Thomas Paine and the Literature of Revolution* (Cambridge: Cambridge University Press, 2005).

Larsen, T., *Contested Christianity: The Political and Social Contexts of Victorian Theology* (Waco: Baylor University Press, 2004).

Lentin, A., 'Anglicanism, Parliament and the courts', in Parsons (1988b), pp. 88–105.

Leonard, S., 'Pornography and obscenity', in Cocks and Houlbrook (2006), pp. 180–205.

Leoshko, Janice, *Sacred Traces: British Explorations of Buddhism in South Asia* (Aldershot: Ashgate, 2003).

Lewis, Michael J., *The Gothic Revival* (London: Thames and Hudson, 2002).

Logan, Peter Melville, 'Fetishism and freedom in Matthew Arnold's cultural theory', *Victorian Literature and Culture* 31 (2003), pp. 555–74.

Maas, Jeremy, *Holman Hunt and the Light of the World* (London: Scolar, 1984).

Machin, G. I. T., *Politics and the Churches in Great Britain 1832–1868* (Oxford: Oxford University Press, 1977).

Maison, Margaret M., *Search Your Soul, Eustace: A Survey of the Religious Novel in the Victorian Age* (London: Sheed and Ward, 1961).

Marotti, Arthur F., *Religious Ideology and Cultural Fantasy: Catholic and Anti-Catholic Discourses in Early Modern England* (Notre Dame: University of Notre Dame Press, 2005).

Mason, Michael, *The Making of Victorian Sexual Attitudes* (Oxford: Oxford University Press, 1994).

Masuzawa, Tomoko, 'Troubles with materiality: The ghost of fetishism in the nineteenth century', *Comparative Studies in Society and History* 42 (2000), pp. 242–67.

Matless, David, *Landscape and Englishness* (London: Reaktion Books, 1998).

Mays, Kelly J., 'The publishing world', in Partick Brantlinger and W. B. Thesing, eds., *The Blackwell Companion to the Victorian Novel* (Oxford: Blackwell, 2002), pp. 11–30.

McCalman, Iain, *Radical Underworld: Prophets, Revolutionaries and Pornographers in London, 1795–1840* (Cambridge: Cambridge University Press, 1988).

McClintock, Anne, *Imperial Leather: Race, Gender and Sexuality in the Colonial Contest* (London: Routledge, 1995).

McIlhiney, David B., *A Gentleman in Every Slum: Church of England Missions in East London 1837–1914*, Princeton Theological Monograph Series 16 (Allison Park: Pickwick Publications, 1988).

McLellan, David, 'Introduction', in Marx (1995), pp. xiii–xxvii.

McNees, Eleanor, '*Punch* and the Pope: Three decades of anti-Catholic caricature', *Victorian Periodicals Review* 37 (2004), pp. 18–45.

Meara, David, 'The Catholic context', in Atterbury (1995), pp. 45–62.

Metcalf, Thomas R., *Ideologies of the Raj*, New Cambridge History of India 3.4 (Cambridge: Cambridge University Press, 1994).

Mighall, Robert, 'Vampires and Victorians: Count Dracula and the return of the repressive hypothesis', in Gary Day, ed., *Varieties of Victorianism: The Uses of a Past* (Basingstoke: Macmillan, 1998), pp. 236–49.

Miller, Andrew H., *Novels behind Glass: Commodity Culture and Victorian Narrative*, Literature, Culture, Theory 17 (Cambridge: Cambridge University Press, 1995).

Miller, William Ian, *The Anatomy of Disgust* (Cambridge: Harvard University Press, 1997).

Milligan, Robert H., *The Fetish Folk of West Africa* (New York: Fleming H. Revell, 1912).

Mitter, P., *Much Maligned Monsters: History of European Reactions to Indian Art* (Oxford: Oxford University Press, 1977).

Molendijk, Arie L., and Pieter Pels, *Religion in the Making: The Emergence of the Sciences of Religion*, Studies in the History of Religions 80 (Leiden: Brill, 1998).

Moore, R. Lawrence, *Selling God: American Religion in the Marketplace of Culture* (New York: Oxford University Press, 1994).

Morgan, David, *Protestants and Pictures: Religion, Visual Culture and the Age of American Mass Production* (New York: Oxford University Press, 1999).

Mumm, Susan, *Stolen Daughters, Virgin Mothers: Anglican Sisterhoods in Victorian Britain* (London: Leicester University Press, 1999).

Nash, David, *Blasphemy in Modern Britain: 1789 to the Present* (Aldershot: Ashgate, 1999).

Nead, Lynda, *The Female Nude: Art, Obscenity, and Sexuality* (London: Routledge, 1992).

———, *Victorian Babylon: People, Streets, and Images in Nineteenth-Century London* (New Haven: Yale University Press, 2000).

Nees, Lawrence, *A Tainted Mantle: Hercules and the Classical Tradition at the Carolingian Court* (Philadelphia: University of Pennyslvania Press, 1991).

Nicolay, Claire, 'The anxiety of "Mosaic" influence: Thackeray, Disraeli, and Anglo-Jewish assimilation in the 1840s', *Nineteenth-Century Contexts* 25 (2003), pp. 119–45.

Nockles, Peter Benedict, *The Oxford Movement in Context: Anglican High Churchman-ship 1760–1857* (Cambridge: Cambridge University Press, 1994).

Norman, E., *Anti-Catholicism in Victorian England* (London: George Allen and Unwin, 1968).

———, *The English Catholic Church in the Nineteenth Century* (Oxford: Clarendon Press, 1984).

Nye, Eric W., 'Effingham Wilson: The radical publisher of the Royal Exchange', *Publishing History* 36 (1994), pp. 87–102.

O'Connor, Eugene M., *Symbolum Salacitatis: A Study of the God Priapus as a Literary Character*, Studien zur klassischen Philologie 40 (Frankfurt: Lang, 1989).

O'Donnell, Roderick, 'Roman Catholic Church Architecture in Great Britain and Ireland, 1829–1878', University of Cambridge, Ph.D. (1983).

———, ' "Blink by [him] in silence": The Cambridge Camden Society and A. W. N. Pugin', in Webster and Elliot (2000), pp. 98–120.

O'Hagan, Andrew, 'Blame it on the boogie', review of *On Michael Jackson*, by Margo Jefferson, *London Review of Books* 6 July (2006), pp. 18–19.

O'Malley, Patrick R., *Catholicism, Sexual Deviance and Victorian Gothic Culture* (Cambridge: Cambridge University Press, 2006).

Otter, Christopher, 'Cleansing and clarifying: Technology and perception in nineteenth-century London', *Journal of British Studies* 43 (2004), pp. 40–65.

Parsons, Gerald, ed., *Religion in Victorian Britain 1, Traditions* (Manchester: Manchester University Press, 1988a).

———, ed., *Religion in Victorian Britain 2, Controversies* (Manchester: Manchester University Press, 1988b).

Pasztory, Esther, *Thinking with Things: Toward a New Vision of Art* (Austin: University of Texas Press, 2005).

Pattison, George, *Art, Modernity and Faith: Towards a Theology of Art* (Basingstoke: Macmillan, 1991).

Paz, D. G., 'Another look at Lord John Russell and the Papal Aggression, 1850', *The Historian* 45 (1982), pp. 47–64.

———, *Popular Anti-Catholicism in Mid-Victorian England* (Stanford: Stanford University Press, 1992).

Peschier, Diana, *Nineteenth-Century Anti-Catholic Discourses: The Case of Charlotte Brontë* (Basingstoke: Palgrave Macmillan, 2005).

Pietz, William, 'The problem of the fetish, I', *Res* 9 (1985), pp. 5–17.

———, 'The problem of the fetish, II', *Res* 13 (1987), pp. 23–45.

———, 'The problem of the fetish, IIIa', *Res* 16 (1988), pp. 105–23.

Piggin, Stuart, *Making Evangelical Missionaries, 1789–1858: The Social Background, Motives and Training of the British Protestant Missionaries to India*, Evangelicals and Society from 1750, 2 (No place given: Sutton Courtney Press, 1984).

Pinch, Adela, 'Stealing happiness: Shoplifting in early nineteenth-century England', in Spyer (1998), pp. 122–49.

Pinnington, J. E., 'Bishop Blomfield and St. Barnabas's, Pimlico: The limits of ecclesiastical authority', *Church Quarterly Review* 168:368 (1967), pp. 289–96.

Ponte, Alessandra, 'Architecture and phallocentrism in Richard Payne Knights' theory', in Beatriz Colomina, ed., *Sexuality and Space*, Princeton Papers in Architecture 1 (New York: Princeton University Press, 1992), pp. 273–306.

Porter, Roy, *Bodies Politic: Disease, Death and Doctors in Britain, 1650–1900* (London: Reaktion Books, 2001).

———, *Flesh in the Age of Reason: How the Enlightenment Transformed the Way We See Our Bodies and Souls* (London: Allen Lane, 2003).

Powell, Ken, 'Popery in Pimlico!: St Barnabas's Church, Pimlico', *Country Life* 178, Nov. 14 (1985), pp. 1502–1504.

Prest, John, *Lord John Russell* (London: Macmillan, 1972).

Ralls, Walter, 'The Papal Aggression of 1850: A study in Victorian anti-Catholicism', *Church History* 43 (1974), pp. 242–56.

Reay, Barry, *Watching Hannah: Sexuality, Horror and Bodily De-formation in Victorian England* (London: Reaktion Books, 2002).

Reed, John Shelton, *Glorious Battle: The Cultural Politics of Victorian Anglo-Catholicism* (Nashville: Vanderbilt University Press, 1996).

Reed, Thomas L., *The Transforming Draught: Jekyll and Hyde, Robert Louis Stevenson and the Victorian Alcohol Debate* (Jefferson, NC: Mcfarland and Co., 2006).

Reynolds, Donald M, 'The "unveiled soul": Hiram Powers's embodiment of the ideal', *The Art Bulletin* 59 (1977), pp. 394–414.

Robinson, Alan, *Imagining London, 1770–1900* (Basingstoke: Palgrave, 2004).

Roskill, Mark, and Herbert Sussman, 'Holman Hunt's "The Scapegoat": A discussion', *Victorian Studies* 12 (1969), pp. 465–70.

Rousseau, G. S., 'The sorrows of Priapus: Anticlericalism, homosocial desire, and Richard Payne Knight', in Rousseau and Roy Porter, eds., *Sexual Underworlds of the Enlightenment* (Manchester: Manchester University Press, 1987), pp. 101–53.

Rowell, Geoffrey, *The Vision Glorious: Themes and Personalities of the Catholic Revival in Anglicanism* (Oxford: Clarendon Press, 1983).

Ruether, Rosemary Radford, *Goddesses and the Divine Feminine: A Western Religious History* (Berkeley: University of California Press, 2005).

Ryan, James R., *Picturing Empire: Photography and the Visualisation of the British Empire* (London: Reaktion Books, 1997).

Said, Edward W., *Orientalism* (London: Routledge and Kegan Paul, 1978).

Saint, Andrew, 'The Grosvenor Estate—II: The Cundy era', *Country Life* 162, Nov. 17 (1977), pp. 1474–7.

Scherer, Paul, *Lord John Russell: A Biography* (Cranbury: Associated University Presses, 1999).

Selén, Mats, *The Oxford Movement and Wesleyan Methodism in England 1833–1882: A Study in Religious Conflict*, Bibliotheca Historico-Ecclesiastica Lundensis 30 (Lund: Lund University Press, 1992).

Shell, Alison, *Catholicism, Controversy and the English Literary Imagination 1558–1660* (Cambridge: Cambridge University Press, 1999).

Sigel, L. Z., *Governing Pleasures: Pornography and Social Change in England, 1815–1914* (New Brunswick: Rutgers University Press, 2002).

Skinner, S. A., *Tractarians and the 'Condition of England'* (Oxford: Oxford University Press, 2004).

Smith, Phillip T., 'The London police and the holy war: Ritualism and St. George's-in-the-East, 1859–60', *Journal of Church and State*, 28 (1986), pp. 107–19.

Smith, R. J., *The Gothic Bequest: Medieval Institutions in British Thought 1688–1863* (Cambridge: Cambridge University Press, 1987).

Spyer, Patricia, ed., *Border Fetishisms: Material Objects in Unstable Spaces* (London: Routledge, 1998).

Stallybrass, Peter, 'Marx's coat', in Spyer (1998), pp. 183–207.

Stallybrass, Peter, and Allon White, *The Politics and Poetics of Transgression* (London: Methuen, 1986).

Steele, Valerie, *Fetish: Fashion, Sex and Power* (New York: Oxford University Press, 1996).

Stumpf-Condry, C., and S. J. Skedd, 'Richard Payne Knight', in H. C. G. Matthew and B. Harrison, eds., *Oxford Dictionary of National Biography: From the Earliest Times to the Year 2000*, vol. 31 (Oxford: Oxford University Press, 2004), pp. 921–24.

Sussman, Herbert, 'Hunt, Ruskin and "The Scapegoat"', *Victorian Studies* 12 (1968), pp. 83–90.

Taussig, Michael T., *The Devil and Commodity Fetishism in South America* (Chapel Hill, NC: UNC Press, 1980).

Thompson, F. M. L., *The Rise of Respectable Society: A Social History of Victorian Britain, 1830–1900* (London: Fontana, 1988).

Tilley, Christopher, 'The metaphorical transformations of Wala canoes', in Buchli (2002), pp. 27–56.

Toon, Peter, *Evangelical Theology, 1833–1856: A Response to Tractarianism* (London: Marshall, Morgan and Scott, 1979).

Tropp, Martin, *Images of Fear: How Horror Stories Helped Shape Modern Culture (1818–1918)* (Jefferson: McFarland and Co., 1990).

Valeri, Valerio, *The Forest of Taboos: Morality, Hunting, and Identity among the Huaulu of the Moluccas* (Madison: University of Wisconsin Press, 1999).

Vance, Norman, *The Victorians and Ancient Rome* (Oxford: Blackwell, 1997).

Van der Veer, Peter, *Imperial Encounters: Religion and Modernity in India and Britain* (Princeton: Princeton University Press, 2001).

Voll, Dieter, *Catholic Evangelicalism: The Acceptance of Evangelical Traditions by the Oxford Movement During the Second Half of the Nineteenth Century*, trans. Veronica Rutter (London: Faith Press, 1963).

Waddams, S. M., *Law, Politics and the Church of England: The Career of Stephen Lushington, 1782–1873* (Cambridge: Cambridge University Press, 1992).

Wallis, Frank H., *Popular Anti-Catholicism in Mid-Victorian England*, Texts and Studies in Religion 60 (Lewiston: Edwin Mellor Press, 1993).

———, 'Anti-Catholicism in mid-Victorian Britain: Theory and discipline', *Journal of Religion and Society* 7 (2005), pp. 1–17.

Ward, Anthony John, 'Society and the Suppression of Vice: The Sociology of Moral Indignation', Brunel University, Ph.D. (1980).

Ward, W. R., *The Protestant Evangelical Awakening* (Cambridge: Cambridge University Press, 1992).

Watkin, David, *Morality and Architecture* (Chicago: University of Chicago Press, 1977).

Wauzzinksi, Robert A., *Between God and Gold: Protestant Evangelicalism and the Industrial Revolution, 1820–1914* (Rutherford: Fairleigh Dickinson University Press, 1993).

Webster, Christopher, ed., *'Temples Worthy of His Presence': The Early Publications of the Cambridge Camden Society* (Reading: Spire Books, 2003).

Webster, Christopher, and John Elliot, eds., *'A Church as It Should Be': The Cambridge Camden Society and Its Influence* (Stamford: Shaun Tyas, 2000).

Welch, P. J., 'Bishop Blomfield and the development of Tractarianism in London', *Church Quarterly Review* 155: 317 (1954), pp. 332–44.

Wheeler, Michael, *The Old Enemies: Catholic and Protestant in Nineteenth-Century Culture* (Cambridge: Cambridge University Press, 2006).

Whisenant, James C., *A Fragile Unity: Anti-ritualism and the Division of Anglican Evangelicalism in the Nineteenth Century* (Carlisle: Paternoster Press, 2003).

White, James F., *The Cambridge Movement: The Ecclesiologists and the Gothic Revival* (Cambridge: Cambridge University Press, 1962).

White, Jonathan, 'A world of goods? The "consumption turn" and eighteenth-century British history', *Cultural and Social History* 3 (2006), pp. 93–104.

Williams, Thomas Jay, *Priscilla Lydia Sellon: The Restorer after Three Centuries of the Religious Life in the English Church* (London: S.P.C.K., 1950).

Wolffe, John, *The Protestant Crusade in Great Britain, 1829–1860* (Oxford: Clarendon Press, 1991).

———, *God and Greater Britain: Religion and National Life in Britain and Ireland 1843–1945* (London: Routledge, 1994).

———, 'Lord Palmerston and religion: A reappraisal', *English Historical Review* 120 (2005), pp. 907–36.

Yagou, Artemis, 'Facing the west: Greece in the Great Exhibition of 1851', *Design Issues* 19 (2003), pp. 82–90.

Yasuko, Suga, 'Designing the morality of consumption: "Chamber of Horrors" at the Museum of Ornamental Art, 1852–53', *Design Issues* 20 (2004), pp. 43–56.

Yates, Nigel, '"Bells and smells": London, Brighton and south coast religion reconsidered', *Southern History* 5 (1983), pp. 122–53.

———, *Anglican Ritualism in Victorian Britain* (Oxford: Oxford University Press, 1999).

———, *Buildings, Faith and Worship: The Liturgical Arrangement of Anglican Churches 1600–1900*, 2nd ed. (Oxford: Oxford University Press, 2000).

Young, Alison, 'Aesthetic vertigo and the jurisprudence of disgust', *Law and Critique* 11 (2000), pp. 241–65.

Index